Maurice Beebe
4/1975

Epitaphs of Our Times

Books by Edward Dahlberg

Bottom Dogs, *1930*
From Flushing to Calvary, *1932*
Kentucky Blue Grass Smith, *1934*
Those Who Perish, *1934*
Can These Bones Live, *1940 (rev. ed. 1960)*
The Flea of Sodom, *1950*
The Sorrows of Priapus, *1957*
Truth Is More Sacred (with Herbert Read), *1961*
Because I Was Flesh, *1964*
Alms for Oblivion, *1964*
Reasons of the Heart, *1965*
Cipango's Hidden Door, *1966*

Epitaphs of Our Times

the letters of Edward Dahlberg

GEORGE BRAZILLER   NEW YORK

Editor's Note

This book makes no claim to being a "Collected Letters"; it would take several volumes to contain even those letters of Edward Dahlberg's we have been privileged to read, and there are probably as many more we have not seen. Nor can this book properly be called a "Selected Letters," for this would infer that we are offering only those epistles which, in our opinion, are the best of the lot. Actually, as many "best" letters had to be omitted, for reasons of space, as are included; the letters to Herbert Read alone, if published in their entirety, would crowd out the rest of the contents. Let us say, then, that what we have in the following pages is simply a Dahlberg epistolatory sampler.

What letters appear in these pages were chosen by the editor without consulting the author. Mr. Dahlberg quite rightly asked not to be involved in any way in the matter of selection.

Perhaps a word should be said of the arrangement—or seeming lack of arrangement—of the contents. The alternatives were clear: the letters could either be published in the order in which they were written, or grouped according to their recipients. Although the latter arrangement inevitably takes on the aspect of theme and variations, since a theme stated in a 1958 letter to A, let us say, is likely to be picked up in a letter to B written around the same time, it still seemed to be more attractive in that it made for a sense of communion rather than random communication. Accordingly, with two exceptions, the letters have been arranged in groups in a progression established by the date on which the first letter within each group was written. The exceptions are (1) the letters to the author's brother, sister-in-law, and nephew, which seemed to belong together regardless of the dates they were written; and (2) the letters to Robert M. Hutchins, which are placed early in the contents because the biographical sketch in the first of these letters may help the reader to place later references.

For permission to use the letters published in this book our thanks to Miss Josephine Herbst, Miss Isabella Gardner, Mrs. William Carlos Williams, and Mrs. Michael Sands; to Mr. Robert M. Hutchins, Mr. Michael Sands, Mr. Steven Sands, Sir Herbert Read, Mr. Lewis Mumford, Mr. James Laughlin, Mr. Allen Tate, Mr. Frank MacShane, and Mr. Stanley Burnshaw; to Mr. Donald Gallup and Mr. Herman Liebert of the Yale University Library, and to Mrs. Mary M. Hirth and Mr. Harold W. Billings of the University of Texas Library. We also wish to thank Mr. Paul Carroll, editor of *The Edward Dahlberg Reader*, for his kind cooperation, and the many others who so generously responded to our request for their Dahlberg correspondence though regrettably, again for reasons of space, we were unable to include their letters in the present book.

E.S.

Contents

Epitaphs of Our Times

Introduction

New York
September 26, 1966

Dear Edwin:

What have I to convey to you but a plethora of misgivings? To begin with I do not know what is in this volume. It includes, I am sure, about twenty-five years of madness, follies, dissimulation, turbulent and incoherent thoughts and peevish and dour moods. All flesh is guileful, and perfidy is a parcel of trust. I am not declaring I ever wished to be a dissembler, or that I have been an adventurer with other people's sensibilities or pocket. But on occasion what was on my tongue was not in the heart; the foot goes one way and the head another. We clasp a foe in our arms and are frosty with a friend. Then it is easier to fall out with those we care for than with an enemy. Human acts are opaque and fickle, and we prize an adversary because he is so resolute and determined and despise a friend feeble as the cony. Please do not think I am sporting with flamboyant paradoxes. I am unsure of everything, and do not know what I do, but continue to do it.

Epistles are hypnotic trances of our unknown selves. One's life is the scrawl of a dream which I hear tolling wretched events.

This is the age of the destroyer and robber; the bread is dishonest, the milk senile, the butter false, and the vegetables and fruit grown in Orcus.

John Ruskin says, judge a civilization by its products. Letter writing today is as artificial and inhuman as the rest. Our mate-

rials are no better than the bastard neologies, which the specula-
tors in the market place and pedantic trimmers in the colleges of
lower learning have sold to the gullible. Our cult is the new.
Could we slough our skins we would do it each day.

We are a young nation, already in its dotage, and the male
does not know how to raise his hopes; he shortens the women's
skirts to awaken him or puts up skyscrapers, those humbug
phalloi, to persuade him how virile he is.

You can mention the pyramids and the pylons in upper Egypt,
and I am not prepared to offer you grubby quibbles. But I live
now, and what was bad and wicked in another age does not
sting me. It is clear we are not producing the cities of Attica or
Heliopolis or a kidney of sages.

I wear funeral weeds; do not blame me. I did not invent this
period, but am only the prey of it.

These letters are the epitaphs of our times; they are for those
who are lost. He who tells you he has found himself is contempti-
ble.

It is now the fag end of April, next to the poet's month of May,
when the blood should be loud and lickerish, but I sit at my
guillotine-desk in a flensed apartment amidst the dirty Gehenna
of this growling auto town. I dwell in the hungry, toothless gutters and belong, like Charles Baudelaire and the poor, to the
fraternity of the *déshérités*.

This is a plaint, as I have said, but what is there to affirm? The
average U.S.A. Caliban would rather gulp down wormwood than
one reasonable, stout nay. I am a negative soothsayer just as
Calchas was who could only predict misfortune for Agamemnon.
Homer is correct, and always right. When a human animal is
uneasy because vague intimations of disaster or the death of a
friend press down upon his nerves he is a prophet. This is true,
since the hands and the cranium can know no more. But if a man
claims foreknowledge of good hap and benefits that will come to
a person he is a mountebank.

Would that I were born in another season and could listen to
Socrates in the agora and meet Euripides and Aristippus. You
may say olden sophisms lie more easy on the stomach than
our civilization. How can I deny it? I am a passionate logician

of the absurd. Of course I should like to be a gull in some
other century. Some days my head is filled with country
brabbling, petticoat matters, and when a hedge acquaintance
greets me on the sidewalk there are the craziest chimes in my
pulses. A message from a friend is manna and quail in my Sinai
Desert.

When nothing occurs, my bosom is sulky and my life is zero.
Then I think a stunted lichen and rocks are more sentient than
skin. Do I hanker for evil tidings? No, it is those mute, level
hours that bite me like spiteful flies. I want something to happen: it is preposterous to admit it. What I am unable to endure
is a cheat who would rather cozen a thousand others rather than
me. Even a foe has title and deed to my affections because he
clings to me. I cannot bear to be utterly forsaken. It is obvious
that everything is important to me, and that I am doomed if I
cannot even create an incident.

Call this a mumpish song of the worms, but what is has to be. I
could be jocund as anyone, and am not invulnerable to the
cruddled buds spoiled by gasoline fumes and the bony, spastic
branches in this garbaged megalopolis. I laugh though I may die
any moment, and as Langland puts it in *Piers Plowman:* "In a
somer seson whan soft was the sonne I shope me in shroudes."

Our diseased haste sorely troubles me. Though our lives are
often briefer than the oak or conifer, everybody is in a hurry.
Who can walk or think, which is what Aristotle meant by peripa-
tetic, without being killed by an automobile? Should you meet a
passer-by on the pavement, he is too nervous to stand for three
minutes; he squirms in his trousers as though he has to pass
water, and informs you he is busy.

Our sick habits are governed by the machine. Does not the
telephone inhibit people from seeing each other, and what else
are the railroads for except to keep the parents apart from their
children? Men are always traveling because they are miserable in
one place unless they can go to another.

The American is the loneliest person on earth, and he is so
ashamed of it that he is sly with everybody.

He drops into squalid familiarities with a stranger, and
after a brace of minutes he addresses him by his Christian name

and then decimates that in order to give his innocent victim the impression there is a close bond between them. In such matters, one is the hunter and the other his prey, for soon as the trap is set the cully is sure to ask when the two of them can meet. The huntsman has caught his hare and earned his penultimate simper, for his instant reply is that he is very occupied.

This conycatcher, who refuses to see you should you request it, arrives when he is unexpected. Open the door for him with a jubilant countenance and he announces he is leaving. Should he be persuaded to enter and sit down, he speedily champs his words about money, the countless appointments he has, and his most recent amour with a crumpled trull on Charles or Jane Street. He can never remove the comic sock though it stinks because he is unable to be earnest about anything.

So he rambles from one fellow to another seeking the snoring and idle chatter that affords him comatose comfort and an easy stool. Charles Lamb complains: "I go nowhere . . . have no acquaintances . . . and I am left alone. . . . Allen calls very occasionally, as though it were a duty rather, and seldom stays ten minutes." What harrows up my soul is the wall between people.

The streets are even a greater jeopardy to one's composure.

Should a brach in rancid trousers crush your foot beneath her envenomed heel, and you apologize to her for hurting you, she takes you for a simpleton and rails at you. Should you open the door for her so that she can go into a shop she does not even mumble thanks but passes through you like a sword.

All this is droll, I realize, and such wounds should be covered with swaddling clouts. There are other ironies in this book. The truth is I have not read these letters because I am afraid of my character and defects and who is courageous or clever enough to see his own faults? Socrates advises every man to know himself, but who can? Heraclitus says that nobody can step into the same river twice, and although people don't change, why do men's acts continually startle them? François Villon confesses: ". . . I know the nun by her veil; I know the sharper by the jargon; I know fools fed on creams; I know wine by its barrel; I know all, except myself."

Coleridge reveals the same rueful truth about himself: "My

mind is illegible to myself. I am lost in . . . the trackless wilderness of my own bosom."

I am true as skin can be, and mourn because the bruckle body cannot be simpler. If these epistles betray me, they did so for a kiss. For I have been a stubborn palmer who imagined he had discovered Cathay or come upon the spices of the Moluccas when he found a friend.

But how often have I imagined I was bound to a person and that both of us had made vows of mutual fealty beneath the equinoctial line, only to discover that our union was vaporous and neutral, and then I am houseless and a mistral blows about my head until I am becrazed.

A man's letters are naked as Adam before he knew Eve, for there is less feigning about them than what is in a work of art. With what apprehension I open an envelope, for first I glance at the conclusion of a missive, praying I shall not see a sincerely yours, kind regards, or best of luck, which are as withered and cold to my nature as the regions about Lake Titicaca.

Consider what a wry face the modern, Laodicean man will make after I have cited Coleridge's salutation and diction: "My dear, dear Southey," or elsewhere, "Convey my softest affections" to another. Lord Bolingbroke pleads for the alms I require, when he begs Jonathan Swift to "love him," and Gay writes in a similar vein to Swift: ". . . as you guessed my thoughts and knew, that I had not forgot you, and that I always loved you."

Pope asserts in his *Dunciad* he lived in the leaden age, but we are in the loveless one. Pornography is rife, and yet the most libidinous four-letter word in English is love. The American hoards his feelings, or has he any? He is the extreme Narcissus; permit me to alter Plato a little to make it pertinent: self-love, "house-mate of solitude." What avails it to explain he is still the undomesticated ruffian pioneer who regards a tender inscription as womanish or only fit for a headstone.

I confess I am fond enough to expect a scrub acquaintance to send me the balm that might ease a mean, gravelly day.

Worst of all for me is a letterless, obituary Sunday, for I am then spleen'd until Monday has covered those twenty-four burial hours in the week.

About a fortnight ago you told me that all centuries were bad and nearly the same, and that the author always had been a lonely figure. How far you are in the right I cannot conjecture. What has been, as Solomon holds, will be, and I am no one, may I repeat it, to argue against wisdom. But I would not have it so, and although I fear people, I love those who will permit it. Boethius counsels his hearers: ". . . for I never yet saw nor heard of a wise man desiring to be an outcast."

It has been my purpose to describe as best I can the epistolary me: I reflect the age to which I am opposed. What especially concerns me is the poet's quandaries. One is either shrewd or noble, a Parnassian sharper or a truthful scribe. As for me I am every man's dupe, and am of the opinion that one who thinks he is so vigilant nobody can deceive him is an arrant knave. For he who has not been humiliated by his own life has never lived. To reword Swift for my own use, may I say I swallow four affronts every day.

A writer who is not dissident is not worth a rush, and though no one will hear the cry in these letters my ears are not surd. Still, I am helpless as the next man, if not so silent. Maybe all I can do is cry out against the times, and though nothing may come of it indignation is necessary, for, as Quevedo writes, all that an author is capable of is to "make people pray for the Egyptian locusts and caterpillars, in exchange for vermin."

It does not matter how often I fail; what is important is that I never joined the intellectual or the academic crowd. The rabble esthete is no better than any other species of a demagogue, or what Prior calls the comma and colon men. Every time a bumbailiff of our venal, literary agora praises a bad book he starves the writer of a good one.

Find such plain dealing, if you can, among our hairdressers of grammar as the following in Swift's correspondence: "The Beggar's Opera hath knocked down Gulliver: I hope to see Pope's Dulness knock down the Beggar's Opera, but not until it hath fully done its job."

Had I at my disposal the page of Rabelais' Pantagruel I would send him abroad to curse these canting dunderheads of our brave new syntax half an hour every day.

I know you never looked for the musty falsehoods of an Iago of belles lettres from me. Our criticism is villainous and ignorant and smells of the stews, and it has been my constant purpose to tell the reader he has been cheated of his inheritance of our imponderabilia by the Philisters of the American literati who pretend the worst is the best and that what is learned does not even exist. Or as Erasmus held: "I have at least stirred the bile of those who would not have the world grow wiser, and only fools now snarl at me."

I believe in the holy logos without which we are a slavish and depraved people.

In the beginning was the *Word,* and then came the god cash, and afterwards the devil print.

My unfamiliar readers, after glancing at the many names of those with whom I have corresponded will surmise I have jolly, roaring evenings at one pothouse or another. However, there are no taverns or chocolate houses comparable to those of eighteenth-century London where one could discourse with John Dryden, Pope, Addison, Steele, or Dr. Arbuthnot.

Still, this *boke* is no dirge; for I am certain there is enough in it that is bizarre and glutted up with passions to amaze a tender hearer and vex to the blood the poetaster.

A cabalist, born in the wrong season, I beseech you, live long, which has eight letters, twice those contained in spelling love.

Edward

letters to

Theodore Dreiser

Mexico City
August 9, 1937

Dear Theodore Dreiser:

I have thought of you very much, and have written you many letters, all of which only existed in my head, except one. That I sent to you the day before I left New York. I don't know whether you got it as I never heard from you. This is not an accusation but a dull stony fact.

Cato took to his sword, and I took to Mexico; Cato was the good deal the wiser. For here I am, alone, sitting in a room in that cash-register monastery, the YMCA. I have been here two months and now I want to get away. Whatever Mexico is, it is not for me. I will divide this letter, as follows, into Travel Notes, Observations, Misinformation, The Priapic Gods Are Athirst, The Cross, and The Chamber of Horrors.

The first day I was in Mexico City, let me baldly confess it, I was enthralled. I myself do not know what I saw or how I saw; but here was a city in the clouds, built on a mountaintop. Here was the city for the poet. By the end of the week I began to see, not with my outside eyes, but with the eyes of my nerves. To begin with, I rented a servant's room on the roof of one of those squat, functional buildings; there on lines hung beautifully pigmented drawers, rectangles of sheets; there desolately pecked rooster and hen; there old Indian women made tortillas, spanking the sour dough between the palms of their hands. Outside of my window was the Revolution itself. There stood the monument of the Revolution, a broad-hipped biped from whose cement elephantine arch projected in neon lights, OTIS! At night

the immaculate plaster of my wall was shadowed with like ci-
phers: BUSH! But do not think I look on the sour side of life—too
much; for my heart was overflowing with nobler feelings. True, I
loathed the mestizo, the half-breed barber culture of Mexico; but
I also loved the Indian. So as I strolled along the Alameda, the
trees laden with reminiscently graduated fragrances, I never let
pass an Indian without smiling, even if the smile was more often
inscribed on my brain rather than on my lips. Or I stopped to
needlessly ask the time or a direction. On one occasion I paused
to contemplate the supple and cadenced carriage of a young
Aztecan dressed in rough blue shirt and workmen's overalls,
thinking how subtle it was for that cosmogonal bête noire to
have made so many different peoples and temperaments. As my
eyes dropped perpendicularly to his shirt I saw pinned to it:
POPEYE THE SAILOR CLUB! Which leads me to say, my dear
Dreiser, that History will accuse not Hitler or Mussolini as the
great vulgarizers of the world, but the Paramount and Fox Film
Corporations.

After three weeks I could no longer bear the great scavenger
city in the mountains immersed in dirty blankets of clouds. I
couldn't stand Diego Rivera's cafeteria serape murals. Nor San-
born's, that monster House of the Tiles, where tired and seamy
virgin schoolteachers go to get their American ice-cream sodas,
and which looks like the Elizabethan Room in the Paramount
Moving Picture Theater. Which, if you don't happen to know it,
is the baroque water closet. I was bored to death with folkloris-
mus, with the cult of the sombrero and the white drawers, with
the Mexican Revolution which was nonexistent. And with myself. So I took myself to Taxco, hoping to leave myself there,
while I remained elsewhere and looked on. Taxco is one of those
quaint poster pueblos, with travelogue cobblestones where
browse pigs, burros, and tourists. It has the thick stable smell of
an old Bible manger. Overlaid with New World jazz. On the
balcony of the bar is a five-piece orchestra which plays together in
complete disunion, a xylophone, a violin, a trap drum, a cornet
accompanied by a small boy who scrapes the guts of a gourd with
a toothbrush.

Taxco has numerous churches, notwithstanding the social
revolution. A dozen or more; some have been closed. In the

square is the largest one, which looks like a stale moldering Hershey chocolate. The interior is no less satisfying. At one end is an emaciated Christ. From his bony wooden brow steams the shellacked mists of suffering and crucifixion. His ribs are skeletally barreled, the knees and thighs bedripped with the rusted coagulations of blood, and the upper loins are swathed in delicate white sexual panties. At the other end is another Christ bludgeoned with war medals. The air reeks of worm-stuffed shadows, dirty incense, and metaphysical urine. A poor Indian in white drawers is kneeling to a pastry-hued Virgin Mary. Iconography rules the world, and we can never emerge from this world until we have departed from that dark charnel house, the Church.

Taxco is colonized by Americans. They do nothing, read nothing, and only defecate, I am certain, when afflicted with dysentery. Also in Taxco is the Polish Minister; he is a little dry flaky man, who clicks his heels and makes his bows, not so much to the people he greets as to himself. The pinochle minister of eleven vest-pocket Latin American countries, he is a fair representative of the kind of diplomatic intelligence which rules the world. I ask him: "What do you think of the Spanish Situation?" He replies: "I think it is quite a situation." I continue: "What is your opinion of the Jewish Question in Poland?" He: "It is a considerable question." I: "And what do you think of Literature?" He: "It has been in existence a very long time."

I need a change, as you may doubtless surmise. Which reminds me of the Indian who came to sell a chair, which he had made, for ten pesos. The merchant who admired the chair asked him to make twelve of them. Whereupon the Indian demanded twelve pesos for each chair. When asked why he demanded more instead of less money the Indian replied: "It is so much more boring to make twelve chairs."

The early part of next week I am going to San Antonio. I may remain there a week, or more, or less. Then I go to Kansas City to spend a few days with my mother. After that to Chicago. Incidentally, if you should happen to know any people I could look up in Kansas City or Chicago I would be most grateful.

Meantime, please accept my warmest regards and admiration.

Your friend,

It would give me very much pleasure to hear from you. I am still
at my book,* having completed an essay on Thoreau. Now working on Whitman, that divine mountebank, savior of the American phallus.

New York
January 4, 1938

Dear Dreiser:

Of course, I am very pleased that you are coming to dinner
Thursday. But Dreiser, I confess to you, as I would to my
own miserable "underground," your letter stung me! One
little pin jab, and I go a-sprawling. What are we made of? What
thinnish whimpering stuff. But to the point, I am wriggling on
it, what do I finally care about being right or wrong. I have
always preferred an imaginative error to a safe truism. Almost
everybody is right about Caldwell, Hemingway, Dos Passos,
Cantwell, Farrell, and so on. For almost everybody accepts them.
I do not. I am wrong. Believe me, to the very cutting truth of the
little ego that is always cutting me, I would leave off writing
altogether if I could not defile the soul with more splenetic
imagination, if I could not degrade man with a subtler thrust, a
more evil brain. No matter, you may say. I don't care whether
you write or not. I'm a realist and I accept. And not churlishly.
I'm not trying to create anything on anybody else's bones; we do
that, as it is. That is why I despise these modern novels of carnage. I have no quarrel with naturalism as such; but I want a
purificatory naturalism. If our times is a Gargantuan vomit I will
loathe it but not grovel in it. I will face it but not immerse
myself in it. I won't add another vomit bath to it.

Another thing, I am no literary geographer; I don't care about
American Literature in that false American sense of the word.
The word European still has meaning for me, and I will measure
our books, our canvases, and our men by the standards of that

* *Can These Bones Live*

rich, mortal, and now wounded, body of Europe. We cry about roots in our country and we become master provincials in our search for them. We want a past and so we look for the bones of Boone and the skeleton of de Soto. This is a good thing, in part; and it will add to our reveries, our dreams. Any quest that will make us dream and yearn more I deeply pine for too. But, finally, the Mississippi is not as psychically subtle or still or mysterious as the Ganges; or the Rhine; or the Rhone. Finally, we do not know Wisconsin—those cool autumn reveries of pasture land, brindled cows and melancholy dairy mills and silos unless there is a Switzerland or a Mont Blanc in our souls. A literature that does not echo some forgotten substratum of a long past and dimly remembered and perhaps never known Himalaya or treeless terrain of fantasy, experience, sensation of yesterday and yester century, is, strictly speaking, no literature. He who does not transcend all limits can never know or even illuminate his own. Melville did this all his life, and he is a veritable Tamburlaine of our imaginative wisdom.

If I wrong Twain and Fuller, and so wrong myself, I live with my error and by it, and with a thrust. It may be faulty but it is better so, for me. In excluding Twain I do not so much insult the Holy Ghost as our autopsical critics. May they do less for me.

However, I shall continue the pursuit. I will read Fuller's *With the Procession* though I die in a consumption of boredom. And may I remind you, my dear friend, in all due deference to your own profoundly earned errors—I respect them, too, and hope to cultivate a few of them and feed my own life with them—that it was you who suggested *Cliff Dwellers* to me. How am I sure? It is the only certitude that I have in this world; for I knew nothing about Fuller until you mentioned him to me; not the man nor a single title.

Now that you have accepted my Adirondack Impudence, if you have, but then you have a vast and memorable comprehensiveness, please also accept my full and warm and courteous admiration. Accept me, dear Dreiser, and you make Tolerance seem unambitious.

Your friend,

Dear Dreiser:

I have just reread your exquisitely felt piece of reminiscence on Randolph Bourne and want to ask your permission to reprint it in the magazine.* It has the subtlest gradations of ripe and mellowed remembrance and remorse and pain, and withal a pervasive hope and gallantry.

I am thinking, of course, of our pleasant and gay talk last week. Though I follow you at almost every point and know a little of the terrors and horrors of the human spectacle, I know too that I would go mad were I to do nothing but look into the beast abysses of men. There is a true and melancholy legend that Shakespeare disappeared and lost his reason before he died. I mean that it is so true in the light of the text of the plays. Madness too is a penultimate protest and contradicts the real nihilist—if there be such a one. I don't believe there is.

Though I believe that optimism is more often passive than not, I cannot go entirely in the opposite direction either. Instead I pursue a desperado philosophy of believing, hoping, and willing, choosing the chivalry of morals even though such a pole star be flaked with the cinder and ashes of Hades. What else is there to do? Why not gallantly decay and so find a seeming bloom in all the cankering?

One thing I want to remark in this little note is that I am so glad that you are not the GREAT MAN. I will instruct myself in the most insidious mysteries of the most occulted modesty; for in so doing I at least dupe myself and offend no one else. Should I ever see my vanity going about in this world in the shape of one of those starveling Christ-ribbed Mexican dogs I will not feed it with my spittle. The reason I mention this is that today I saw a real and beautiful person who suddenly assumed leviathanic proportions.

If you are free some day next week it would be good to see you; and if you have time and inclination to write me, it would

* *Twice a Year*

be good to hear from you. In any event please let me know about the Bourne piece.

Meanwhile, your friend and admirer,

New York
April 22, 1938

Dear Dreiser:

I have been up to Cambridge and only got back last night. I have thought of you a good deal and spoke of you to several people who deeply care about what you have written. I also succeeded in picking up a copy of *Forgotten Frontiers* and find it full of material that I can use.

A drearier sloven place than Cambridge I do not know; it is far worse than one of those darksome pen and ink abstractions of the Depression, those emptied and dismantled mill cities, like Fall River or New Bedford. These, like the fleshly ruins of a onetime superb Carmen, excite sorrow and wonder and amazement because they have fallen; and whatever has fallen wounds and saddens us and for that reason alone we never tire of commenting anew upon the misery of man. But Cambridge never had an Original Sin and so never had a Fall or a Redemption. Cambridge is a gray plaster-of-Paris town with a metronomic pulse. Within Cambridge is that fiscal Franciscan secret order—the Secret Order of High Finance Education. The Harvard man has that evil pustular monastic look to him, that nasty glazed masturbatory eye. His whole demeanor is an admixture of calculated lymphatic inattention and zeroidal learning. That slow walkathon haberdashery flounce has a caste meanness that in its way surpasses anything I know. But so much for cash-register education in America.

I have been reading so much that books for the moment cannot feed me and so I am going back to write, to redo the Bourne essay. Nothing that I do ever quite satisfies me; but as I have no mania to rush into print I don't mind. I learn as much from not writing as I do from the perilous mistakes I make while doing it.

One thing I have made up my mind to do is never to solve or solder impossible contradictions on paper that cannot be mended or put together in life. And my book is full of that. I know it and it bothers me, terribly. I don't believe too much in the "superstition of progress"; yet I believe just as man from day to day must create his own atmosphere and fiction of free will and speak in demonic absolutes or succumb, so must he *act* as though man were not an eater, a cannibal, and as though the most planetary and remote and ridiculously foolhardy ideals could be achieved. One has two choices, either to be Jesus or the Ass upon which He sat as he rode into Jerusalem. I prefer to be both and am reasonably certain that I can carry a divine burden as the Ass better than as the Jesus.

Dear Dreiser, it would be good to hear from you, and better, if and when possible, to see you.

Affectionately your friend and admirer,

New York
April 28, 1938

Dear Dreiser:

This morning I have been pondering all the subtle and less than heinous follies I could commit and so I begin by writing you. To begin with, whenever I send you a letter I am never quite certain whether I am living in this mournful and yet so sweetly budding April world or in some anaesthetic, ozone, and metaphysical realm. For, as I never get a reply from you, I long cease to ask myself not whether you received my last fatuity but whether I really ever wrote it. So I ask, begging your memory, did you get a letter from me, which I seem to have written to you last Friday? I put this craven question to you, for I know I shall never be silent and sequestered and so secure. Actually, I am the most insecure person imaginable. Each letter that I write is an ache or doubt, misgiving and inchoate sleeplessness. What inane attitude did I strike, what preposterous yearning did I dissimulate, what loathsome poison did I distill? It is inconceivably worse, of course, when the unfortunate recipient of my most pathetical pulings decides that it is better to take an ambling spring walk, sit in the nutritive afternoon sun, eat a peach, read Hamlet, take a nap than answer such a ninny letter. Who can argue against such Jovian wisdom, who would? Nobody, but me.

This is just a note, less than a letter, nearer zero and so purer. Incidentally, I bought a copy of *The History of American Idealism* which I expect shortly to read. These days I am as lazy as a July worm; right now am pecking away at notes to rewrite my Bourne essay, which is, in effect, an anti-war piece. The Shakespeare I rewrote and will redo again, for it is not yet what I want. The Thoreau, which I completely rewrote, is, I believe, satisfying. I see in the papers that some one came all the way from Sweden to make you write another novel so that you can get the Nobel award. I know a good one too. A friend of mine who teaches up at Harvard recently tried to get a scholarship for three hundred dollars but was finally rejected because he did not have a Ph.D.; and so I suggested that he go out and borrow ten thousand dollars so that he could get the Ph.D. and so acquire the three hundred dollars. I know all sorts of little doggerel ironies, but then you are not interested.

Your friend,

Boston
September 24, 1938

Dear Dreiser,

I have been in Boston in a furnished room, writing and eating my piece of limbo. What else is there for a writer to do among these Yahoos; frankly, I do not know. I only know I have become more dour, sullen—more nihilistic, and yet more psychically total than I have ever been.

I have thought of you often, and wanted to write to you; but doubted greatly whether you would care overmuch to hear from me; you have mammoth tenderness in your books, but strange and mephitic reticences in your human relationships—that is, with me, I should add. The last time I saw you at Mount Kisco I left you with a mournful sadness; some of the conversations that we had—and there were some rare insights you communicated to me—had a personal fervor and quickened pulse. But that last one on Rabelais was dreadful, particularly my part in it; what fatuities, what high-grade nonsense I uttered, knowing all the while what a poor ridiculous fellow I was while doing it. But then, what the brain knows rarely gets to the heart, and when the heart knows a thing it does not have to trouble the brain about it, since the true heart has all the thinking, all the aches, all the mounting blood in it.

I have wanted to get off alone, nakedly alone, as one can be in a cheap room or in a bare tiled cafeteria, cold Arctic white and dismally scoured clean, for I have wanted to prove myself, as that most pained and beauteous immortal Keats said, to prove myself upon my pulses. And so here I am, walking like a shade among the diluted ghosts of Boston, living psychically compressed between the tumorous growths of pulseless stone buildings, and treading those bitter and arid wafers of balding macadam. I look at our cities, the Death Wish of flowers, trees, foliage, color, and wonder how soon it will be before we all go mad, before the American breaks out and spills blood if only to have pigment in his life!

My own manuscript now has enough substance to be called a book;* what I showed you was a puny and ill thought-out scaffolding; what I have since written I deeply believe. Of course, I doubt whether I will ever find five people to agree with me. The only criticism that matters is but deeply awakened self-love; a man who does not love his truths has none to give to anybody else. So I propose to sit upon my own dunghill and like Job scrape the sores off my body and soul with a potsherd, and let it go at that. My book will be I, and nothing else; which reminds me, once Henry Seidel Canby wrote an article in a book making a perfervid plea for anonymity among American writers, but did not fail to sign his own name to his essay. As it is, most of our

* *Can These Bones Live*

literature is about as anonymous as it can be. I notice that
Thomas Wolfe has just died; I made what appeared a very
brutal remark to a man here the other day, by casually remark-
ing that Thomas Wolfe's death may have been a loss to his
mother but none to American Literature. But mistake me not,
when a real spirit has been quenched out, I feel orphaned,
alone—more lonely in this naked bursting world than before; for
no two or more original spirits are ever in competition with one
another; it is the mediocre who starve us and pilfer what they
can.

Soon I will have to look about for a publisher to whom I can
market my throbbings and my aches, and that frightens me. For
there is not one man of taste or integrity in the whole publishing
field who will take a book on its artistic merit and sights. My
book will make enough people angry, that is, if enough people
ever hear about it. But you know, so much better than I do, how
the *New York Times* can take a book and lower it in its back-
page burial plots, after which there is nothing else to do but go
back and write another book for the *New York Times* literary
morgue, page twenty-six and on and on.

Of all the men you have mentioned to me, those of the immediate past, I think the most gifted one was Harris Merton Lyon;
your title is very pat, de Maupassant Junior, but he had more to
him than that masturbatory keyhole gossip of tales. You know, I
don't think people compromise; I believe they merely unfold
themselves. Merton Lyon has a quote from Job, the one book in
the whole Bible for me, new and old, which tells or foretells his
story and all others in our American Parable—"Cannot my taste
discern perverse things?"

Stieglitz has really recovered; he is a Lear among the American
Arts, living there with those bare white walls among those magical and immaculated vulva flowers of Georgia O'Keeffe, he is
really one of your apostolic figures, out of a page in *Twelve Men,*
but no provincial Diogenes or Plato. He will be remembered,
tomorrow, of course; did not De Sanctis say that Fame is remote-
ness? Do you know a single celebrated genius right near at hand,
who, I should add, does not enjoy the gimcrack myth of a reputation? This I conclude with another story. A group of Russian

readers were discussing a very gifted author, one dwelling upon the shadings and nuances of his prose texture, another emphasizing his imagery and his heroical adjectives, while a small and pugnacious fellow with the splenetic temperament of a phthisical tailor was with poor success withholding his own spittle. Finally he spoke up, "He's no genius. Why, I know him."

If you have the mood and the mind to write I wish you would, and if during the two years I have known you, and felt in you a friend, rightly or wrongly, you have not found me too much of a bore and a violent ordeal, or an ordeal in Violence, do let me hear from you. As the men say to the women they are about to leave in Chekov's short stories, "Please do not think too much evil of me."

By the way, did you enjoy the Lawrence book on American Literature I sent you last summer; I think he is about the only man who ever wrote about us who had some mortal juices in his loins and some direful but star-fated truths to tell. And yet the puling little hacks speak of it, when they do, as an inanity—so go and write a book!

Meantime, I send you, as ever, my admiration and warm affections,

                                                            Your friend,

letters to
Robert M. Hutchins

New York
September 17, 1958

Dear Mr. Hutchins:

I have your charming note; like Prince Myshkin, I thank you so very much for liking me. As for my autobiography,* I think of those profound and mournful words of Schiller: "Life's an error, and knowledge is death."

If you can translate the water of this world into the wine of Cana, I shall be most grateful, and if you cannot, I shall still be most grateful—if only for knowing you.

I was born in a charity hospital in Boston, Massachusetts, in 1900, July 22nd. At seven I was in a Catholic orphanage, and at eleven until I was well into my seventeenth birthday I was in a Jewish orphan asylum. I have always been loyal to my beginnings, by which I mean I have always been an orphan.

I was a vagabond when I was eighteen; though I had a wonderful mother she did not know how to guide me, and I was living in Kansas City. I have the sort of homesickness for Kansas City which Odysseus had for Ithaca, I for my past wretchedness, and Odysseus for his porkers and Penelope. At twenty-two, by the time I had been tutored by want, sorrow, and solitude I had read about all the English translations of the great Russian writers, Tolstoy, Dostoevsky, Pushkin, Goncharov, Andreyev, Gorky, Lermontov, Gogol, and Chekov, along with the French and George Gissing who was the idol of my heart. I refer, in particular, to *By the Ionian Sea* and *The Private Papers of Henry Ryecroft*. I was also immensely shaken by Tolstoy's *What Is Art?* and

* *Because I Was Flesh*

though I had resolved to be an American writer when I was eighteen and lost in the Mojave Desert, I thought that if literature is so decadent, I must not write at all.

When I was twenty-two I went to the University of California at Berkeley when goats browsed near the campus. They were a great comfort to me because they ate all my lecture notes and were able also to digest them. I discovered, much to my amazement, that graduate students considered me a very educated man.

I did two years' graduate work at Columbia University, because I was a kind of job-lot student who refused to follow the dull curriculum.

I did special work in the doctrine of the Logos with Professor Anathon Aall from Oslo, and also studied the *Summa* with a priest, a scholar, at the same university. I had a year's work in Middle English, but can say that I got more out of reading Chaucer myself and studying the glossary. I admire Skeat very much, and also have some real feeling for *Piers Plowman*. I took a B.S. in philosophy and devoted most of my time to the pre-Socratic school, Anaxagoras, Anaximenes, and Heraclitus. From Empedocles I learned one thing that has never departed from my nature: "The blood around the heart is the thought of men."

I taught high school for one year, and with my savings went abroad. I determined to extirpate my brain, that poor, leaky vial, and wrote a harsh naturalistic novel, *Bottom Dogs,* with a Preface by D. H. Lawrence. It was done in a limited edition in England, followed by three trade editions. In America I had a fantastic reception though a wizened audience. Edmund Wilson, whom I do not particularly admire, once said that it was "distinguished but dull." I think it is just dull. After three other novels, one done with drawings by Augustus Peck, I dropped into the pit of Acheron, a long oblivion, and everybody forgot about me. For seven years I worked for Rachel, and after studying our own remarkable colonial annals and the ancients I published *Can These Bones Live,* which may be weak-eyed Leah rather than Rachel. How can I tell since I can only make animal conjectures about everything. Meantime, I had printed a good deal of verse in the small magazines. In *This Quarter,* when it was published by Ethel Moorhead, half of a very thick periodical was devoted to my work. This woman, an Irish feminist, and a devout friend of Ernest Walsh who died of wounds he received in World War I, and who would have ripened greatly, I believe, had brought out the first works of Joyce, Ezra Pound, Kay Boyle, and Ernest Hemingway.

In 1950 our remarkable friend James Laughlin bought the English sheets of *The Flea of Sodom,* done with a Foreword by Sir Herbert Read. He had also written an Introduction to the English edition of *Can These Bones Live* seven years after it was printed by Harcourt, Brace. My last book, as you know, was *The Sorrows of Priapus.* I just received a letter from Allen Tate whom I have never met who says that I am "unique in our time." I hope so.

This is not brief, and please forgive me for prattling; even Democritus of Abdera was a gabbler.

I also taught at Hunter College for awhile, and at New York University. Young, callow, and inflammatory (now I'm just callow and inflamed), I went to a faculty meeting, and not hearing one learned or good remark I made the mistake of saying: "Why, this is a capitulation to football culture." However, in 1950 I was asked to be a Visiting Lecturer in the summer session, giving talks on American Literature, and never touching that abominable carcass which is sometimes called a textbook. I was also a humble academic charwoman at Brooklyn Polytechnic College for over three years, where I gave courses in composition and in the *inhumanities.* I am a zealot and did all within my abilities to teach, that is, to talk lucidly and truthfully, and often with a good deal of success. There was also a year spent at Boston University, where I taught writing (an oxymoron) and gave other courses. I was, I believe, the most talked-about man there, very popular among the sensitive students, but the bête noire to the bursar and the sundry deans. The truth is that I never did anything scandalous except to tell the truth. They even asked me to return, but refused to give me any sort of advancement, so I declined.

I have human fervor, and whenever I meet anybody I do all I can to drive him to a sage book.

Please forgive all these heterodoxies. I am not trying to be clever, but all the gall and hyssop of my past seems a little droll to me.

Be sure of my immense appreciation of your identity and your large heart.

This may not be a shrewd letter. I have always said that one is either noble or shrewd.

I also happen to admire you greatly. Laughlin says that the most waspish people he knows are those for whom he feels the most genuine friendship, Ezra Pound, himself, and me. You could add Socrates since he is our contemporary.

My deepest thanks and warm-hearted esteem.

New York
November 5, 1958

Dear Mr. Hutchins:

It was deeply good to see you though I have abundant misgivings about talking to a Human Being in an office. America has become the Office by the grace of the Bank. I am an irascible and vehement man, and I ask your pardon for these faults. Matthew Arnold has said: "Righteousness was to the Jew what strength and beauty were to the Greek, or fortitude to the Romans."

I have read several of the booklets printed by the Fund for the Republic but find they are done in a phlegmatic and almost lifeless prose. A writer should employ a language that can pierce the heart or awaken the mind. Style ought to have some kinship with mountains, seas, glens, orchards, furrows, if it is to have a symbolic and human value. I find our academic factory vocabulary repulsive because it is exsanguious. A melancholy author can lift up the spirit of man solely because he knows how to write well. For myself, one line in Luke or Isaiah has far more importance than a thousand chapbooks on statistics.

It is not my intention to give anybody an affront, and I see no reason to mention the names of the authors who composed these booklets. I am sure they have moral natures, and if there are no

organs, hands, feet, eyes, or Heaven or Tartarus in their style it is
that they are the prey of American education. We imagine that a
scientist must use a barbaric diction, or that an economist cannot
appeal to a reader unless he uses the stale professorial jargon. I
have only one trade, and that is to try to be Human, Ecce Homo,
and to talk to other people as flesh speaks to flesh, as worm
touches worm.

I cite some of the phrases, quite typical of all of them, which
weaken the soul and send all human hopes to Erebus: "The cycle
of shift from individual possessory holdings," "governmental or
quasi-governmental purposes," "this unbalance is about to be
redressed," "the 'passive-receptive' column of our diagram,"
" 'chewing up' control of those corporations," "Sears Roebuck is
socializing itself via its own pension trust fund," "the last vestige
of his power to legitimate a management by a vote," "possessory
private property in this area has been metamorphosed," "power
pyramid," "management pyramid," "some misrepresentation or
falsification on their Personal Security Questionnaires," "at the
levels thought necessary without compulsion of the draft," "to
keep down the ominously-rising 'manpower pool,' " "trained reserve personnel," "a 'control factor' over the manpower pool."

Now each booklet is the same and written in a dingy, soulless
style. There is no energy or intellectual affection in such prose,
and I do not think that anyone is going to be persuaded in such
impoverished and corpse-like words. We have forsaken ritual,
custom, symbol, by which we have disemboweled our thoughts,
and expect, somehow, to nourish another man and even make his
pulses tremble when we write as though we had no bowels ourselves.

There has to be love in a book if it is to be useful to society.
"Affection is the energy of society," says Aristotle. And there also
has to be people or a strong and pungent sense of them in words
which we employ to persuade others. I find, however, the academic vocabulary is as peopleless as our commonwealth. You
have walked along the streets of our modern cement towns, and
seen nothing but houses with shades drawn, and gazed with a
desponding wonder at our machine-made buildings and synthetic and fraudulent colonial dwellings. No one sits on the porch,

which has vanished from our lives, and where American families sat in the dusk or in cool Indian summer evenings. Now you see no one, nothing but a few miserable tin cars squatting next to the curbstone.

I observed, as I told you, Mr. Hutchins, that among your people who counsel you, and with whom you discuss our tragic American dilemma, there was not one poet, essayist, or imaginative intellect. Have we forgotten the effect of Tolstoy, Gorky, and Gogol on the Russian people? Is it not odd that you, our most eminent American educator, who said, and with so much truthfulness, that the greatest occidental Buddha for a student was a wise book, has not one good book-man near you? Why does such a man who fought so valorously, and as an impossibilist, for the reading of Great Books, absolutely shun the writer? Is there the insidious or sleeping belief that a poet or novelist cannot write well and reasonably about trade unions, the usurious corporation, liberty, defense, and war, though Tolstoy, Ruskin, William Morris, Herzen, Kropotkin, Saint-Simon, Luke, and the Hebrew prophets have done this with far deeper feeling than ten thousand drab chapbooks on human tragedy, whether it be penury, or our false gods of comfort, pragmatic and stomach convenience, and cupidity.

Randolph Bourne, a humpback, whose life in some ways resembles Kierkegaard's, who also had a mishap in body, wrote the bravest essay against the state that I have ever read. He was the son of a New Jersey clergyman, and a tender legend in my soul since I was a young man. I know of nothing so piercing save Tolstoy's *Patriotism and Slavery* or Kropotkin's *Fields, Factories and Workshops*. Alas, Bourne was dead at thirty-two, long before he had time to ripen his identity, and to come to that "transvaluation of values," which he and we so urgently need. I wrote at least four essays on Bourne, hoping that his books would be republished. Finally, someone did, but the essay on the state was not included. We fear to print what Jefferson and Franklin once felt and wrote, and his book was no more inflammatory or prophetic than Thoreau's "Civil Disobedience" or Turgenev's *The Diary of a Sportsman*. These men were not legalists, statisticians, economists. They had pitying flesh. My bowels, my bowels, cries Isaiah.

As you know, Jefferson and Franklin gathered all their knowledge about a tender commonwealth from the French physiocrats.
Jean Jacques Rousseau was their demigod. Both of these men
recorded their fears—both knew well enough that the curse of a
people is trade, and they longed for an agrarian civilization, in
simple, bucolic words. In a sense they were Vergilian economists.

I remember how deeply affected I was by reading *The Note-
book* of Sherwood Anderson; one small phrase, deeply imagined,
opened my eyes and gave me the strength to see; he wrote of the
cruel rubber-and-iron towns, Akron and Youngstown, Ohio.

There has never been an organic connection between the poet
and the state in America. While Moby-Dick was feeding on
pelagic grass in the Pacific the other Leviathan at Washington
was devouring the populace, and the two great Whales never had
any commerce with one another.

I do not doubt that these men are idealists, but what we need
today are men with "windmills in their brains." Besides, there
are no ideals which are not translated into the most valorous,
Quixotic conceptions. As Herzen says: "There are few nervous
disorders more recalcitrant than idealism. Idealists are cowards
about facing the truth." Herzen does not mean that such men
lack personal courage, but that they lack absolute intellectual
vision. "Audacity, more audacity, always audacity," cried Danton.

I know you are not afraid to fail, and these are the only people
I deeply care for, and who I believe will bring love and understanding to our great and lost people. Once Sherwood Anderson
said, leaving business and dollars behind him to be a man of
compassion in America: "Now I am going out to walk on the
bedrock of a stream." Thoreau in a more truculent vein once
remarked: "I want to get the Concord, the Merrimac, the Massachusetts out of my head so that I can be sane a part of each
day."

Can we change the American by giving him new laws or refur-
bishing the old ones? Will one more statute alter his habits or
quiet his nature, make him more pensive or loving? Who can
know the laws we already have? Go into a courtroom, as I said to
you, Mr. Hutchins, and will you hear the words, bread, want,
and suffering mentioned? There are so many laws that only a

sottish man with a brutal intellect or memory could even remember a moiety of them. There are probably all the ordinances or tenets anybody requires to be found in the Four Gospels, in the Sibylline Books, or in the fragments left us by Pythagoras. It is enough to know the Rig-Veda to comprehend that we must not injure those who are already hurt, and to care for others. In our colonial period almost any American farmer, cordwainer, or mechanic was a close reader of the Bible and Shakespeare. We then had remarkable craftsmen, just prices, and stable habits, without which any commonalty is insane.

What is the source of our national suffering? The other side of our indifference to others, street and store insolence, our lumpish apathy. What is underneath this American numbness, but anguish because we do not know what to do with our lives, our time, or our wages. We have the least regard for our women, and they, utterly perverted, have become hard and despotic and arrogant. We are today a wounded, lost people. We leaped from the wilderness and the frontier, which gave us moral sinews and fearless men, into a decadence without ever having attained a human civilization that is sane, civil, and moral. Look no longer at the pages of Suetonius for Domitian, or at Herodian for the depravities of Heliogabalus, but simply walk through our immense macadam meadows or saunter down Eighth Street about midnight when every hall is occupied by a male prostitute. Mary Magdalene is dear to me, and William Carlos Williams has referred to the Virgin Mary as that glorious whore. Tolstoy remarked that the poor and the prostitute we will always have with us, but he was not alluding to men who sold themselves to men, and are the symptoms of a crepuscular and dying country.

How are we to survive television, more horrible and pernicious to the nervous system than the Salem witch trials? Who is going to give us an antiseptic newspaper? The newspaper is the ten plagues in Egypt, and how are we going to avoid this Stygian infection? What moral vaccine is there against our tabloids which have become one of the principal pastimes in the United States? The television, radio, cinema, and the newspaper have taken the place of a communal life. Our isolation from one another, the national tragedy of separation, has given us a malady far worse than disease, earthquakes, floods, or wars. We are afraid to touch anybody because he might be diseased or homosexual. Go into one of those vast sepulchral markets, where people hardly talk to one another, and where self-service prevails, and you quit it more wormy than Lazarus. After one has bought canned peas, or pallid, storage carrots wrapped in cellophane as the dead Pharaohs were garmented in papyri, you go to the cashier. Often a sour, wordless man or woman drops the coins into the palm of your hand so as not to touch it. But unless we exchange human germs, or otherwise we dare not kiss our mother, father, or wife, we will expire, diseased and cankered, in absolute solitude. Why do we have self-service? The answer is very simple: because no one wants to serve anybody nowadays except himself. We are getting a spurious folklore from trade, cupidity, and all the wretched shibboleths of the cartel and the savings bank. In the *Cyclopes,* or the fragment of it that is still extant, Euripides tells us that the worst sin of that anthropophagous monster is that he labors for himself alone. Cicero once asserted, "We are not born for ourselves alone."

Had we heeded Ruskin or the Luddites we would do all in our power to struggle against man's implacable enemies, new inventions and novelty. When everything is changed every week or month the whole nation is unstable, and the people become testy and hysterical. Greed does its vile work with the greatest efficacy when change is the basis of everything in the commonwealth. Change is the revenue of the cartel but the infamy and the degradation of the people. New prices every other day, different fashions in raiment, bizarre shirts, jackets and skirts destroy national remembrance. For who can remember what he paid for a pound of peas last month, or know whether he is a parcel of synthetic, homogeneous society, when he wears what is old-fashioned or when his speech, culled from Shakespeare, Skelton, Donne, and Samuel Daniel, is a cause for a smirk from a street-urchin. The street-Arab is as likely to be a professor of American Literature in one of our colleges as he is to be a rough boy in our economic ghettos. The late Alfred Stieglitz said: "A lustrum is now equivalent to a generation."

We must not be idealistic but perceptive; Dreiser had already

thought that America was a hopeless country. Are there remedies
for our ills and our inertia? What is base is to do nothing, and
what is mischievous is not to attack the windmills of our own
century. Herzen has written: ". . . looking idly on while people,
convulsed by some general madness, run amok and destroy each
other in frenzy, while an entire civilization, a whole world, is
collapsing, amidst chaos and ruin—that is beyond human
powers. There is nothing to be done about Vesuvius, but in the
world of history man is at home; he is not only a spectator but an
actor. . . ."

The Americans are not familiar with their own epical annals.
They do not know their own authors, and how—without a
knowledge of our colonial beginnings when we were strong and
had stout moral principles, and with no acquaintance with the
writings of our demigods, and the valiant deeds of those who
were the fathers of the American Conscience—can we revivify the
populace? The Miracle Players in Medieval England went from
town to town reciting the tribulations of the Apostles, the woe of
Abraham when he was making ready to kill his son Isaac. This
was a kind of intellectual guerrilla warfare, engaged for the weal
of the people. This same kind of democratic Passion Play must be
re-enacted throughout all the states to awaken the people. The
populace must know the wisdom of Thoreau, Melville, Veblen,
Debs, Emily Dickinson, Emma Goldman, Bourne, Benjamin R.
Tucker. We waste our entire national wealth so long as our new
world heroes remain unknown to the American. The life of that
Nazarene socialist, Eugene Debs, could be done as a one-act
Miracle or Chester Play. Bourne too is legendary drama that
must no longer be hidden. Thoreau's wondrous pilgrimage
would hearten many, and even be a guide for our wayward apprentices in letters. What we need is some kind of playhouse in
which the lives of Thomas Jefferson, Daniel Boone, and Andrew
Jackson could be portrayed. Chapbooks, too, containing the
record of their mythic lives should be available to the nation. For
we must remember that the culture of the state has never been
the civilization of the people. But this should be a portable playhouse or theater which can be taken into the streets of all towns
and cities.

What didactic poetry is there in the knowledge that Jefferson shuffled about in a frayed dressing gown and rotten slippers in his heavily mortgaged house at Monticello. Was Jason or Odysseus any braver or more truthful than Andrew Jackson who left the White House with ninety dollars in his wallet, half of which he gave to his foster son so that he could pick his cotton? A few pages out of *In the American Grain*, by William Carlos Williams, could quicken the multitude and give them rebirth which cannot be done by countless pamphlets dealing with statistics. There is an enormous tragedy too in the annals of the American Trade Union Movement. Give the people the Living Tragedy, and not dead statistics, if you are to restore their faith and a longing for an Iliad or a destiny. What good are new or old laws, bad or better ones, so long as the populace have no historical aims or beliefs in the destiny of the American nation? The life and the image are of far greater worth to a commonwealth than any amount of corpse-like facts no matter how true they are. Christ can heal the lame, the palsied and the blind, but the legalist, the accountant, and the economist cannot. Politics is what do you have to pay for a pig or a bag of grain. You have read how many books on the Reconstruction period; what the churls in Congress said was insipid, for the history was being written on the soil, the plantation, and in the mills. What is most important is where the Negro slept, in a stable, or upon the furrow, or in a ditch; how much a loaf of bread cost him, and whether it was mealy, sour, and corrupt; what did he pay for shoes, or had he any, and did he have a shirt to shelter his beaten and houseless back.

No, it is not new laws that will bring about the revivification of man, but values and ethics that are kindred to valleys, peaks, brooks, the family table and the marriage bed.

There is no legal approach to man, only a human one, and only pulsing flesh can relieve people who are harmed, harried, and enslaved. The beggars and the Ishmaels understand best the hurts of the heart. We have to teach the American to understand suffering, and even to suffer; surfeit dries up the veins and the hams. What the American must do is to disburden himself of the terrible plethora of commodities he does not require for his life or fate. The late Eric Gill said: "God bless indigence." The ideal of Sparta was neither wealth nor poverty. The greatest temptation in our mechanical wilderness is to buy what one does not need. Spending, like waste, is the recreation of the people.

Though you are Anglo-Saxon, and my own parents were European, I do not regard you as an alien! We are all immigrants, striving hysterically to be a synthetic nation. We will be in time. When Aeneas came to ancient Latium he brought with him the Palladium, Pallas Athene, which is Wisdom, the whole heritage of Troy. We too must honor the old gods of Europe if we are to have our own. Not by a humbug parochialism will we come into an American culture. Someday we will have an indigenous civilization, but we can't invent one. Homer sang the customs, the wars, and the loves of the Greeks, and probably did not invent a single piece of history. Ilium, Ithaca, sandy Pylos and Agamemnon were there. He was the pure vessel of two thousand years of hymns, feelings, proverbs, and meditations. When Sir Herbert Read went to Greece many years ago he sent me two clymenes he plucked from the tomb of Agamemnon, and from that time on I began to understand the *Iliad*.

We must teach the American to be quiet. All the troubles of man come from his inability to remain in one room, said Pascal. It is so rare to find a person in his own apartment that I wonder why he allows his landlord to fleece him because he's paying rent for rooms he hardly occupies.

I appreciate your most kind offer to let me do a booklet. I should do all that I could to write a good one, for there is no decency in impugning what you think is bad unless you can do it better.

I should like to write about America as an American author; to do some kind of memoir on my own feelings about our homeland. I prefer, of course, a strong negation to a weak or myopic affirmation. "We destroy one sanctuary in order to create another," said Nietzsche.

I have a very genuine regard for you; I think you know that. We really perceive more as animals than we do when we imagine we are thinking.

It may be that your next step should be politics. I have every belief in you, and what would give me the deepest pleasure is to see Robert M. Hutchins as the President of the United States.

We have two depraved political parties, and there must be a new one, not one organized by our dinner-pail trade unions; wages without vision or, I should say, more earnings without Golgotha or Truth is wicked. We have a police cartel, a police university, and in some sub rosa and insidious sense a police literature, all of which comes from cupidity and the ferocious cult of sameness.

You have my copious gratitude, and my affectionate esteem.

I earnestly pray that I can see you outside the office. I walk through the doors of our modern sleek offices as though I were entering the jaws of Cerberus.

New York
December 2, 1958

Dear Mr. Hutchins:

I wrote to you yesterday, and I am still very troubled about our conversation. I wish, also, to add another name to the list of authors I think would be of use to you. There is Mr. Jack Jones who did a long essay showing how dadaism and communism have brought about nihilism today. Some of it is exceedingly well written; but he too at times submits to the cowardly jargon of our times. Though I reproved him very strongly for this, I at once sent it to Sir Herbert Read, who also finds some very fine thinking in it. I believe, myself, that Marxism has set back literature in America and throughout the world at least a century. However, I have been influenced by Mr. Jones' conceptions. It is his resolve to eradicate Marxist shibboleths. I wish you would, please, mention him to Mr. Ferry, along with the other names I have suggested.

I am deeply sorry that I offended you because I think you should occupy humble quarters. In London as well as in New England the old clapboard houses were used for business, and that made barter or trade far more civil and easy. Seneca once said: "I have not yet come into my own frugality."

But have we forgotten the lessons of *Walden*? Was Thoreau

less of a Christian than you? You know what a remarkable impression Benjamin Franklin made upon the French when he went there in a homely, democratic garb. Nothing so nauseates me as a Soviet ambassador, surrounded by bodyguards, and living at the Waldorf Astoria. Nothing is too good for the proletariat, say these liars. But there are many things that are too good for people.

Can you redeem everybody? Could Jesus heal Iscariot or the rich man who went away because he desired to keep his possessions? Is Saint Paul, who believed that there were men who were depraved by nature, less of a Christian than you? Jesus says that a camel will sooner pass through the eye of a needle than a rich man go to heaven. A very misanthropic remark! But was Christ unchristian?

When the people of Verona saw Dante they used to say: . . . there is the man that was in Hell.

You say that you are content with yourself, and pardon me, I feel that is not a Christian sentiment. Whatever it is I imagine I know, but may not know, has come through suffering. The only real thoughts are the suffering ones. It was Heine who said that every time a man thought it was Golgotha.

Pascal, I think the greatest of all Christian thinkers, was in great despair about the human race. What woe there was in his, "Man is malicious," and in "No man fears himself enough." We often mistake acerbity for hatred or a hardness of heart, without pondering the weight of human sin there is in not perceiving man as he is, though you toil all the days of your life to mend him. I cite Carlyle: "What a paltry notion is that of his *Divine Comedy's* being a poor splenetic impotent terrestrial libel; putting those into Hell whom he could be avenged upon on earth. I suppose if ever pity, tender as a mother's, was in the heart of any man, it was in Dante's."

The Four Gospels are just as good for our republic as they were for ancient Israel. When I see a pope in monarchic garb I faint in the wilderness.

There are many ways of being a Jew, too. The purest Hebraic poem to come into the world was *Rejoice in the Lamb* written by a wondrous Christian scribe, Christopher Smart.

Mr. Ferry infers, or so I think, that maybe good style cannot be conveyed to people; God knows, he has ample proof for his remark. But is it true that we must write badly to communicate with others? When I say badly, I do not mean a simple, plain grammar. How complicated is *Moby-Dick*, much of it done in a species of Elizabethan blank verse, and now read by hundreds of thousands, or *Walden* itself. These men were in limbo when they lived, but I confess I do not quite know how the Word who is flesh is scorned, but the author who is a corpse is not.

I have suggested that American publishers do not know how to reach Americans. It is true that when Huebsch, Liveright, the Boni brothers, Thomas Seltzer, and at least seven to eight other true and good men had little money themselves, they had far better taste, and also that they did not sell fewer volumes than they do now, when publishing is only done in an expensive, recherché manner. More money goes into maintaining opulent offices than into the printing and making of a book. They have killed the culture of the land, for they are Houses of Mammon, and should be overturned no less than the tables of the money-changers that were in the Temple.

In short, when publishers had little money, they sold more truthful books than Plutus, the big business publisher today.

It may be that you have a more intelligent way of distributing pamphlets than the book merchants do, and I don't doubt that at all.

Since publishing became luxurious see what has happened to bookshops. They are infamous greeting-card stores, littered with trash. The only decent and civilized people left in the book business are those who have shambly stores on Fourth Avenue. Do I want La Rochefoucauld, Saint-Simon, La Bruyère or Dio, and I am being literal, I have to go to used-book dealers. Should I desire to procure Strabo or the elder Pliny or Alexander von Humboldt, do you imagine I should have the least luck in buying these on Fifth Avenue? Suppose I desire Whiston's translation of *Jewish Antiquities* by Josephus, where do I get it, in a meretricious book house which looks more like a Greyhound bus—or in the shabby stalls on Fourth Avenue? I found a rare Guerrera, a fifteenth-century Spanish monk who did some mar-

velous chapters on Heliogabalus and Otho, in an immense loft
glutted with all sorts of volumes that would entice a fevered
brain. You can't even get literary staples in the new, gimcrack
bookshops, Ruskin, Burton, Coleridge's *Letters, Sartor Resartus,*
the *City of God* by St. Augustine.

When we spoke about colleges and renowned and truthful
work that was done there I had no intention of not giving you all
honor and respect for what you had done. At the moment, in a
desponding mood, I was considering American education today,
nor would I speak dishonorably of the work your brother has
done. I was ignorant of it, that was all.

You think I am unjust when I say that the booklets are written
in a jargon that is not dissimilar from that employed in our
universities. But I beg you to recall some of the citations I had
made in one letter to you. The educated vernacular is unmistak-
able. You assert that you are successful in getting these chapbooks into the hands of many people. May I not in the like
manner suggest that millions of people go to colleges and read
more or less the same intellectual patois. We have a vast public
for pulp, or for comic strips, as Mr. Ferry said. What does it
prove? And how are we to revivify the people? Can we by disgrac-
ing the herd mind, the academic herd mind or any other, it does
not matter, give them the simple ointments of human grace?
What you think you achieve by compromise you lose. Marx said
that ideal was a bourgeois word; such a remark offends my whole
trembling being.

I only make these comments with some forlorn hope that you
might just a little heed me, and not to be unsavory. Since I have
nothing but gratitude toward you, and can only alienate you by
trying to be as truthful as I know how, I beg you not to be vexed
with me. You may even be indifferent to me. Remember, please,
you have great influence in the world, and I have none. Helpless
myself, I can only help the maimed, the palsied, and the blind
who come to me, and many do, and unchristian as I am, I have
scurried through the streets to get lucre for people that I could
not secure myself. Writers ask me to sponsor them for Guggenheim awards which I was never able to secure. A fine Scotsman,
thirty-three, educated at Glasgow, who has a wife and a newborn

son, came the other evening, and I felt utterly mean and vile because I had not the money in my pocket to offer him. But I am doing my best to get money for him through some organization that would not do a thing for me. Am I generous; no, whatever virtues I have come from a nervous disorder, and perhaps, great solitude.

This is probably a bad letter, but I cannot say anything better and doubtless I should never have spoken at all. Simonides said that he often repented it when he spoke but never when he had not.

As always, my affectionate esteem.

letters to
Michael Sands

Dearest Michael,

It had been my intention to write you long before this; but I remained so briefly in one place that I really had neither the space of time nor the table for a letter.

I had a good weekend with Richard Aldington and his wife in Washington, D.C.; he read some memorable passages out of his *Memoirs,* to be published in January, on Ford Madox Ford, Lawrence, Norman Lawrence; he wanted me to remain longer, but they had rather compressed living quarters in a hotel there, and I felt it would be a burden to do so. I was in Chapel Hill with Paul Green, the playwright, and a number of professors and their wives; they arranged an evening for me, and I did most of the parrying and talking, and it was very gay. Then I moved on to New Orleans, again by bus. But what had formerly seemed so fragrant and mellowing in the old French Creole quarter now was debris and human offal. I really did not bother to look up anybody; but got into a bus, and for three continuous days and nights traveled and ate arid American miles until I got out to Los Angeles, weary, done in, and yet not nerve-spun as I had been in New York. I have seen a good many people here already; been taken out. Had a pleasant Christmas dinner with a scenario writer and his wife and some people. Last evening a bookseller who had sold a good many copies of *Bottom Dogs* and *From Flushing to Calvary* took me out.

I may go up to the ocean and the dunes to thaw out on the beach in sun, brine, and soft blowing air; I have no plans, but am leading an easy vegetable existence, not thinking of anything,

talking to people, amusing them when I can, and being enter-
tained as much as possible. I should have galleys of the book* in
about two weeks now; that will be a delight; for I have waited
long for this.

I got a hasty note from our beloved mother; that was forwarded to me from New Orleans.

How long I shall remain out here I do not know; right now I
certainly don't want to hazard the evils and wickedness of the
New York climate; I still have uncomfortable electric pangs in
my shoulders and back, but already the sun, the lucid light, has
eased me, and I hope in the near future that I shall enjoy some
deep blessed health.

Dreiser is out here, and I may yet visit him; it is rather dis-
comfiting for me to do so, in a way, because his books no longer
mean much to me; yet I would be very pleased to see the man
and talk to him.

Well, Michael, I look forward with pleasure to have a line
from you; so soon as you are able, let me hear how you are, what
you are doing, and whether the gods are kind to you, as I deeply
hope they may always be. I send you with this my warm, deep
love,

Your brother,

Northmoor, Mo.
April 12, 1942

Dearest Michael:

Mother is deeply delighted with the furniture; there are three
chairs, the studio couch, the chest of drawers, the table. She has
been living here with such trashy things; I have told her that she
must cease living for the property, and live for her life. And she
is very contented having me here, and hoping very much that
you will be able to come when you get a vacation. I can say
emphatically that she is eager to sell the houses; she admitted

* *Can These Bones Live*

that years before she had not, but now she despairs of remaining here, alone, any longer. She knows that after the war there will be another fat ruin of land and houses, and so wants to make a sale now, in the next few months.

Now, I must tell you about the plumbing; she has never been able to secure a plumber. She had, however, to pay a hundred and fifty-five dollars for a roof, as the old one was in such deterioration, leaking badly, and she had to have the walls papered, and the three houses painted. I think she told you that for two months the three houses had been vacant, and so with expenses, most necessary for her own convenience, and for sales, and living, since she was deprived of her rentals, she had to use the money you so generously sent her for the plumbing. She did not like to tell you this, Michael, as she did not wish to displease you. And of course I have not had the heart to rebuke her, as I know, really, she was narrowed down to niggard circumstances, when the houses were empty. Besides, I am watching her closely; she takes medicine for her heart, and goes to the doctor for her other ailments, most harrowing burdens for her. Otherwise, she is in a good mood, speaks of you with feeling and tenderness, and is always grateful for your devotion and many gentle kindnesses to her. She would rather have, Michael, a spring coat than a dress, and would like me to go with her to choose one for her. It would be simpler for her to get the size and style she wants right here and there are some very fine department stores in Kansas City.

Now, as to my own plans; I am staying on for a bit longer; will remain here until the end of the month, or nearly so. I want to give her as much pleasure as I can. Of course, as you know, it has been an affliction to me to give Doris pain, but I have had to do this. My life was becoming dingy in New York; I got to have less and less relish for the few people I knew there. As for the writers of the day, those meager and skinny souls, I cared not to see them at all. What I will do, I am not sure; I may if mother should sell the properties want to return, and get a little house for ourselves, you, mother, and I an hour and a half or so from New York; or should I plan to live on the Coast, we might find something there, and perhaps you could secure a transfer. But we will do nothing without first talking it over with you, to see how you feel and what you wish to do. But these are uncertainties, and yet soon they may not be, so we must resolve them, or at least know that they are in our lives.

I am working on my notes each morning; go out little, even at night; I have no impulse to see the University of Kansas City blockheads. I read in the Bible a great deal; Job is my instruction and vineyard; Isaiah is my wisdom and weariness; Ecclesiastes, the solace of my vexed spirit, which I can pour out alone better than in company.

We will continue to make the effort to do something with our lives, while ripeness is yet here, and when I say this, I am thinking of you, of mother, and of me.

Mother embraces and kisses you; give my affection to Minnie, and take for yourself my devoted love and many thoughts for your own consolation and life.

Your brother,

Northmoor, Mo.
July 26, 1942

Dearest Michael,

This is a tardy thanks for the gracious gift you and Minnie gave me for my birthday; but full thanks to both of you for it. I have been busy unto weariness. I arrived in Northmoor just to find poor mother in a most hapless condition. She had fallen again, sprained her thumb, arm, shoulder, back, and had scarcely eaten food for three days, she was so helpless. I have been lackey, hospital orderly, cook, janitor since. Cleaning up the house has been an ordeal. After all these years I decided to take mother's fate, and her engine of will, a relentless, sorcerer's volition, into my own hands, and to cast out the rags, litter, scum of a genera-tion, and put it in the fire of Gomorrah. I had bought her a lovely mirror hand-wrought in Santa Fe, a Chimayo purse, more rugs, Mexican glassware and pitchers. By the way, I sent you another Navajo, quite a little larger than the previous ones, which I hope will fill your apartment, bedeck it in the gay man-

ner I hope you two will make it. I trust that neither of you will
go out and buy trashy new sets of furniture, supported as they
generally are on those heavy legs which remind you of the vari-
cose bourgeoisie. Look, if you will take my counsel in this, at the
small antique shops, for early American pieces, a chair here, a
table there, nothing uniformly demented and of an insane sameness. Know that your rooms will be a faultless painting of your
own spirits, too often a libel and a curse.

I also went out and got a gas range for mother; she has been
cooking on a kerosene stove, which when it does not explode,
does not burn either, except the food. And she has had new
linoleum put on the floor of the kitchen, and I have thrown out
into the heap old chairs, the nails of which perforated and punc-
tured two pairs of pants of mine.

Besides all this, and I am done in by night, I write in the
mornings, playing on the machine, lovely, lovely Beethoven's
Sonata in F Major, or Mozart's 40, or the Bach Concerto. You
see, I made a little coup for myself in Los Angeles. For years,
twelve or more, a batch of D. H. Lawrence letters, written to me,
were lying in a drawer, and of no use, and no sentiment to me;
they were doleful reminders of callow, ugly days, *Bottom Dogs*,
and so on; anyway, I sold them for one hundred and fifty dollars,
a great help to me.

Taos was fragrant with hay, cows, clover, but the pressure of
the altitude at this moment was too much, and it is enough of a
task, heaven and hell's to write a novel, without combating
mountains and windmills as Don Quixote ever does. So I came
here, luckily for mother, as she was, to repeat, in a poor state of
flesh and health.

I will stay on till mother repairs herself; then may go on to the
Ozarks, always going where I can write, and I can write anywhere, and in any season, but give me not too much havoc or
abuse.

I write to nobody these days, save you.

Tell me, whether you and Minnie got the rug, and how it
pleases you. You know, so many of the Navajos just like all other
manual arts are done in the conventional patterns, and I have
made a particular effort to find what is gay and mirthful, not

usual. If you are not using your Navajos now, have Minnie
sprinkle them heavily with moth flakes, then wrap them in newspapers, tie them, and around that bundle wrapping paper, and
tie securely, so that they will not be eaten up by pests, moths.

I think of you often, and always with love. My full, warm
devotion to you and Minnie.

Your brother,

letters to
Steven Sands

Dear Steve:

I am hastening to reply to your letter since you are leaving on the sixth of September. Should you come to Soller, I am enclosing directions; otherwise, you will have much difficulty in finding me. The address you have is a post office box. I live about two kilometers from the town.

Education is very bad everywhere; Oxford is no better than a provincial backwater college in Iowa or elsewhere. A professor is a man who has suffered from academic senility for at least forty years. What choice have you? Not much. I think I told you a university diploma is a trade degree. What can you do with a B.A.? Nothing. You'll need a Ph.D. in order to get a job at a college. I should counsel you to do that as soon as possible; otherwise, by the time you are thirty-five or so, you will be regarded as a man in your dotage. I can say that I have been old all my life, and it was always well-nigh difficult for me to get work. Being a writer is to be permanently unemployed. Oh yes, I have been an economic slave of literature, but the rewards are niggish and dispiriting. Now, I am not telling you this to dishearten you; but it is far better to see than to pretend.

The truth is you can be lost at any age; you are twenty. About a year or so ago I received a letter from a chairman of the French department of a Southern university. He sent me a book of sonnets he had published, but never thought I should bother to reply. Of course, I did, and I hope I have been useful to him. Indeed, I have tried, and shall do the same for you.

Most of the people, in fact all of them you mention who are

professors at Columbia, I have never heard of; history, like everything else, is a rapid-transit course, not a study. The teachers
themselves have the scantiest knowledge of the subject they are
endeavoring to convey to the students.

But let us return to the point: should you desire to be a writer,
you will have to teach; otherwise you will be a very hungry man,
and an ailing one, like myself.

I think you are doing what is absolutely right, in endeavoring
to be as close to your father, Michael, as you can. This is the
century of nihilism, when the son rejects the father, and that is
very wicked.

Another matter: a truthful writer neither tries to be simple or
difficult. You have an unknown audience, and your only concern
and passion is to be honest in good, just words.

When you return to New York you can, if you want to, meet
two or three of my friends. There is Abby Schwartz, the artist,
but not abstract. I hate abstract painters, homosexuality, and
idiocy. Josephine Herbst, who has been a close friend and admirer of my work, and a remarkable author herself, you might
find extremely interesting. She is robustious and without affectation. Her struggle for lucre in this devilish world has been hideous. She did a marvelous book on Bartram, the eighteenth-
century American naturalist.

Meantime, I shall look forward to seeing you; it is very hard to
entertain another person, or to give him good advice.

Your uncle,

Soller de Mallorca
November 29, 1963

Dear Steve:

You had not heard from me because I had a severe attack of
influenza. A day before I fell ill I wrote to your mother and only
yesterday managed to get off a reply to your father, Michael.

Your perplexities are great, and difficult to heal, impossible.
To be a human being you have to die not once but seven times a

day. You said you had to read Camus and Sartre; but remember every six months or so a new genius will be announced in the tuppenny press, and you will have to read that. If you read all the trash that is published, according to Thoreau, you won't have time for the good books. Now, I gave you an unusual list for your study; take my counsel: get them as quickly as possible, and the more good volumes you get into your belly, the less your torment will be. I don't expect you to become phlegmatic, sure of yourself. Only your doubts can save you from becoming a Philister.

One other matter: when you commenced to correspond with me you were anxious to relate yourself to me as my nephew; now I notice that you have dropped that, imagining that if you call my brother Michael or his brother Edward that that brings you closer to him or to me. It does not. All that is a parcel of our creed of vulgarity. You can still address me as Uncle Edward and I will not be writing you stuffy letters because of that or adopt a congealed and fossil style toward you. You've got to be connected with somebody, not unnaturally, but by affection and values.

Don't give up your room unless you are absolutely certain that you can find other quarters that are more suitable. You can locate a virgin nowadays more easily than a good room in Paris. Be sure to give me Helion's address, his full name, so that I can write and thank him for being so kind to my nephew.

Your education is another matter of great moment; I told you when you were here that no matter where you went by the time you got your doctorate you would be senile and a total ignoramus. Of course, you can't take that kind of curriculum in history; you would be crazy in a few months, and I should have betrayed instead of helping you.

Dear Steve, this morning I have so many letters to reply to, so that you must forgive me if this appears a little meager. But along with this goes my love and Julia's warm regards.

See what happens to your application at Oxford. My own papers, letters, and notes are in sundry American university libraries, and I could write to people in America for you, but you would still be taking rapid-transit courses in the inhumanities.

Write whenever you wish to, and don't imagine that I am
indifferent or not completely aware of your woe. Remember that
I do not know the answers to the thousand miseries of mankind,
but that I have some experience with them, and all that I can do
is to convey that to you, and you can then take it for what it is
worth.

One more piece of advice if that does not sound pompous:
don't read to win an argument, no real person ever won anything
in this world; don't read to be au courant; study a book, eat it as
one of the Hebrew Prophets says, like honey, so that it may
moisten your bowels and your mind.

Soller de Mallorca
January 2, 1964

Dear Steve:

I am very glad that you have found more suitable quarters;
what you say in your letter is very good. When you can read
Villon in French I shall indeed be very proud of you, and go
about saying that you are my nephew and how lucky and honored I am. Learn French, and then Greek or Latin. I learned
several languages including English, and it all came to nothing,
which is the result of modern education. Each time I want to
compose a sentence I have to see how Chaucer or Sir Walter
Raleigh said it; otherwise I am in a hopeless situation.

Be sure, please, to give Jean Helion my affections, and tell him
how much I should like to see and admire his work. But Paris is
too expensive for me. Could I find an apartment where I could
cook, and if the rent were not thievish, I should go there for
several months with Julia. But I have to remain here, and prices
are soaring every day in Mallorca. The only cheap dwelling place
is Hades, but I am doing my best not to take up quarters there at
this time. I am quite patient in this respect and willing to wait.

My two books* should be published in February. Don't think I

---

* *Because I Was Flesh* and *Alms for Oblivion*

am going to be such a simpleton and send you the books, and
consider myself fortunate if you tell me they arrived and that the
day in Paris is wet, and that you have lost a button from your
shirt. I once gave you a book, and as the Mallorquin says, it was
por la basura. Recently I got a letter from my literary agent in
London, and he said he never praised an author. I told him not
to worry too much about laureling a writer, and that even if he
gave a poet or an essayist an encomium it would not hurt the
latter's feelings. But people are so devious; this man is the literary executor of D. H. Lawrence, and Lawrence, when I was
twenty-eight told me to get an agent, and not to be the idiot
he had been. I listened to his counsel with the greatest gravity,
got a literary agent, and though I had to place my own book, I
also had to pay him for nothing. So you see, my dear Steve, heed
my advice, but take it at the peril of your own good fortunes.

It is good of you now to admit that you are my nephew, since I
am told that I am a craggy, difficult man; you can keep this a
secret, and not be so indiscreet as to go about and tell people
that we are related. Besides, nobody has a mother, a father, a
cousin, an uncle anymore; all that is done with; let NOTHING
reign, for nothing lives.

You could use my name as a reference, but suppose the letter
falls into the hands of an English pathic, you are undone, and
will never be admitted to any college, and might then get an
education.

As I told you, I don't know where you can be best uneducated;
but read the books, that is good avuncular advice; read, read,
read, and read.

Julia and I came back from Barcelona; I was at the clinic and
the diagnosis is that I have severe anemia, and that is why I did
not reply at once. I had a sweet letter from your mother, and a
very fine sweater from your father and mother. I hope you are
not such a nihilist as to call them Michael and Minnie. Mother
and Father are still savory names, and it dilates the heart of a son
when he says Father or Mother.

So much, my dear Steve, for cantankerous admonition. I liked,
to repeat, your letter very much; if you have a feeling heart to go
with your quick mind, why some day you will write a book and

some scribbler in the *New York Times* will assert that you are
the nephew of Edward Dahlberg, and just a cranky idiot. But
never mind, you are young, whatever that means, for ideas decay
in youth just as quickly as in older people. Meantime, Julia
sends her fond regards and I give you my love, and when you
write again I've got all sorts of advice for you which I never
took.

Soller de Mallorca
January 30, 1964

Dear Steve:

A just commonwealth depends upon the purity of the language of its poets. Of course, there is no justice, and I am speaking of a republic that is not dominated by the rabble. Sir Philip
Sidney makes good reading for you, and so should Edmund
Spenser; both are somewhat tedious, but the language will refine
your soul. Myself, I prefer Sir Walter Raleigh's verse, and
Wyatt's. But I am teased by Sidney, Spenser, and Samuel Daniel.

I am asking my publisher to mail you a copy of *Because I Was
Flesh*. You should know it, for we must try our best to understand our origins; what ancestors howl in our ribs.

Paris is brutal, but where can one go? Rousseau said that after
he had been away from Paris for a fortnight he was as good as
dead to his friends. If you are alone in that city it is hellebore.
The reason that I suggested Alliance Française is that I thought
you might have some feminine companionship. Without a
woman I find any city an inferno of progress.

Sir Herbert is now in America, and I will be writing to him in
a very few days, and see whether he knows some people there.
Those I have met there are homosexuals, narcotics addicts, and
café flâneurs. Or you just encounter poseurs at the Dome or the
Select.

I earnestly pray that you are accepted at Oxford, anything is
better than the army. Should you have trouble, for God's sake
don't return to the States so that you are beyond the talons of

some brach on the draft board. I should not like to see you go so far from me, but I realize what a wretched experience military life would be for you.

Meanwhile, I do nothing, a sordid and mad occupation. I am still between books, and do not know what I shall do next, perhaps a volume of adages à la Rochefoucauld which will bring me a hundred readers, or one on women. Stendhal wrote a marvelous book, not a boudoir essay, called *L'Amour*. You should read it, so that you will make your mistake later rather than now. At twenty you know nothing about women, but you don't realize it; at forty you know nothing about women, but imagine you are not as ignorant as you were; at sixty you have no knowledge of women, and can be enchanted for no more than two or three days. After that it is ennui, two bored people staled together.

Wish, my dear Steve, I could be more useful to you. The tragedy of being alive, or imagining that you are, is that you can do nothing for others, or almost nothing.

letter to

Mrs. Michael Sands

Soller de Mallorca
November 15, '63

Dear Minnie:

I have your kind letter and your generous offer to be of some use to me, but really there is nothing that can be done. Am still stumbling about, as Steve doubtless told you, and some days I seem to mend, and others am in the dumps. Steve spoke to me about David and I at once surmised that his great affliction was feeling. You can't have emotions and prosper in this world. That he has not done very well in school is of no moment; all the boys who went to school with me and were then considered brilliant turned out to be dunderheads.

A letter just arrived from my brother Michael; tell him that I love him and will reply very shortly; I owe Steve an answer also, and will get that off tomorrow. Believe me, I am immensely pleased to be of any advantage to Steve. You can't obtain an education in a university; that is one certitude, and in the course of four years you are not likely to meet one human being. I have been battling the curricula of Caliban that is offered at all universities for many years, and oddly enough I get more attention and notice in the U.S.A. academies than I do in the papers which I also detest. My position in American Letters is incongruous: papers and letters and books of mine are in more colleges than I know; above a week ago I was informed that I was well represented in the Lawrence, Henry Miller, Lawrence Durrell Collection at the University of California at Los Angeles and in other archives there. Letters of mine, many, are in the Alfred Stieglitz Memorial Collection at Yale University, and Texas University gives me enormous amount of regard. What does it all mean? My brother Michael knows that if I had not had a monthly pension I would long ago have died in the gutter. As I told you or Michael, the University of Minnesota is publishing this February a volume of essays, *Alms for Oblivion*, and Oxford Press in England and Unwin in Canada are buying books from them. Myself, I have not received one penny for the book. But don't imagine I am complaining. One French writer said: "If I had my life to live over again I would shoot myself." I totally agree with such a salubrious opinion, but at the same time no matter what the risks were, and they were infernal, I would only be a writer. Making a book, good or bad, is the only cure for any disorders I know.

That brings us back to the other quandary: what should Steve do? I told your quick, intelligent son that what you and Michael were doing for him was marvelous, and I am grateful to hear that he thanked his father many times. And, of course, you. Tell me, how can I tell a young man, who must needs take hard-earned money from his father and mother, to pursue poverty? And to decide to be an author is to resolve to be poor. I thought of a middle way, being no man of compromise myself. It was and is my firm belief that Steve after two years of intense study of French (don't let him make a Cook's Tour of Europe and just squander your money and his life) should return to some university and get his doctorate. Sure, by then God knows what a college will have done to his mind, nature, and ethics; but what choice is there? Most work is odious; if somebody had told me that I had to be a drudge in an office or die of want, I should have preferred the latter alternative. But I cannot so advise my nephew. Assuming that courses in idiocy do not utterly deprave him, he can earn his bread as a professor and at some time or other do an honorable book on some sage of literature. I have gone all the way, but look at the ill health I now have, and if I discovered to you the years of darksome penury I have had even after I was forty, you would wince. Meantime, be sure, I will do my best to counsel him. Will he take my advice? If it is good, probably not, but I will be pertinacious.

I am very glad that both of you enjoy the strength that is needed to keep alive in this earth. Steve said quite proudly that his father is a handsome man, and of course that pleased me very much.

Meantime, you have again my thanks and affections. My one seeing eye still troubles me, and that is alarming. Suppose I cannot in the close future study learned books, I am then good for nothing. But shortly I go to see another eye surgeon in Palma, and if that is a bootless errand, I shall, after recovering my strength, arrange for a sea voyage to Barcelona.

letters to
Herbert Read

Wellfleet, Mass.
June 8, 1948

Dear Herbert:

I thank you very much for your letter and for your book. It is a sweet title; I dream but cannot wear Joseph's robe. I am cast into the pit by varlets who are not even my brethren. The hapless tidings you give me deplete me; for the instant I could lie upon the ground in the Cave of Endor beseeching the ancient crone of Israel to bring up Samuel's form so that I might know my fate. I think you know I do not care for the repulsive lucre reputation of the day, and that I do not hanker after many readers. What if I said to you it is of no matter what happens to a publisher? Am I to repine because Caesar cannot fleece the multitude again? Is it important that we feed Pilate and worry when the money-changers are not prospering? Am I egotistical? I do not believe that is significant either. "What is philosophy?" asks Plotinus who replies, "What matters most." Do you care about the dove-vendors? Are you bowing to the citizens of Gaza? If we are to crop some thyme or verdure or holy grass from the meadows of Amos, in what granary are we to store them? You recall how Schopenhauer once said that after you take out of life literature, art, religion, and philosophy, what is left? The simple answer would be, Routledge or an American garage. Does that mean that I am not grateful to you and to Ragg, especially to you? There is no debt in my spirit to anybody save to those who love. Nothing stands between death and our miserable, sluggish country but human fervor.

As I wrote you a week ago, you go on, my good friend, in your own droll way, lecturing about literature and art, while a man who feels, or as Lear says, speaks feelingly, cannot get his book published. Do you know the Indian in Thoreau who, after offering his baskets for sale to a lawyer who refused them, replied, "What, do you mean to starve me!"

You recall how you asked Richard Aldington to return to England so that human values would not altogether perish. Alas, as we know, it is Richard who has died. But what if he had come back, and given you a little book, a prayer to his Muse, and you would have told him, "My dear Richard, a hundred young men, seven of whom may become poets, visionaries, with Elijah's chariot burning in their hearts, will read this. But what you have is not a mural but a diminutive primitive panel. The size, my dear fellow, is most unfortunate. We live in an age of rush, and people have not got time to read eighty or ninety pages. Will you please send me a book of a thousand pages." O my dear Read, you too deal in wondrous occidental goods; you share the salesman's point of view. Pray, what point of view? What the manslaughterers have not defiled he will pollute. Does any man love the earth; he will murder him. If a man has a pensive countenance, he will rush to Caiphas at once.

No; my dear Herbert, I say you are more at fault because you know and you feel, and you have not got jibing intestines. Call me a carping Jeremiah who goes out into the streets with God's balances weighing the human heart (and I do it with the certainty that man exacts of the Angels and not with the sureness of coarse flesh); I know, if I know anything at all, that my folly and my madness are as they should be. There is no idea, or gall or vinegar or Golgotha or holy frankincense save what one man of spirit can share with another. "I am alone, and they are all together," says Dostoevsky. This is your truth and mine. If we choose any other way we lose the miracle of human spirit and are empty, and how easy it is to be void of the Angels, and when one is prone or, to repeat, emptied one is unclean. That is what I fear most.

If you could get some one, Routledge, or any other publisher to bring out my little book, *The Flea of Sodom,* how good that would be!

I am deeply pleased that you are with your charming family

again. Winifred really regrets that you could not come here.
Were it summer and we could talk about Strabo and Livy while
kelpy Poseidon raked in Zeus' foam, ay, that would have been
Attica and Jerusalem. I keep your clymene and the fond smile in
my soul I have for your spirit.

Your friend,

New York
February 10, 1949

Dear Herbert:

Thank you very much for your letter. I think that going about
to view the ruins of each country is a rude avoidance of thought
and human feeling and produces characterlessness. Going somewhere else is Western sickness and a sham activity of the soul.
Men who do not want to think as much as they ought to, or as
their natures demand, travel. I wish that you would be more
constantly in the company of Christ, Tolstoy, Shakespeare, Plato,
whom you wisely cite but whose wisdom you reject.

You know that *The Mint* has been printed and that "The
Rational Tree"* does not appear in it. It is a long time to wait
for Grigson, who so fervently admired the piece, to forget about
it. Plato writes in the *Republic* that "a soul which forgets cannot
be ranked among genuine philosophic natures." Both of you
have really forsaken me. Of course, I know you are far above a
Grigson, and it is even foolish to say it. I want you, above all, to
know that I do not covet the attention you are receiving; I live so
meagerly and even dimly in the world that I know about such
things rather vaguely. In some ways I am resigned not to be
published, and brood on oblivion with the same comfort and
piety that man considers the rites of the worms. That does not
lessen my intellectual anger against you, which is not sick or
splenetic. For what reason are you seeking more influence? Can
you bear being a director of a publishing house and behave no
differently from any other man who abhors literature? Did
Goethe neglect Schiller?

I read *Education for Peace* with great care. Your prose, because

* An essay in *The Flea of Sodom*

you deliberately violate the form of your own nature, is far beneath your aesthetic purpose. Why are you in a greater hurry to achieve what Plato in the *Laws* and Tolstoy in "Patriotism and Slavery" were so patient in making. Your book, were it more private, and less the breeding ground of public phrases of our sham cultural thoroughfares, would affect the human spirit. Your volume has not the soul of one of Tolstoy's letters about the Dukhobors. The reason is not that you are a less gifted stylist than he. You are probably better educated than Tolstoy was, but he was more on guard against the world than you. The more of the world there is in a sentence the less character there can be. One empties the other, and the two cannot live together save one die. Perhaps your naturalistic submission to death makes it impossible for you to have as many deaths as an artist must have for those probing pangs of rebirth.

Your feeling for the *Laws* is deeply discerning and true learning. Although Plato went three times to see the despot Dionysius he did not write a pickthank prose. You beg the world, and toady to it, to accept your book, and you make it as acceptable as you can to the academic roustabout and knave. Your design and your phrases are mortal foes. You say you esteem modern psychologists, and I blush to repeat some of the garbage words you take from them: "psychosis differential controls," "shock-absorbers," "team-spirit." What a sick, prostrate English this is. Your citations from Gill, Miller, Jung are barren platitudes. Look at your citation from Jung: "One goal is within our reach, and that is to develop and bring to maturity individual personalities." Does one have to read Jung to learn such an evil banality? I say it is evil because it seeds other hackneyed words in the minds of the inexperienced. Are not the two guardians of an ideal commonweal or book shame and fear, and have you been under this divine tutelage without which men make monsters of themselves, and even write base books for lofty purposes?

I beseech you, as a friend to your spirit, do not write an automobile and garage prose in order to persuade more people. There is no difference whatever between the gas-station attendant and the psychologist you respect. I again implore you to use the remarkable *Laws*: "The absence of grace, rhythm, and learning is clearly related to an evil style and an evil character."

What you say about music is altogether discerning; there is very little in the book I do not adhere to; what I refuse is the wanton violence against your own identity and gift, and perhaps your sly hankering after fame—the infamy of the market place. Your book belongs to practical action; it will be read and admired and forgotten about right away. Do you deeply want to prevent a war, perhaps not the impending one, but some slaughter or carnage in the future? Write, then, *Endymion,* or *The Death of Ivan Ilych*; repair to Yorkshire, as you said you wanted to do, and MAKE A BOOK.

"We have to live art if we would be affected by it," says Herbert Read. Please do so, and make your life those ritualistic "sacrifices, games, the song and dances" which will yield you heaven's grace.

My letters to you have been unheeded, rarely answered. Would to heaven you could find Arion's dolphin to carry you out of the coarse shoals.

The other day I saw almost the identical words that are in my own soul in Melville; they are simple and reverential; let us both kneel to them: "Do thou too live in this world without being of it."

I send you my real affections and love for your children.

New York
March 17, 1949

Dear Herbert:

Your letter is a benefaction and I thank you very much for it. My own epistle to you about your book was, I fear, waspish. I did not intend it to be so. I am, I pray, the affectionate friend of your Muse, and no less than Socrates I have had the deepest urge to protect your own Daemon. We have written to each other for two years, in which time my zeal for your own oracle has not abated. I do not object to negatives as you do, nor do I find it destructive or baneful to accuse Pilate or revile the world or condemn a people. If you object to sharp censure you will have to silence the negative tongue of Socrates too. You are hardly by character an Athenian Dykast who is ready to commit himself to such a role. The abhorrence of negations is a part of the desire to be comfortable and sluggish and pragmatic. This distaste, so incongruous in you, for emphatic denial is the buckler of common sense and opinion or Plato's doctrine of the multitude. Do you know how often Plato chastises the rout in Book V alone of the *Republic*? Herman Melville, after reading *Timon of Athens*, speaks most severely of the world. Would you then reject him as a teacher? Then you must ostracize Luke and Shakespeare and Nietzsche and Heraclitus. You must say these men are not teachers; if you say so, Herbert, you are no learner.

You must forgive me, but as kind and good as your second letter is, it is an annulment of the preceding one. You conclude the earlier epistle by telling me that your heart is now ready for such counsel as I have given you. In the last one, you feel it a grave fault in me that I have not the stomach for the evils of the world and reprehend them. I must add here that Goethean words, like finite and infinity, are too general to be examined, and the sentence you cite from him cannot be defined. However, I do not wish you to believe that I am unmindful of your burdens; a wife and five children are a boon and an enceladic Aetna upon one's back. I, too, have come to a juncture in my life when I do not know how I shall get the two fishes and the five barley loaves. I know that goodly, honeycombed men were low menials of base words in Grub Street. Kit Smart must have been such a porter of phrases before he was able to write his Paschal Lamb verse and *The Song of David*. We must somehow keep our force, though, for the human spirit. And do not be vexed with me, if I reiterate that you cannot do so, Herbert, by writing a hundred letters a week to people who are craven. Read, instead, the *Laws* which you understand so fully, and the *Phaedo,* which is a piece of philosophy that appears to have been conceived by Charon as he was oaring men to Hell. I mention this because you again in shunning those deep, uneasy, and yet God-like negations in man's soul, reject the principle of death at work in all men of spirit. I believe that the appetite for cessation in the poet is as dominant as his craving for the living waters. It is also my feeling that where death is not constantly a destroying principle in the soul there can be no awakening or rebirth of poetry. Is not this the Platonic doctrine of generation? Does not Socrates or his beautiful pupil say in the *Phaedo* that philosophy is the study of death? However, I love the pomegranate seeds as dearly as Persephone does, and all that I am saying is that it is the nature of the poet to think about death.

If you can get my little book published I shall be so indebted to you, as I am already for your great goodness to me in having gotten *Sing O Barren** published in England. You may not know how rejected I am in America; no one could be more a literary untouchable than I. I want you to be steadfast to my vision, and disloyal to any lies I may utter consciously or not.

I never cease to ponder how prose should be written; the good line is as elusive as Proteus. The Word escapes me no less than this wily god of change eluded Menelaus at the Nile. I ask the oracular Proteus of the river and the sea whether a sentence should be a predatory tiger, a water hog, or a mild Pythagorean bee.

I am very distressed to hear that Benedict is not well and pray that he will mend soon. You know how much heart-blood for frailty I have, and how it hurts me to know that such a tender stalk of human innocence is afflicted.

Do you think you can get my Ms. from Grigson?

I send you, Ludo your wife, and the children my love. If you want anything for them, please let me know.

New York
November 15, 1951

Dear Herbert:

Your visit has sorely troubled me. I must tell you very clearly that I do not approve of your way of living. Frankly, I should rather have the hatred of the vulgar literati than their counterfeit laurels. I know then, at least, what I am, but how sure are

---

* Title of the English edition of *Can These Bones Live*

you midst so much adulation in a period of such poverty of affection of the role you are playing? Do you think it is good to go to the foes of art to heal the artist? I don't care what money you get for whom, what you are doing is at the bottom a sin. Nothing can convince me that you are an anarchist in spirit or in mind or in the living experience at all, while you are sought after by all sorts of institutions and the adversaries of human love. You very curiously insist upon repose; what you are really saying is that you don't want to be bothered. You want rest. According to Thucydides, the Athenians were born to be unquiet and to trouble others. I should not have to remind you that Socrates was regarded as a gadfly; you will answer that you know it, and every schoolboy knows it, but neither the schoolboy nor his teacher does anything about it. I must then say that knowledge that is not action is gross and evil. What kind of an anarchist are you? I have never known in my life that an anarchist got on with the well-to-do people, the exchequer gents of the arts. Ibsen has said that what is important is not to find a definition of art, but to oppose those who are against it. You imagine Ibsen to have been a very reposeful, idyllic nature. Plato, despite many dialogues, which are the fiercest attacks against the Sophists of his day, you reckon to have been wholly detached. For the plays of Hamlet, Lear, Coriolanus, Timon, you have the little academic word, projected. It is a barbarous word, hardly seemly out of your mouth.

I want to mention a number of particulars which are at the bottom of this letter, which you will doubtless reckon to be thorny and acrimonious, and which will not give you that laxative ease you desire with others. Though the *Symposium* itself makes for charming reading, we know that the relationship between Socrates and Aristophanes could hardly have been altogether jocular. So much affection had I for you that I ran to the railroad station time and again simply to spend twenty or thirty minutes with you. When I was doubled over with pain, and loaded with codeine and at least four other sedatives, I came out to say good-bye to you at the airport. Of course, you may add in reply that you were busy with the bankers of arts and letters. Tell me, Herbert, have you known at any period, except in some anomalous instances, of poets and seers being sought after by the money-changers of literature? In the time that you were here, not once did you have the humble affection to ask me when you could see me. People are far too skilled in the world to bother about such matters with me, knowing that I am a fool for people. You think I am wrong about Eliot. There is too much of the well-fed votary of Helicon in him, and real seers are waifs, or Ishmaels waiting for the angelical waters to spring up in the wilderness. Maybe what is wrong is that he no longer has to wait. It is a terrible evil to have everything.

You have, you say, a wife and children to support; well, may God give you that manna, but somehow or other you must remain in the wilderness, for if you cease to feed upon the locusts and the honey, your spirit will die. You are now, as we all are every instant of each day, on the verge of losing that life which you so urgently prayed for. One may not be able to go a second time to the simple rocks and pour the oil of sacrifice at Beth-el. I like your Coleridge who dropped to his knees every day to pray to his God. Your agnosticism is too much of this world; I would prefer you a little mad, and much more unacceptable to the "dirty bourgeois" which Cezanne could not tolerate. The more of a poet you become, the more I will love you, and not only are you not too old to river and source your gift in the Greeks and Sumerians and Amorites, and to make some sort of *Timaeus,* but you must begin to do it now. I am much like Periander you cite in the Kierkegaard essay; I am wise and live like a maniac; but you live too shrewdly and that is the worst error of a poet. No poet can afford not to be a maniac. Madness is his stuff, his goods, his ecstasy, and it is better that he be a foe of the world, though that may be a great harm to his table and bread. Maybe you need a little more failure; I should like to see you turn angrily against the Pharisees, and the Pilates of literature. I should like in some way to dare you to attack what is mean; how will you go to the angels when you consort with the liars? Take care for you will get the lentils you are busy for; be on guard, lest you be gentle to the Philisters who have made me so testy. What deeply troubles me is that a man may commit a thousand adulteries, or be a thief, or be Cain, but if he harms his spirit, he shall no longer thirst. You must always thirst, and first and last be in the company of those who are athirst. Otherwise, you lie to yourself, and may deceive many people. Keep apart from the bourgeoisie of the Muses. As for solitude, it is a great pain in the heart, but a man must remain in the wilderness.

Do you know that the two letters you received from me and which I sent to you at Princeton, you returned to me. You are a Jung man but very dirty waters never flow into Hippocrene. I am talking of Jung as source.

Well, I must find my bitter bread; it is not that I do not labor for it. No one will let me. If I had some health and some of Pilate's money in my pocket, I could write a book to make Zeus envious, for I have thunderbolts in me, and I cannot cast them. So much for me, but do not be a friend to those who put their heel upon Prometheus' fennel stalk. Remember that the greatest enemies of art and literature are those who write and paint, and that the bursar members of the faith of art would rather slay a poet than not get their annual six percent. Rlene sends you her love and I sign myself a believer in God, a man who kneels to whatever is holy in living, and the friend to what is gifted in you. "All that is not Helen is dross," and each day we must throw out the trash to look upon Helen.

New York
November 24, 1951

Dear Herbert:

I have your reply to my letter, and though I tell you that I am very troubled about you, you may also find this "amazing." I am no more trying to change your temperament than I am endeavoring to alter your style, both of which I admire. I recall another visit to America which did not give you the ease you now feel. I had not heard you then laud the rich nor set aside the Greeks or the Hebrew Prophets as unintelligible. Why should I be surprised to hear you have a very good opinion of Goethe? I cited a line from him in *Sing O Barren* with much feeling. Will it make you uncomfortable to remind you that Goethe was an ardent admirer of the "unintelligible" Greeks? May I ask you why one civilization is more unintelligible than another? My own reading tells me nothing of the sort, for I find an unusual similarity in all high cultures. What perversity in you makes you of a sudden turn against Hellenic ideas? Was not one of your own books deeply influenced by Plato's *Laws*?

Let us admit that you are not going to find that physiologic ease with me that you appear to have gotten from the rich. I am glad that you can quietly till your seven acres of land. I, however, must till my seventy square feet of room, and I would be content with this provided your good rich men made it possible for me to live altogether. Why is it that you know so many moral rich men, and cannot find one who would support the very little literature we have in America and in England? I called Laughlin, by the way, and he told me what a fine letter you had written about *Bottom Dogs,* and then asked him whether he would please give me some sort of contract for the book. I had hoped he might give me a hundred dollars, which would be very needful to us, and he told me that he could not consider anything at all at the moment. He said that you would speak to Frank Morley and that he would wait on that, and maybe he will do something. He has been promising to bring out *Bottom Dogs* since 1939.

I think, Herbert, it is a fault in you to assume that you know America as well as I do, or can measure the acts of these men whom you, with your innocent eye, reckon good. You see that although you will not believe what I tell you about these people, you will have to take the word of history. Were these same people, with different names, kind to Poe, Melville, Dickinson? If wealthy people are so kind, why did Poe have to go hungry? Why was Melville driven into brackish deeps, and why was Dickinson altogether shunned? You call me a case, and that is very charming of you, but even if I were one of your cases and even if there were many poets, cases, untouchables whom the rich avoid, why is it that you cannot get them to help these dirty waifs of Helicon?

How, pray, did Nietzsche make so much of the "unintelligible" Greeks? And why was Blake so sourced in the Hebrew Prophets?

You admire both these natures, and yet have scant use for the men who seeded their vision.

Without wishing to offend you, I must strongly urge that the art bourgeoisie is the most implacable foe of vision, and that art itself is fast becoming the enemy of truth. I hope this statement does not amuse you, for it does not make me very sportive. Don't the rich fete and party you, and give you all sorts of accolades, and you are such a quiet lamb, knowing how to hold your tongue, which I do not know how to do, that they will not know what you think and will as a result regard you as a very amiable and lovable fellow quite fit to be a member of our sham society for art Philisters. Suppose that I am just a testy, unpleasant man, but that my books are really good. Why then don't they consider the work? But notice, none do, and that most of those who are apathetic or even antagonistic to my few books are people I have never met. Have you tried giving some of my books to your kind, rich friends?

You see at one time I could cite some Greek or Jewish thinker to support my own views, but seeing that I cannot do this, I can only remind you that Hamlet would be just as good a book for you to go to for my feelings as the ancients. I could also advise you that the great English writers did not have your disdain for the ancients. You will say that you know this, and of course you do; the trouble with people nowadays is that they know everything, but never act on any of their knowledge.

Now, my dear Herbert, I am not one of your cases, nor do I intend to be. If your conscience tells you that it is good to come to America and be in the company of rich, dissembling people who are starving the oracles, that must be your exchequer Golgotha. I propose to go relentlessly writing in that fiery furnace in which Daniel's three friends, and William Blake, burnt, for those that do not burn will have no flaming ecstasies. In my own iconoclastic way, I will be a fool of a Quixote, considering that Jeremiah, and Socrates, and Plato, and Philo were really intelligible, and follow them to my grave. It may cost me the bounty of the good, innocent eye of the rich and those who are clever enough to see so innocently, but I do not intend to call evil good or the sweet bitter for benefits from you or anybody else. I urge you, for the sake of your own nature, to employ that gifted style of yours for better uses than to tell me or maybe the young and the callow how Nazarene and sensitive and artless the money people of art are.

You have come to a crucial path in your own life. You have found a lovely prose. What are you going to do with it? The people you reject, I mean the ancients, have summered every poet of the old and new world. You refuse Socrates and accept those people who give you physiologic ease, but the seers of the past looked everywhere for men of intellect and learning. Do you imagine that I or any man of feeling am going to believe such sophisms? Do you think that Horace and Smart are to be set aside for Jung and Freud? You also have a high regard for Smart. He was a miserable urchin of the Hippocrene founts, and he found his balsam and vision in the New and Old Testament. You tell me quite significantly that you don't want to go mad, and I tell you, as Hamlet would speak to your soul, I would rather go mad than be Polonius, and there are as many Poloniuses of the arts as there are in trade, and they are more subtle and vulpine, because they are dealing in the goods of the soul. Woe to those who cheat us by selling us such cunning wares in the name of art and the spirit, and I repeat that art today is the greatest enemy of the spirit, and that it is nearer to money and to what is the black angel in our lives.

One last word, for you see, I do not pretend that your letter is amusing. How many cases have you on your file who require help? I mean how many Edgar Poes or Edward Dahlbergs are there in America or in England, for that matter, who must be eased by being printed. Why is it that almost anything you write you can get published, while I cannot? Does your kind of anarchism tell you that this is just? I am quite willing to commit myself to limbo, but I should like at least to see my words, just those that are living, in a book. I believe they will be of some use to young people, who are so debauched by waste and a lack of moral judgment in all places, particularly in the art realm.

Well, Herbert, you will take this letter for bitterness toward you. I am only bitter that the one man I thought would not defend what is ailing in human beings would not take the side of

the art burghers against me. You admire Cezanne, and you tell
how he broke with Zola because the latter had become a "dirty
bourgeois." Do you believe that Cezanne was right or just acerb?
Or were you being a gracious chronicler of human foibles, altogether detached, refusing to make any moral judgments? Why
then bother about war manifestoes? Why not be detached?

I must remind you that you were abashed by Richard Aldington's reply to you, and that you are now very dangerously doing
or preparing to do what he has done. He, too, found wealthy
company a great deal to his liking, and had no relish, as you told
me, to return to poor England. You have far greater gifts than
he, don't debase them for the people or for the rich; use them for
truth. Rlene and I send you our love.

I am still pondering your Chinese citation, and reject it not
because it is "unintelligible" but because it is trite. Nor can I
turn to you rather than to Christ or to Tolstoy in considering the
rich. The rich do not keep their wealth because they wish to do
good with it; they keep it because they have envy and bile and
greed. Does it not seem a little singular to you that these Elysian
and calm natures will not even finance the publication of a
single book of good verse? You said you made appeals in my
behalf and that you were unsuccessful. I do not in the least
doubt this and am sure that the ear of the rich to whom you
appealed was as deaf as the adder's. You may think I covet your
reputation, or want even three thousand readers, or that I am
not content to live here with Rlene in two small rooms. You have
a pelting comprehension of me if you believe so. I simply want to
be printed, and it may seem just a little odd to you, despite your
great contentment with your lot, that you have all sorts of books
published in America, while I cannot even get published in my
own country, not even for nothing; for should some one say to
me I will bring out your book, but that I cannot afford to pay
you, I would gladly consent. That this is the truth you cannot
doubt, since that is just about what I received from the publication of my last book.

Remember that you insisted upon coming over here as a poet,
and may I then, please, remind you to behave as one toward me?

What you are suggesting is not the counsel of a seer, but are the commonplaces that I hear everywhere in this cruel land, and may I also beseech you to believe that I understand America better than you ever can. It is my country, and I have studied its beginnings, and I know its people, rich and poor. The late Otto H. Kahn, a banker who gave much money to poets, said that in all his life he could never persuade one person of wealth to give anything to a writer. As for the *Freeman,* do I lie there? Do I debase my values? I may be ejected from there at any time, and you know that I have been ailing, and have had very much pain, but as Quixotism has become a cheap, trifling thing to you, you will scarcely appreciate the irony that I go on writing what no one else will do in this land. Besides, a man may tell the truth anywhere, even in a book published by a capitalist. It is not he who prints you but what you have to say that matters. I have never in my life been a pecuniary anarchist, nor can I find what you write in your letters in Kropotkin, or in Proudhon, or in Herzen, nor in any other radiant thinker, and if I find this new exchequer ease between you and the rich rather anomalous, you must pardon me for saying so. I have no bile toward you nor envy. I repeat this, because you are likely to confuse my differences with you with such low feelings. Were someone to ask me now, Would you rather be Edward Dahlberg or Darius, I should answer at once that my gift spares me the greed you think the rich do not know. But I must now return to my dear, beloved, unintelligible Greeks. My love.

New York
January 19, 1952

My dear Herbert:

I am very glad to have your letter though deeply sorry to hear of your gloom. I suppose I should tell you not to be despondent and simply to affirm what is good in the world. You see with all the affection I have for you I cannot believe that it is good or gentle or poetic or affirmative to hide what is wicked, base, and indecent. Nor can I extirpate at least one half of the intellectual

faculty of man in order to shed vague vapory yeas while the earth
is rotting. What you say of England can only be grim knowledge
to any man of conscience. But then you bother about Hitler
while, if I am to take your counsel, you should be affirming
Edmund Spenser, the Vedic hymns, and the sacred Tigris. Naturally, what you say in your epistle regarding Hitler is true. I
know also that England is being ruined by American imbecility
and dollar savagery. Should I conceal this and say write an article for the English telling them how generous we are to nations
who have had floods, earthquakes, plagues?

Some years ago you reprehended Aldington. He was then a
friend of mine, but today he is not. I do not mean to say that I
would not be happy to see Richard. I would, but should I tell
him that you are a negative Heinesque spirit in rebuking him? I
regard T. S. Eliot's poems as evil, but I admire some of Marston.* Am I to consider your friendship for him in valuing him as
an author?

I do not believe that when the world is in crepuscular rot as it
is, the poet should abolish his moral functions. I can find no
power in man more urgent than his understanding. I consider Eliot as a poet a robber of other men's gifts. If you think I
speak harshly just read Coleridge's *Biographia Literaria.* I fear
you may find a great deal of that asperity you reckon so uncomfortable in my nature, and he is not a Jew or a Greek or even
ancient. I consider all the fustian books that are being written
about Eliot absolute dross and cant. I should say the same about
Pound, for what with the shortage in paper, and penury in
England, and specious plenty in this infernal land (I mean
Amerik, and I think you may pardon this despite your mood
for seraphic and vestal yeas), there is not enough paper, and
human will or faith left for obscure men who are gifted.

Let me go a little more into detail: Do you realize what a
paradox you present? What you say of English poverty is most
lamentable. I have the greatest feeling for the English poets.
They have been my mentors and seers. You can hardly only
expect of me the noblest of sorrows for English desolation
at present. I should go so far as to say that if England falls

* Philip Bourke Marston (1850–1887), author of *All in All* and *Wind
Voices*

into ruin poetry in the world is lost for a thousand years. That matters to me very deeply. What then? First I must decry the credo of waste in America that makes English misery possible. That is the labor of the negative spirit which I regard as great and necessary as the affirmative. The yea in man is a lie and a great fault without the workings of Mephisto in him. Then I must see what our Parnassian votaries are doing to ennoble the human spirit? I can then only judge them as your Coleridge does, for I find that each one of them is more interested in a wild, Medic metaphor or a startling, illogic image than he is in the heart, the head, or even the arm or the foot of the human beast, man. There is another folly and contradiction which you do not appear to perceive, and that is that the American poet is in worse straits than the English. Is that a cause for anger or dismay in me? Should I be vexed that your own situation is Elysium compared with mine? Now for heaven's sake, don't accuse me of envy, though God knows how envious and spiteful and mean-hearted is human flesh, and I pray that I should drop to my knees twice each day as Coleridge did, should I have the least greed. All that I am telling you is that I do not know how the American poet manages to get bread. As for the pomegranates and the palm groves of Jericho, these are not for them.

You must know, Herbert, that a poet can manage almost any denial save not getting his songs sung to other people. I am so pierced by the ancient Essenes because they lived together and that word has come to have a saintly meaning for me. You do not seem, then, to appreciate my position. We have been more close to the bleak, scathed gutters than you know, nor would it be worth your while or mine to narrate our plight to you. I can only say that I thank heaven that you have a home, your darling buds of spring, your children, your wife, Ludo, and what I covet more than the barley loaves, a way of getting your words into balsam-bearing plants, a book. That is why I am, for one matter, so vexed with the rich. I know that there can be no pleasant commonwealth either in England or in America or anywhere as long as some have a base and indecent superfluity while others have not eighty square feet of room. You urge me to believe, or even, to imagine that the rich are kinder than the poor. You say they are without the greed you see in the penurious. I say this is miserably untrue. You come from the poor and so did I, and I imagine that you have done far more for others than the rich, and I venture to say that I have labored for others in my own way.

I say this further: any author who has moral goodness, must, if he is more fortunate than others, work for them. Otherwise, we are all doomed.

As for reformation, why, I think we who are quick rather than dead and sere are always trying to reform our faults. Mine are very many, and since my best teacher is my baseness and foolishness, I cannot at any time overlook what goads me to vice if I am to be worth anything at all as a human being.

Your citation is very beautiful, and I honor it. Would to God I could act upon it, but I must try, no matter what our limits be, or whether the greatest hoax in our lives is that free will does not exist. This is a terrible jest and tragedy, and though I grant the smallest amount of will to man, that is the source of poetry, love, friendship, and the Five Acts of Man.

What you have done for Zukofsky is of great moment. It means that he has some hope. Take away from man his expectations, and you give him the tomb.

I must repeat, Herbert, lest you misunderstand. I want you to have the laurels, the house you require for your good family, and what monies you need. I wish for you more fortune than I do for Rlene and me. I only ask you to remember what the rich have forgotten, that their abundance is a turpitude, if they do not use it for others. As long as we work for the obscure, we are the greatest dupes in the world, and it is only the deceived who are savants.

Look, another matter, we are all easily stung, and I know that at times I am absolutely astonished at my own damned defects and gross sins. Everything bothers me, but let God or Chance give me any bounty at all, and I run out to do a kind act for the devils of Gadarene.

You know I am a zealot by trait, and I must be so or perish as a writer, and I would rather be poor and yet somehow find the Gates of Jerusalem and the grapes of Galilee than run the hazards of being contented.

We both send you our love; we have at the moment nothing

but that, but I pray to God that we somehow keep our rooms and have a loaf so that I will have no envy of any man, for I have a crazy, humble fervor for the little. It is the much that I fear.

I am, I hope, your friend, and I only ask you not to sting me by advising me in my hapless condition how savory are the rich and what malevolent male Hecubas are the poor.

New York
March 4, 1952

My dear Herbert:

Thank you for your very good letter, and for the enclosure. Today I picked up *Poetry and Anarchism,* and read with quick pleasure any number of nimble and sane remarks on the artist. It should have appeared in this country long ago and many a Marxist buffoon might have retired with a blush had the book been known. I like the Freedom Press. You know I don't, though, care much for Picasso, though not for the fatuous reasons of some ninny Marxist. So much I think, also, that is cubism or surrealism is just another excuse for artistic senility and the most savage illiteracy. I have by no means read all the volume, and do not imagine any words I may have to say about Picasso is the result of niggling egoism, for there are wise allusions to Gorky and Shelley, and I shall really go to the back to cite something from it for a critical piece I may be doing for the *Freeman,* alas, not of the same ilk or of a similar race of ideas as the Freedom Press. I am, I hope, always an anarchic poet, having that discipline you respect, and which you say Wyndham Lewis calls the symbolic discipline of the artist. You know in the Vedic hymns it is said that when the wind is blowing from the pupil to the master one should not teach or hear, and I have the greatest veneration for all these alleged superstitions in the Upanishads and in the Apastamba because they imply order, good laws, justice, and respect without which we are cannon-ball barbarians, ammunition writers, and very deceitful and covetous. I am very pleased that you know that I take joy in whatever you feel or write and unlike so many of our vain tribe of poets do not regard a well-written book by another man as a menace to my identity. More men consider a wise saying, or an aphorism that is uttered by a perceptive man as a reason for the most gorged spite, and they go about the world like Achilles sacking every remarkable book.

I wish, my dear Herbert, you would comprehend my feeling about those booby writers or votaries of the Muses who are in the American Academy of Arts and Letters. No such institute is anything anyway but a cabal against the singing cicalas. Please know that I live here, and see what is happening to this most dismal automobile populace; books that one would care to read are becoming anachronistic. You know we are a commonwealth of collectors, for after we demolish a habit, a tender Shaker chair, or a nineteenth-century table we look everywhere for one to put it into a museum. Now a buggy is a relic, and soon a horse will be, and if there is any way of placing civility, say, a handshake or a thank you in a museum, these too will soon be embalmed and archived for greedy people to see and to admire.

The ancient Medes taught their children to ride, shoot, and to tell the truth, and though we were formerly a mesa and cowboy people we have lost all our wild, primeval arts; we are essentially perhaps only moral when we are close to savage, forest habits. Now we have what Bismarck called ink shooting and most of our scribblers are the greatest liars. That is why we have the Academy of Arts and Letters, and don't regard me as too peevish, for I hate not them but their harpy practices.

For the past five days I have been at work on a small novel. I am doing something on the comedy of education, and have moved with so much gamy speed that it is almost half-finished, that is, a first draft of it. This is droll rather than waspish, and it may make you and Ludo laugh. I have titled it, "The Diary of a Social Man." I must in a few days return to the bitterness of bread and write so that we may have a few onions and the Pythagorean vetch. I had the most piercing inward push to do this, and unless I am prattling and indulging in nincompoop arrogance, imagining this is good and has that animal health without which writing is a shameful velleity, you may care for it.

We were glutted with the newspaper funeral stories of George VI, and we are great fools here for regal fatuities, and everything you say in your *Postscript to Posterity* is altogether true. As you so well know, the cult of the nonentity has become an international theology.

I imagine Sophie must be a gracious darling by now, and it is very good to hear that Ben is so prescient and with such a nimble faculty. O what sweet grass is a child and a man in whom that has grown sere is wicked.

Chamberlain tells me that my pieces are attracting more attention than anybody else's in the literature section, but I am still a canonical lazar writer for them and have to extort any check they owe me. You know Spenser's epitaph for Thomas Churchyard, "Poverty and Poetry this tomb doth enclose."

As for my health, dear Herbert, I am still ailing, and each day I have some outbreak; we have a terrible sinus climate, and the air, if you will pardon me for saying so, is as bad as the discharges of the Harpies who spoiled Phineus' table.

I had almost placed a book of verse. Charles A. Pearce, the publisher, is an ardent admirer of mine, and I was already writing some affectionate acknowledgment to you, hoping to send you the book with it, when he told me the others did not want to do it. I wanted you to know that despite my querulous habits, and my testy differences with you that I do not reckon past kindnesses as "alms for oblivion."

Rlene has not been feeling very well, and what with our infernal money maladies and my own sickness, we get quite depleted, but when I can make a droll line, or have the strength to send you and Ludo and all the children our love, I do not count myself an orphan in the earth. Your devoted friend,

---

Santa Monica, Cal.
January 13, 1954

Dear Herbert:

Your letter came as a gift. I had nothing during the holidays to give my Rlene except my indigence. The Paschal Lamb drawing of Benedict is a delight; the inscription in the pamphlet I shall

hold as dear as water the gazelles dig for in the Gilif Desert. The
pamphlet is laden with thoughts. I cannot help it; I come more
and more to regard aesthetics as a Phoenician ivory box. You
have used some very moral words in your books, but the word
itself is a claw to your apprehension. You know I have a niggard
regard for Eliot's poems, but I believe his conception of originality is discerning. Had he been even the pard or the lion
among the ruins of Erech, or the tiger asleep on a Theban pylon,
he would have been loved by the Pleiades and the Sisters of the
Muses. I am not sure how far you impugn Eliot. I have much
rain in my desponding head today, and it may be that I have not
read you well.

I believe Adam would have accepted Lu Chi, and I had hoped
you would in your own mood take up his cadence of justice and
speech. Thoth is the god of the alphabet and also the scribe of
Truth. Hermes is the deity of language and is death. Now how
much death there is in the living rock of art I cannot feign to
know. And how one makes a line that strengthens the will, which
is the verb, is an enigma. The adverb, less potent, is the gentler
breathing of Ephesian John of the sentence. What is my buried
self as I write cannot be fathomed. Should I cast aside my head
when I write? How? I have little faith in that vain feathered
eagle. When you say that Cezanne read no more than the newspapers I am sorely perplexed. I do not doubt this, but Michaelangelo always had Cavalcanti and Dante in his mind. What dis-
turbs me is that we are living in a day when learning is the booty
of the jackal and the academic simian.

There are many things in the pamphlet that are discerning. I
am of your mind when you say so well and plainly, "Every word
was once an original work of art." Of a truth too the image comes
first and is Adam and Eve in the intellect of the artist.

You reject the pathic phantasms of Dali as I do, and at this
point I thought I understood your intention. It may be that
Vivante is right in asserting that art is a conquest of conscious-
ness; art or writing, the same, as you aver, is the lion Nimrod
holds next to his breast. Art preys upon the intellectual hunter
for forms. Letters then, to repeat, have as their tutelary messen-
ger, Hermes who beckons men, who are the senile forms to Tar-

tarus. He is the awakener. But, my dear Herbert, you should do it as a poem. The earth we can grasp, the sea enforces the eyes, kelp is the health of the nose. All this is the handiwork of God, and palpable. Days and hours and seasons can be graven in the palm of the hand or on Achilles' shield. Suppose you are right, that the head is a coxcomb, and of little use in creation. But your whole pamphlet petitions the faculties rather than the senses or those obscure regions in men which know more than Ham or Japheth or Magog.

Your pamphlet is too long to be discussed in a small epistle, and if I err or am roundabout do not be vexed. Language, as you remark, has fallen into the hands of the grub and the store churl. Poetry can seldom exist in the gutter jargon of the present. Eliot is again correct when he says that Pound is best as a poet when he is archeological. The use of the baby-trade dialect of today is a symptom of the fall from grace. I think that Dido and Carthage heal the Shakespeare you quote; you may not agree. You yourself are nimble, and most apt when you employ the word, hired, but hasty when you follow it with quality. You are again in the realm of absolutes, and I salute you when you write, "The greatest enemy of originality is, perhaps, the Zeitgeist."

You weigh the verse of Coleridge as Minos would, but what you see in the trite "Rime of the Ancient Mariner," I can never understand. Sensibility is a ruse, as you understand; you have indicated in *Phases of English Poetry* the hiatus between passion and sensibility. A flautist will seldom risk a pithy saying; the psalmist has both the senses and the Deity. If I have to choose myself, and I grant you I cannot, no matter how many sage books are grass in my chest, I will sit down each morning as I do, and toil to ransack the sun or to parch the discouraging rheum as Sirius does, but the result will be just a little out of my hands. I pray before I work, and then go down into some mummy pit of a book, and what I resolve to do is missed. Dust or sky or ruddle swerves my decisions. Still, to flout the intellect is foolish; it is unnecessary because it is the most derisive of all of man's inheritance, save his fate.

I admire the *Phases of English Poetry*, though I regard Schiller's work on aesthetics a mountainous bore. Most books dealing with beauty rather than the doxologies of Xenophanes or the epic battles of Gilgamesh, are a fox that eats the heart.

You regard yourself as a philosophical anarchist, but the word moral is hellebore to you. Granted that you are doubtless the sole anarchist in modern annals whose prose is a young lissom doe, that word should not be the prey of the canting monsters in the world.

I should write you more regarding Originality. In the ancient world of Judaea the families of Asaph and David were harpists, played the sackbut and the sistrum, and they knew more than we do about the dove of Semiramis, or the unguents of Rahab, but they were also moral visionaries. Never were men so unlearned in the Rig-Veda and justice. I urge you deeply because of your gifts not to write about the viol unless you also include the worm. Do you think that Euripides was indifferent to ritual, another word for the laws of Zeus, or that Prometheus is not a great Moral Hymn? Of course, should a beadle say it I would be as wroth as Xerxes was with the Hellespont.

Too many people paint, too many write, and the world of art is not even a good whore. Few are the grapes of Jericho or the manna of the wilderness Tarfa Bush in poems. What America requires most urgently are Moses and courtesans who would cost less than a pound of butter.

I give you counsel I might not take. I live in frigid solitude, no Scythian zone could be so peopleless as my world. I see no one all day; people here are as unlearned as wild beasts; seeing anybody has become a jeopardy to my soul, its fluid already broken and poured out into the earth that no longer hears. Once Unamuno said that if one is in the wilderness the woods hear. Maybe.

I should like to send you a manuscript, not long, which I titled "The Sorrows of Priapus." It has to be rewritten and repaired. I no longer know what is good; what else have I in Erebus and in obscurity but an animal guess. The other is a poem I have worked at for many months, and not yet finished. Here I have used as my image and reference the Tuat chamber of the Pharaohs, the Nineveh of Sumer and the bull of Aschour. I earnestly appreciate your willingness to read them, and as soon as I have them in some order I will mail them to you.

You have as you know, my love; my heart is like one of those Hagarnes in the east of Gilead, but if it is ophidian remember it is more steadfast than osier or blood. Rlene, of course, also sends her love to you, and thanks you for the dear inscription. May health be yours and Ludo's and Benedict's, Tommy's and Sophie's. I was deeply distressed to hear of the Cooks' tragedy. I quarreled hotly with Ludo's sister, but never disliked her. Her rancor was as undisciplined as my own. Our dispute was over Eliot's *Quartet* which I regard as mediocre. But really it was all just male and female blood; I am a misogynist who would be the morsel of the winds were it not for the Shulamite more precious than the balsams of Punt.

Your devoted friend,

Santa Monica, Cal.
January 23, 1954

Dear Herbert:

I have sent you two letters of late. One you have in reply to your own ripe epistle which cured my heart. You are now in America, and I feel that at least one friend treads the light here. Maybe, too, you can now appreciate my own hermetic solitude. You know that I give you homage as a writer, but feel hindered because you are so involved in that art which no man understands, namely, how or when the soul is prepared to utter the cry of the widow, Isis, pecking the salted delta, or when it is utterly niggard, and has no sentience at all. There have been months when I should have brayed, had I feigned that I were a stone, or I would have deceived myself had I pretended that I was a nettle tree or the desert tamarisk. I imagine that the greatest Satan that either God or dust must wrestle with is Void. For in the beginning was not the Word, but Nothing.

Now I am constantly thinking of the pamphlet you sent me. You were or still are a philosophical anarchist, which means that justice is a great concern of yours, and that evil dismays you and quenches your strength and day. I am sure that ignorance is a dragon that you do battle with in all the seasons of your conscience. What the nostrils understand may also fill the jaguar, and that is sometimes called art or aesthetics or Babylon. The ears are not always soothed by truths, and often when they are most gratified they are two wild asses. The eyes are unstable pools and seldom perceive a Buddha, a Lao-tzu, or a humble Cato in the furrow. All the senses are the gifts of Proteus. I am merely saying that hearing and touch are often so perverse that they are not the steadfast witnesses of affection. The senses are, alas, more often Cain than Abel.

Do not imagine that my misgivings represent a denial of the image, or that I, too, am not the prey and the booty of phantasms. Each of us has enough of Iscariot to be on guard each day of his life, for the worst foe is not another man but one's self.

Granting that you have already written books that one will always savor at any time in one's life, what now is the purpose of art creeds, if I may employ such a vexsome word. If I write a book on aesthetics will I advise you how to make a strong line? Can I even be sure that while writing about art I myself may not be writing badly? Will an apple, the mandrake of Haran, or a Cezanne tutor the soul as some hymn to Ra inscribed on funeral papyrus? First there is Nothing, then the Word, and afterwards the Apple. Otherwise, you have the jaguar arts of the present day. You may disrelish the word, moral, because it long ago fell into the hands of the beadle with nitre in his spirit. However, philosophy and poems are composed of a double vision, the apple that gladdens the imperfect and loveless eye, and the waters of the intellect, dream and death.

If men of your gift are going to be aesthetic mandarins, who will counsel the raw acolytes of the alphabet and of painting? You know I am not a pamphleteer, nor do I expect you to be writing books on Kropotkin. Political natures always write the most dreary volumes on authors. What I object to most is that what you deeply know you do not seem to know continuously. A wise man utters the same truth until he is given the hemlock of Golgotha. Heine once said that every time one had a thought it was Gethsemane. That is a tragic conception of literature to which I hold.

But where are we? I loathe the church, the communists, and the capitalist blackguards who have the gullets of Tantalus. What happens to me? The communists, who are no less the enemy of the Tree of Knowledge than the servants of lucre, have given each book of mine the crypt. I think you know that I derive the least pleasure from the encomia of the gutter ignoramuses of the papers. No people can survive the scurrile American newspaper. All I can hope for is notice enough to warrant the publication of another small volume whenever the Deity or Fate or the Earth that must wax and wane will allow it. Can it be said that I am just hidden away in the winds and in secret places by the Marxists? Ford Madox Ford, whom I care for as much as I do you, sent *Sing O Barren* to Ransome. He wrote the most ardent letter about it, but said he was too much of a poltroon (his word) to print any part of it. He would not even review the book. After receiving his very warm letter, also calling me a prophet, I wrote him several times but he never answered. Why, I do not know, except that my book was an embarrassment to his soul. He would not protect or deny it. *The Flea of Sodom* was not mentioned in the *Kenyon Review* either. I challenge any one on the earth today to say that this book does not warrant the deepest attention of one who is interested in the art of writing. What is the matter? We return to justice without which the arts are the devils by the tombs. I have grave faults, but do I kill conscience, which is Abel's blood, a book? Am I one of the sinners Milton impugned in the *Aereopagitica*? Do I have to write like you to get fillets or for you to be like me to be cast into the ditches of Tartarus? Suppose I disagree with some judgments of yours; shall I then be your hangman, or worse, so skulk that no one ever hears of your book? How will we have a better, or a less criminal commonwealth, if people, feigning the greatest love of letters, shed the blood of the first book which they cannot take to their bosom? What then is the reason for the malice of these ravens that root upon the acacia tree?

You saw what happened to the *New Republic*? Your chidings were dross upon their palate. Not only will they not accept me as a contributing critic, but they will not mention my name at all.

The *New Republic* is supposed to be the country cousin of the city Marxist. Why do they suppress books and cry out against censorship? When *The Flea of Sodom* appeared someone sent a copy to Josephine Herbst. I had not seen her for two decades, but received the most charming letter from her in a Washington, D.C., hospital, saying what health and sun and greening things there were in the book. When she came to New York she called the *Tribune* and asked to review the book. Miss Van Doren, of that iniquitous family of Parnassian realtors, said they had a review, but none ever appeared. These people filch my soul, my bread, my portion, in the name of liberty, a free press, the survival of culture.

Laughlin has become an ardent admirer of my work. I sent him entreaties; of course, he will print one poem of mine in his annual anthology where I will be interred. I have come to be very fond of Laughlin. I go to and fro in the earth, not because we are poor, but because my work is hungered and athirst. But the false St. John the Baptists of communism and liberalism and manic greed have no hunger or thirst. The truth is that neither Marx nor Kropotkin nor the impostor Bakunin can give a man a soul, a heart, a truth.

I am sending you some manuscripts in the next ten days. There is a long poem, "The Burden of Cain," which I should like to dedicate to you. I had much reason to think that Laughlin would publish a book of mine, and I had intended to make acknowledgments to you who have been the steadfast friend of my mountain strivings. Another matter. I have never wanted you to think that I regarded past kindnesses as already paid for.

I have also done about a hundred typewritten pages of a book in essay form, titled "The Sorrows of Priapus." What is Eden in one's work or chaff in the widowed winds I cannot pretend to know. Maybe some of the things I send you may contain that salt which is the Angel of Ocean. I don't know.

Both Rlene and I send you our devoted love. I pray that Ludo and all the children have health of cassia and the aloe tree.

Your friend,

Dear Herbert:

Your letter is the ore of Ophir, and I shall never cease thanking you for it. I would have replied instantly, but I have been tormented by an acute gastric disorder. Besides, we have just moved into a rough and humble flat of the sort you see in Chelsea. At least this does not smell of money and Philistia.

Now I must tell you that I am concerned about you; do not damage your health. Mimnermus, who was tired and bored, said one ought to live to be no more than sixty, but Solon, much wiser, thought eighty the right number of years for a savant. I pray you will have ripe faculties longer. But you must seek a quieter life. Don't go to India next to give an award to three ceramic artists, or fly, like Nimrod, to Chile to present a nosegay to a muralist. I earnestly wish you would give over all these swollen efforts for painters. There may have been a few who were worth it; but everywhere you go today there are modern art committees, tumid funds for illiterate abstractionists and paint cannibals, and hardly a soul reads Porphyry or Augustine or *Piers Plowman*. As I have said so often, there is no road from modern art to the *Dialogues* of Plato or to Erasmus. Bosch is great because what he imagines in color can be translated into justice. Of course, he is marvelous for other reasons, too. But we cannot avoid the age, and we see that men are raving because they do not know which way the wind blows or where the equinoctial regions are, or whether a savage living by the waters of the Magdalena is not more human than an auto-citizen of the occident. Art either must be a teacher or infamous; maybe in some other time a hyacinth will breathe as much deep uses as the coca tree of the Moluccas, but not in a day when to kill the soul is the most greedy pleasure of men.

You know I do not like to prate about what is good in one time, believing that what is of most value to heaven and earth in one century has the same weight in another. You can move from garlic and cummin seed sold at an honest price to Euripides, but when leeks are scarce, and vegetables are sold at capricious costs, you are not likely at all to produce Eudoxus or the great apostate Julian. We need the word more than beauty; the beauty artist is really not concerned with the geometry of the spirit; for him aesthetics is the stibium pot. It may be that *What Is Art?* is a prophecy rather than a correct appraisal of Rimbaud, Mallarmé, Baudelaire. But was he so wrong about these men? The barest few have escaped. Do not imagine that I read all of Baudelaire with cold eyes, or that I have not been affected by him. He taught me to use adjectives cleverly, to exaggerate the possibilities of wit, to simper a little at male whoring in syntax, and to be a misogynist. There is almost no sympathy in Baudelaire. Yet I do not exclude him—his savagely dismal life with a Negress as a sole consort is his defiance and cross. Someone told me of a Jewish poet from Poland who went about in rags to remind everyone of what the world had done to him.

I rejoice in the emeralds, the ebony, the chalcedony of Eden, but unless they are angels or the rivers of Paradise, goodness or compassion, we are back in the cultus of the beauty parlor of literature. I marvel at the obelisks, and it may be that the rosy-faced Sphinx is Rhodopis the courtesan, but the hieroglyphs on the granite are great moral injunctions.

You may be right that my disgust with sex is Hebraic; still I do not set aside the Nile at flood, or reject the exuberance of the tiger or the flights of the frigate bird. Enthusiasm is a remarkable thing; there should be no shame at twenty or thirty, but eroticism at fifty is quite another matter. Poor Lawrence was an intellectual onanist, and so was de Maupassant, and one went insane and the other was worn out before he could comprehend his talents. I do not believe, my dear Herbert, that Lawrence ever understood them. Like Poe whose waste he comprehended, he himself is much more trash than genius. You imagine he was not influenced by Stein. May I ask you, when did you last read *Mornings in Mexico*? Pardon me, but he was. I had unusual feeling for Lawrence, and do but take a look at his acolytes. Do you imagine genius rightly understood could have such a large influence? What baited so many women, and nearly all zanies; lewd cult skirts? He seems to have attracted not Ariadne by whose thread we somehow manage to come out of the labyrinth but Schopenhauer's volitional and short-legged bipeds. He hated will in women, and I never saw one Lawrence female who had not a brutish tongue and the arms and hands of the man-hating feminist.

I cannot tell you how grateful I am, dear Herbert, for your words on *The Sorrows of Priapus* and on the verse. All your suggestions are good, and I thank you very much for your critical markings. I shall in all cases follow them. You know I am not ashamed to tell you how indebted I am to you, and one of the reasons I wanted to dedicate something else of mine to you was to make another public avowal of the benefits I have had at your hands. Without your help, could I have survived? I have great doubts. A man can shake hills and rivers and ravines, and this is the battle of the soul, but without one nod of approbation from a trembling and gifted mortal, the earth will fall upon his head and break his intuitive life.

We are very discouraged; I write and cudgel my head and walk in Tartarus. America is very likely to be a fascist land in a lustrum; you know I have been mortally punished by the communists; they have killed my books, mired my table, and my lot, and yet I cannot observe these investigations without being very troubled. There is little doubt that despite all the Marxian gibberish the Russians live more sanely than the American who is a lunatic. Should there be a war every American will be expected to regard the Russian as a monster. How am I to expel from my heart all the joys and didactic sorrows I have derived from Gogol, Tolstoy, and even from Andreyev who was a little ikon of mine when I was twenty?

The intellect is always the target of the dictator, and every man of mind, Marxist or anti-communist, will be in a labor camp should this country go to war with the Soviets. It is a mirthless jest to think that people regard me as a reactionary or a statist. They don't read me, they simply assail me, kick my bones and head. What am I to do?

My very good friend, Herbert, should I get a publisher for *The Sorrows of Priapus,* let me, if this is good in your eyes, dedicate it to you. This time I should like to say more than just For Herbert Read. If Laughlin would bring it out in a small limited edition, that might find more curious readers. I still have writing to do on it. But first I want to do the critical essay on your work. I have to wait a few weeks until Shapiro returns. He has some editor there now, but I fear to ask. I don't want a refusal, not that he may have little regard for you; he may simply refuse for no reason at all, or because I attacked Aiken! I would regard it as improper to ask you for some of your books unless I can do the piece which I am most eager to do.

How much longer do you remain in America? I shall feel like a waif when you are gone. Is not a writer the most miserable beggar in the universe? Look, I am on my way toward my fifty-fourth birthday; we haven't a penny and each time I write a book or even a piece, I acquire fifty unknown enemies.

Guard your health, Herbert; there is no day in which you are not on my mind. I pray for every good soul in the earth, and it may be that five spirits can redeem the wounded ground. Maybe the tears of one heart can heal a corrupt holm oak, be medicine to an ailing heath. I pray for you and Benedict, your hearth in York which warms you and your precious family, for every good fireside is Christ and Lazarus. Rlene and I send our loving devotion to you.

Your affectionate friend,

Santa Monica, Cal.
March 16, 1954

Dear Herbert:

I sent you a letter, special delivery, above a week ago. Since then I have suffered from that most horrid of human afflictions, torpor. To be supine is to be dead. Stendhal spoke of the dead blank.

As you know, I have not a soul to converse with; when I am at work I don't mind too much. I labored over "The Garment of Ra" for months, always dreading to finish it. Once it was completed, I knew I would be altogether vacant and more hurt and senile than any shade in Erebus. So long as I work I am least alone; otherwise, I drivel for people, knowing that they will harm me or just pretend that I am a wretched nobody in the universe.

My dear Herbert, Shapiro returns, as I told you, the first of April. However, I have already written two letters to *Poetry* magazine, asking them to let me do an essay on you. They are friendly toward me, but wary of my rough and grum feelings regarding most of my contemporaries. Had not Swift, a crabbed and most affectionate nature, as his epistles divulge, said there were no more than three geniuses in a century? I have one note from them, but as yet no promise. I imagine the acting editor wants to ask Shapiro whether he wishes me to do it. This morning I sent a longer letter, explaining in detail the kind of piece I wished to do.

Meanwhile I read, finding that the woes and the myths of a Chipewayan Indian are as extraordinary as the tragedy of Ceres.

When do you return? We are trying to sell our books so that we can put aside some money to go abroad. I cannot bear the land. Its history is a lodestone, but the present populace is a Hecate.

If we are lucky to get out of here, somehow, I want to do the essay on you, and to finish *The Sorrows of Priapus*. The second part will have to do with the North and Central American Indian. I should also add the natives of Orinoco and the Niger, and the animals of Patagonia and Tierra del Fuego.

You say, my good and dear friend, that disgust with sex is Hebraic. I imagine this revulsion comes in the late season of all races. The Rig-Veda celebrates the abstemious rites; Socrates has two wives, but only to beget just citizens for Athens. Epictetus is no Hebrew, and for that matter, the Huron sibyls are vestals, and so are the shamans of almost all the tribes of North America. Animal ecstasy is a remarkable experience provided it is not spent like the short-lived amorous sparrow. Still, I am not so sure that nearly all our evils—lying, deceit, love of gain, ambition— do not come from that shameless sac. I do not imagine that a spado is therefore more noble. Man cannot do now what nature has not prepared him to understand. There may be creatures in the marvelous deep who are wiser than man. The leviathan is herbivorous, and no matter what we say or think, a vegetarian or grass-eating beast is more palatable to our imagination than the cruel and gory carnivore. Ten years ago I was not so bifurcated in my own feelings. But I saw that a man could read the most amazing savants in the world, and then be the sorriest dupe of a chit. This, too, was the feeling of Burton, hardly of Jewish origin. I am, of course, as you know, referring to the *Anatomy of Melancholy*. Whereas George Herbert was in temperament an ascetic, and so was Izaak Walton, Sterne, the cleric, was definitely not so. How man regards the nuptial couch will always be the sign of the poet, the philosopher, or the brute.

I cannot tell you how much your letter meant to me. I still stand on Pisgah looking at the grapes of Canaan. This is very likely to be my fate. But I do not complain that I shall never have much recognition. I simply want to be printed. How can I overcome the scurrile newspapers? Or how can I be shrewd? It is nobler to perceive than to be Iago.

Do you believe the nonsense about Shakespeare? Do you think he wrote for the common pit? I don't believe such craven legends. These are the coarse myths the Philister disseminates to ease his own squalid mind.

I write you this morning, Herbert, for a very plain reason, namely, having thanked you for your great heart-kindness, you may not assume that I should be content and have no need to thank you again or thrice. Thanks is as eternal as God or the tomb.

How is dear little Benedict, and have you altogether mended your health?

The morning is the best portion of my life; late afternoon is good for the perusal of a sage, the evening is for waste and uglified emptiness of spirit. Would that my whole life were daybreak. How strong the Cordilleras are upon whose back the dawn rests. Do you bother about travel literature; it is marvelous to go everywhere without troubling to rise from your chair. My own life is more uneventful than that of Kant's.

Rlene is weary these days, and I am so helpless. It is not the stupefying struggle for a roof and bread, which is evil enough; we wait for some angelic windfall, a letter, a jot of good tidings, and often for weeks the world is surd. My whole combat, aside from writing, is to make something happen. For months I try to bend destiny a little, and am only lamed in soul, and swinishly dejected. Low spirits are the acorns of the piggish heart.

Well, we both send you our devoted love; please kiss Benedict for me.

Your loving friend,

_____

Santa Monica, Cal.
August 7, 1954

Dear Herbert:

I send you all my thanks for your letter to Laughlin. There is little rest for me; it is said that the South Wind makes its bed in a cave at Cyrenaica, and I am sure that the elements have more quiet than the human animal. Now you are going off again. I had hoped you would find it more natural to remain where you are, since you gave so much of your strength to travels in America. You go everywhere because you cannot help it, and I stay here for the like reason.

Do you believe that any man is civilized? Except saints, who are beside themselves. What am I writing for? One should take one's books and the pages thereof, and cast them as incense to the four cardinal points. But I brag, implying that my books are myrrh or the copal of the Indies. But to return to the uncivil two-legged animal, man. I become more misanthropic, though not abhorring life itself, which I regard as an infernal sin. An artichoke, mountain moss, or wild celery draws tears from my head otherwise no better than stony Niobe. Whenever I do something that is not base or boorish or choleric I marvel at my act, and wonder how I could have been so delicate and fastidious. You mention the Noonday Press. I knew of their inceptions, and one of their versifiers came to me, asking for advice which I gave and which was not taken. I thought it quaint that these people should seek what is in my head, chaff or otherwise, and never ask me for a contribution.

It would give me the least pleasure to have this book done by the Noonday Press. I do not care to become a clandestine writer, or more so than I am. You have much more ease and suppleness than I, and can afford to let a small press do one of your books. I toil so to make a book, and it takes me at least a lustrum to write it, and then another two years to find a publisher for it. I think this is the most important book of my life, and count this, too, as the words of a braying Balaam, for though ultimately I have the least faith in the words of a human grub, I am not enough of a rock not to be vain or to want to be heard. People who praise me here kindle my suspicions, and then I wonder what is wrong with my book; people who refuse to give me their accolades I imagine to be coarse and foolish. Have you, my dear Herbert, as fuddled a cranium as I? I hope not; part of this is bizarre, but the nether crust of these words is tragic. I abhor conceit but envy the peacock; I would go meek, but pray for the feathers of the macaw. I believe in God, but I skulk, and I do not trust either my elbow, my neck, as obdurate as that Pharaoh's who would not let Moses leave his realm, or my foot. What saves me from canonizing my own principles is the nihilism that defeats the worms, for who can feed on nothing, or sing after such a meal.

I expect to be in London in the early fall. I hope to have my book done in the next few weeks. It may take longer; one can hurry nothing, another man, a page, good or bad, and least of all fortune, evil or barren or wondrous.

We have no thought to live in Paris; I have met enough painting and word whores in the United States without looking for more of the same genus. The American cormorant of the arts is, perhaps, the worst, for he goes alone, and eats himself, provided there is no one else at hand. In Patagonia the great predacious eagles sit upon ledges, and in the hot river valleys of Brazil, they sleep in flocks on the branches of the coca trees. They are together, and seldom harm the living, which is far more noteworthy than the habits of men, who forget the dead at once, and always punish those who are alive.

Now, you go to Istanbul; I think I like to travel best at home, and prefer to go to Tartary with Marco Polo. Kant never left Königsberg, but had the most intricate knowledge of the map of

London. Byzantine art is remarkable; does it not sometimes astonish you that the greatest manslaughterers in the world dote on murals and edifices. Burckhardt writes of one of the Roman emperors who had a morbid passion for building. Heliogabalus, the Phoenician pathic, was exceedingly artistic; once he gave a banquet for many friends whom he cast into a bed of roses which was so deep that they were strangled to death by the perfume. You wonder why I mistrust painting, especially the modern canvas which is as close to a conception of the hole as man can apprehend. It may be that one cannot improve man, and the most astounding painting or hewn stone will not allay his appetites. Do not imagine, my dear Herbert, that such a gifted nature as Plato, and with such knowledge of legend and image, was a senile fool, for having immense misgivings about art and poets. Socrates, too, was right, that poets do not know what they are talking about, and cannot explain their best books or understand when or why they write bad ones.

I shall never turn away from words because I imagine, art fop that I am, that I know how to kindle them; still I shall never scorn Plato, or imagine that I know anything better than he did. I think it is not only arrogant to assume that we are wiser than Plato; I believe it is wicked, and stops our own ripening. Suppose I make a book that will be read a century from now. Do you believe it, I care least of all. For what will it matter, and who will profit by it, or be less miserable after the reading of it? Some wight, who writes as I do, and walks the streets more diseased by solitude than Kit Smart or Lucifer? Bedlam is the lodestone of every man who thinks and shakes mountains with a book.

There is wry weather in my soul, and I pursue knowledge and fables that make dust laugh. Rlene will not be abroad until next June. She begins teaching in September; you know what education is in this country; well, what shall we do, O Herbert. Well, you go to Istanbul, and may you see one human face that is not a snare, while I sit here, and imagine that I am tranquil because I go nowhere. Some publisher abroad ought to find these Quiche Maya myths as astounding as the emeralds in Eden. There must be a skull in one of these book markets that will not deny me. Soon I shall be writing of the great hot rivers, in the lower Americas. They are closer to creation than the timorous streams, the river Europas, the small, doved waters of Venus, and Daphne, or Cape Sarpedon which are the tears of Zeus. By heavens, I shall have to find one. I am deeply delighted, my dear Herbert, that the Harvard Press is doing your book. You know, as your heart may tell you, and this is the animal we trust the most, that I rejoice in your good fortune. You need fame and money for your wife and family; I require much less. The forests of Nod where Cain dwelt may be better for me than the gold of Nineveh.

Again, my dear friend, you have my loving thanks; I mentioned your name to two people: a young man in England doing a book on Lawrence, which is to consist of memoirs by people who knew him. Did you see Aldington's book on Lawrence? I will always like Aldington, although I fear he has something double in him. He did a gross, Gaza book on Lawrence abusing him for perceiving the truth. For whereas Lawrence often wrote badly, the living man who walked in the sun, and thought about Sicily and Tenochtitlán, was rarely wrong. He attracted a miserable crew of women. I am glad I am no phallic writer, if all you get for a great deal of sexual adjectives is a brach that a burning Paul or Don Quixote could not stomach.

I also told a poet here by the name of David Ignatow, an earnest and truthful heart, who is editing a Whitman issue for Beloit College, that you might give him a poem. He was very eager to have something from you, and so was this other person. I did a poem on Whitman which he thought very good, maybe it isn't, I don't know, and I thought of dedicating it to you, but then I wondered whether it was good enough.

May I please send you the manuscript as soon as it is done? You have read the first part, and I have mended lines you thought were the humor of the jaguar, or worse, and cast out others. I am praying that you will care as much for the second, which happens to fire my own flesh the most.

Maybe, my dear Herbert, you can think of some English publisher who would care to print me. I have, as you know, unpublished, *The Sorrows of Priapus*, the verse, and half a novel, which you did not care for, and I am sure there was much brutish writing in it, and it may be that I shall throw it away. I hear that Eliot, who has always published his works in England, tells

Americans they should not look at this little isle as their Helicon.
I am astonished continually by the lack of self-knowledge men
have. When I was an orphan, the superintendent, who earned a
handsome wage, and wore long, flowing clerical trousers, always
told us not to make ourselves slaves of our stomachs. We never
did because there was no food there either for a carrion-feeder or
a hungered Lazarus. Besides, the orphans were greater savants
than he for they said, were it not for the fact that they had lost
their mothers and fathers, he would not be earning six thousand
dollars a year, along with laundry, lodging, and fillet of sole.

Your house in York is a place of family mirth and though as
you say, it may weary your good, dear wife, Ludo, what an Elysium is such fatigue. The barren really suffer from weariness, and
there are few on the earth so mean and bilious as childless
couples.

My devoted love, my dearest friend, and Rlene sends hers; we
think of you very often, and you are a hearth to a lonely pair.

Santa Monica, Cal.
August 14, 1954

Dear Herbert:

I sent you a long letter a week ago, and hope these few words
may reach you before you go to Istanbul.

Perhaps you could suggest some agreeable, but inexpensive,
hotel in Chelsea or Soho. I abhor middle-class streets; for money
does not even smell, good or bad; it is just wily like Laban the
Syrian. Do you know what I should have to pay for a room and
breakfast? Should I take meals where I live? I have not been in
London since 1929, except for a week in 1933, after my bleak
experience in Berlin, arriving there two days after the Reichstag
fire. I should ask you about tips; what you give a cab driver on
the way from Victoria Station to a hotel, and what is a just price
for room, or where to eat. You remember the wretched meals we
had in New York, or I should say the miserable, congealed sand-
wiches.

May I please send you the finished manuscript; it won't be ready until your return; you have read the first part, and you won't have to bother with that. I would also be very grateful to you if you would eradicate bad lines, or curtail a sentence that is too lengthy, or excise a paragraph you do not believe good.

I am thinking of going to see Mr. Malcolm Kirk at Peter Neville's, and of looking up Mr. Peter Owen. Have you any suggestions? I was told that Sir Geoffrey Grigson, when he was here, wanted to see me. What do you think? Every day is a vexation, but should we for that reason abhor the day, or cast it away? Alas, the books we make are what we would do had we the virtues, or the will for each sun. In Paradise there was no evening, which is the time when the will is weak and men are the least energetic.

I have a letter from Edmund Wilson; he is trying to get me a scholarship from the Guggenheim Foundation. He is certain to fail, because I am not untalented. How foolish and stupid must one be to attract lucre? I met Edmund Wilson about a half year after I first made your acquaintance in the winter of 1929. He is a kind man, and has enough character to have escaped some of the worst blemishes of trade. Some of his judgments about books are thistles and chaff in my head. You told me once he hated you, but he has mentioned you a couple of times, and always in a civil manner. Of course, I do not know what he has written about you. I fear, should I start reading some of his opinions that will be the end of our connection. Still, I like the man, and I pray that he does not assail you; that I would find hard to endure. He has just returned from Israel, and is doing a book on old Hebrew culture. He comes of the American wizard stock, the Mathers, Increase and Cotton, who burnt the women at Salem, for loving the flesh and expressing their thoughts about those diabolical white churches in Massachusetts. These albic devils, church beadles in immaculate raiment, were a pair of lascivious wights, ransacking the gowns of women to see whether they had privy teats; 'tis a good and profitable occupation provided you go to such scholarship for better reasons. One English medieval author writes that fornication is a kindly sin.

Are there some people I could look up in London? I should

want to see Frank Flint; he may have too much wormwood in his blood by now; negations must be azury, or else we kill what grows, and murder God of whose body we have wheat.

The pair of us have been ailing, but we go to Poseidon for the herbs of the sea, which are fuci, that the earliest men ate. Frankly, I am utterly perplexed. No matter what, my dear Herbert, it is very hard to put words together that are not fatuous, grum, ill-shaped, or predatory. Thoth has an ibis-shaped head; others say it is like a hawk. I fear the hawk letters, the jackal alphabet, the lissom gazelle sentences. I grow more and more to fear art and literature. Did this trade improve Ezra Pound? Am I worse, and surely not better, than I was as a child?

Rlene and I send you our loving thoughts.

Your devoted friend,

I wish I were as sound as a bundle of faggots; Marcus Cato says that what is most important are good stalls, and stout pens; Christ had a well-made crib, for his father was a carpenter, and that may be sufficient to give a man good principles. But the city is a lousy, bleeding manger.

Santa Monica, Cal.
March 1, 1955

Dear Herbert:

I read your letter with a desolate heart. Eliot is a wild son of Ham, and he will not last; when his books are chaff in the wind you will have pensive readers. The evil he is is in the rabble titles of his volumes, *Murder in the Cathedral* and *The Cocktail Party*, which are a claim for cash. As for Wyndham Lewis, you know my mind regarding him; he is the Main Street intellectual pamphleteer, and a master to noddles; what he attacked was done in such craven newspaper prose that he added one wrong to the existing one that he impugned. I do not have to read his latest foolishness to know him, but as you ask me to do so, I shall promptly get the periodical and satisfy your soul which I know to be in the right.

You must not, my dear Herbert, write anything in haste; even a man of your character, softened by the Graces, cannot afford to impair his style. Your lovely essays in his book they will omit to assail what is weak. If I may gently remind you, Kafka is not great. He has all the scatophagous faults of the unlearned. The mongrels, poodles, and canine phantasms in Kafka's dreams are symbols of ordure. Nor should you, my friend, mingle names promiscuously, Dickens, Henry James, Tolstoy, Coleridge, Browning.

Your feeling for Kierkegaard and St. Augustine I altogether share. But after you cite Pascal you go to Sartre. Should I mention Clement of Alexandria along with a sterile beadle who happens to reduce a visionary parable to a common sexton's notion of the universe?

Cast each thought with the greatest slowness into Vulcan's limbeck so that none can harm you except an eminent blackguard.

Neither you nor I can take any hazards with Mnemosyne; she is a frail mother, having exhausted herself bearing nine daughters. I do not trust my mind at all; even with Luck at my side, I have not the bravery to write without consulting at least threescore sages. We entice Wisdom who will not rush into our arms.

I am deeply pleased to hear that what suggestions I have made regarding our proposed book* are agreeable to you. You see now what cant and deceit there are in these writers. Dr. Johnson has said that to attack a bad author is a benefaction to mankind, so my good Herbert, let us be Promethean benefactors! Now here is a brief outline of our epistles which you can change or amplify as you wish:

1. The Disappearance of Morality from Modern Letters: Thoth, the god of the alphabet, has vanished. Saturn has fled with his rustic cruses filled with pious offerings to the Universe. Let us not forget either that hardly a man has had a civil meal in

* *Truth Is More Sacred*

a novel for at least seventy-five years. Here we can cite many passages from the Poets of the Greek Comedy, and you can mention works with which you are more familiar than I am.

2. Ignorance and pedantry: The drying up of great authors, Lucian, Erasmus, Montaigne; for the pages of modern books are like the parched oracles Plutarch mentions.

3. Sophistry in language: The emphasis upon words rather than ideas which should take care of the form. Plato has much to say about such rhetorical babbling in the famous *Dialogues*; Solon says, "Look to the tongue, and to the words of the glozing man." In the place of understanding and philosophy, we have grammar and culture exercises, or as Philo expresses it, "For already some men, ensnared by the charms of handmaidens, have despised their consort philosophy, and have grown old, some of them in music, some in geometry, others in grammar, the most in rhetoric." Language today is more dead than Lazarus, and even void of the corrupt grass and mold with which he was covered. Nimble, rustic words have been replaced by a specious trade vocabulary, the humbug shibboleths of science, medicine, psychology. You know, as you have said in the article on Literature you sent me, how vapid and vulgar are such words, introspective, subjective, objective, without spirit or even a pudendum.

4. The glimmering away of myth and parable and the cult of fact.

5. Tragedy of the Exterior Man: Reading of the ancients, when they are examined at all, by Eliot, Pound, Graves, either for external purposes or for show or to make eccentric judgments. Graves is a warm adherent of Pausanias because he was an Irish prizefighter; Pausanias wastes pages upon winners of the decathlon; we read Pausanias and Pindar to learn more of the Eleusinian mysteries, where Demeter was born, or if the Argo constructed at the Port of Deucalion was not the same vessel of Isis built at Thebes. Graves attacks Pound and Eliot only to admire late nineteenth-century American humorists, which is great foolishness. Nor do we study Eusebius to prove that Jesus was the nephew of Herod, or examine Homeric apocryphae in order to write a senseless book claiming Homer was a woman. Please see, that like Pound, the attempt is not to instruct, but to

astonish, and that the conclusions are wild and as predatory as Esau. The *Cantos* are the result of outside speculation, and not of the inward man; Socrates prays to Pan that the outward and the inward man may be one. Along with the misreading of authors of the past are the plagiarisms of the literary clerk who pilfers like a scrivener or a copyist, without making what he steals a part of his own nature and psyche.

6. The lack of any kind of Philosophy in Literature: Kepler, Thales, Anaxagoras, or the great works of the Naturalists, Buffon, Humboldt, Linnaeus, are no longer the rightful booty of a poet or essayist. This has brought about a decline in symbols; prose, like the Kosmos, is a great warm animal.

7. Trade in Letters: The venality of Eliot, Pound, Huxley, the Hollywood mystagogue.

8. The artist as Prometheus, who was said to have invented mankind, and then lived apart from that race of Cush and Nimrod who peopled the earth. But the books of Prometheus are warm-livered, though laden with the snows of the Caucasus; all great truths come from the Nile or from Mesopotamia, and all the Greek heroes from Deucalion, who is Noah, and Danaus, and Inachus, are of Asian origin.

9. That Mercury and Hermes are the same, and only he can quicken language whose heart is heavy with death; Thoth, who each year was wafted from the source of the Nile to Borsippa, is a ceremony of the grain that dies, and then reawakens. This mystery, too, has gone out of books.

Of course, my dear Herbert, we will not omit some of the lesser votaries of the harp, C. Day Lewis, Sherwood, Trilling, Edmund Wilson, as well as remarks on D. H. Lawrence, Richard Aldington, who also wrote a vehement attack on the cutpurses, Pound and Eliot, but again without furnishing us with wisdom, philosophy, ideas, and emotions of worth to novices and the youth whose reading goes back no further than Henry James. Pound's own eccentric reading can be seen in his rejection of feeling, the whole Hebraic and Christian legend and learning in favor of Robert Browning.

There are many others too who may be valued or cast into limbo in a line or two, and let us employ mockery, wit, ridicule,

for that stings much more than hyssop or gall which these men
cannot drink, for to quote your Kierkegaard again, to make use
of your own citation from him: ". . . they are at the outside."

Well, my dear Herbert, you know you have my love, and that I
am always your steadfast friend; when I have any words of criticism regarding a line or a passage or a chapter, I do not run to
seize the nearest trumpet, but tell them to you. Then if I am to
weigh your faults, never, I pray, mindful of my own, I do not fail
to mention your good works. Often I have been a gadfly to protect your own nature, and to remind you that it is blasphemous
to cite Pound or Eliot fourteen to sixteen times in one piece. I
give such homage to the Universe.

What think you of "The New Dunciad" as a title for our
book? I believe such a volume will cure our souls, which is the
reason for being an author. We must not omit La Bruyère from
our pages; he had sense which is entirely wanting in the critical
pages today, I believe. I told you Edmund Wilson has just discovered Genesis. He also took pains to give encomium to a
female novelist because she was the first one in America to write
about parturition. These are droll knaves and I think we can
make that sport of them which justice and wit require of us. He
has a whole volume laden with such buffoonery. Maybe there is
some moiety of truth in St. Augustine's remark, that a fool is a
protector of the wise.

I give you the pledge of my soul, I shall be just, but I shall
satisfy your own head and wit, when I cudgel these low-born
stylists. It is said that Zoroaster was born laughing; let us make a
book so.

There is no doubt that modern man has taken his leave of the
English of *Piers Plowman*, Gower, Waller, and even the plainest
of men, a fuller, vine-dresser, muleteer whose words now seem
like a golden age of letters. Homer venerated customs and
phrases of the highest antiquity, and would on occasion use an
obsolete word, and with some wariness we too should not be
averse to taking up an archaism.

Again, you have our love.

Your admiring friend,

Santa Monica, Cal.
April 5, 1955

Dear Herbert:

I have been thinking about your various suggestions regarding the epistolary essays. First, I think you are altogether right in saying that we should confine ourselves to the important malefactors of Hippocrene. These are the names I deem worthy of our attention, and you can add, or subtract from the list: Joyce, Pound, Eliot, Wyndham Lewis, Robert Graves, Henry James, Gertrude Stein.

At the instant, I am rereading *Ulysses*; this book is the principal assassin of our century, for the Greeks, returning from Troy, were no greater beggars than the readers after leaving *Ulysses*. Adopting an epic title, the novel is entirely anti-Homeric; Joyce can do no more than thinly veil his banal writing by inverting his sentences, and cataloguing old names which he does not know how to use. Lawrence was clean compared with Joyce, who has the miserable lust for the repulsive found in the lower middle classes.

Joyce has annihilated a whole generation of values, degraded ancient myths and has already had the effect of the Chimera and the Basilisk on another growing generation. The same is true of Pound, Eliot, Lewis, Stein, Lawrence. Joyce's intellectual deficiencies are enormous; Whitman, unable to explore ancient books and poets, did no more than cite them; but Whitman was savory, neither offending the nose, the mind, and altogether avoiding those scatophagous passages with which *Ulysses* is laden. I want to oppose Homer, the epic and the eponymous, to Joyce, the apotheosis of the little. The sinking of the Colossus began with the Titans in Homer and Hesiod, and now we have the villainy in the little.

But these are amorphous thoughts, and I am writing this in haste to catch you before you take your journey to the continent. Also, I am following your suggestion, and am starting the first epistle of our book within a week.

Meanwhile, I continue with the reading of modern books, and though as you know, my elenchus, like that of Socrates, is in large measure negative, the first letter shall be about health and love, and such warm gods, that a sacred literature should have, and which are seldom found in modern letters.

The emphasis on words instead of ideas and legends dominates poetry at present. Joyce has a few interesting ruses; leaving the butcher stalls, he has Bloom follow a trull with great fluxional hams; or coming from a shop, the proprietor's name reminds him of Gennesareth, and the wastes of his life call up visions of that lake, and also of the bituminous waters which breed no fish or weed. But he does nothing save to mention the lake or the asphaltic waters. There is another problem, the failure of the Father in our literature; Zeus, Osiris, Apis, Serapis, no longer honor the anti-heroes of our imaginative works, and the authors are lickerish and scatological, instead of carnal, mythopoeic, and virile.

Herbert, will you please tell me where I can reach you. I may have two epistles for you before you return to London, or at least, I earnestly hope one.

We both send you our warm love and blessings. You have my prayer for your health and safe return to your homeland. Ay, the Lotophagi sleep and gender, everywhere, with no thought of their wives, children, houses, and the earth from which they sprang.

Again, love,

letters to

Lewis Mumford

Dear Mumford:

It was very good to see you. You were very kind about *The Flea of Sodom*. You know how few readers one has. No matter how many people see the book so few perceive it, and not because they are not intelligent. Even sensitive persons are too arrogant to acknowledge another man's perceptions, or just too nihilistic. This is a sad subject, and at the moment I prefer to be droll, and recall Auden's attack; what the sons of Gomorrah won't do in the name of syntax. It may be that I shall get a chance to mention it in my column in the *Freeman*. I want to because it is too good to hide and, alas, too sick. It is all a part of homosexual aesthetics which is the desire to make everything into the hole that came before the first six days of the Creation. It is healing to know that you care for Tolstoy's *What Is Art?*. That marvelous man will never depart from my nature.

I am also of your mind regarding painting, and I am not so sure that the Jews were not altogether correct in prohibiting all graven images. How quickly man erects a pillar to himself, and most art is brewed in the belly of Moloch. I have the greatest regard for Bosch and for Goya, and yet I think we should forget about them until man has returned to the Word. One can make a sloven idol of painting, sculpture, music, but how debase Proverbs or the Psalms. Every true religious poet is an arsenal for the will. It would be almost impossible to garble Traherne, or the *Areopagitica,* or even Defoe's *Meditations.*

Dear Mumford, I wanted to get a few words of affection to you and also of appreciation of your own good, sharp faculties. All of us live as city cenobites, and it is the tragedy of our literature. As long as the American author is a Bartleby the Scrivener, we can never have an unusual commonwealth. I cannot mend it myself, but I try as best I can to record my own sick solitude. Books, books, we pine to make that which separates us from others, and maybe disfigures our own lives and ends. It was Origen who said that every sigh is for the end, and a book is a sigh, and if good, always eschatological.

It takes a long time to misunderstand people, and it may be that we shall talk again and labor for this sweetest of all human delights.

I am still at work on the little novel. I must say that it is deeply kind of you to say so willingly that you will read it when it is done. Should this book be published first, I want to make my acknowledgments in it to you provided it is a good book; for no one has the right to give another man a mean or average fate by putting him into an uncivil volume.

I send you the warm Trades, and the May sea-rivers that run from the Gates of Hercules to the Antilles.

Santa Monica, Cal.
April 17, 1953

My dear Mumford:

Your exceedingly kind letter reached me at Berkeley. I thank you very much for what you say about the poems in the *New Directions Annual*. The best title for that yearly product would be "No Directions." I urged Laughlin to ask you to edit one of the *Perspectives USA*. He wrote me a very civil letter without referring to my suggestion. I told him you would bring a human wisdom and culture altogether wanting in that periodical which is expensive waste. But then, as you know so well, waste is our bourne and touchstone. I am very sorry I failed. I am not one of the pathics or flâneurs of this little sodality of letters. I print my work where I can, and it is hard for me to find a page open to any thoughts I have.

What you say about your position as a writer pierces me. Many will regard the fact that your books are bought as sufficient; I know it is not true. The American has no memory so that what he admires or feigns to praise he does not even recollect. Besides, living as we do in a culture in which fact is the main god, a writer is expected to produce books very rapidly to prove that he is an author. One has to prove one's self to everybody each month and year because no one recalls the last book, but is only seasoned by the latest one. That, too, and you know it sorely well, is our faith in the new and our Stygian distrust of the old.

I have been reading some of your pages in *Technics and Civilization,* and Auden is certainly foolish in asserting that you do not write well. I think your prose is exceedingly good. It is bare and often austere, and no one can find fault with a plain style. Not in obscurity, but in plainness, is wisdom, writes Euripides. Your feeling for modern products when the art is not added, as you say, is deeply fetching. I come, you know, to your book, not with a hostile attitude toward your faculties for which I have the greatest regard, but with a great uneasiness about the machine. You know the late Anderson felt so, and though he did not have your reflective abilities or culture, he, as Thoreau said, argued from his hands to his head.

The influence of Veblen upon you I also esteem, and I think you have gone beyond him. The only reason I do not speak with more sureness is that aside from the small book of lectures I reviewed, and some pages I have read with great care, I am still a niggard reader of yours. I can tell you I should like very much to do a long essay on your work. It would not matter that I am of the mind of Ruskin and Morris. What is important is that I respect you, and there is very little to respect at present. I am so at odds with the times, and out of patience with the congealed abstract alphabet that is taken for the liver of Prometheus, that I live in almost impermeable solitude. I do not relish this, but this is the result of my feeling and nature. If you know anywhere that I could write about you, that is, a medium that is good, I should be very glad to read your works as searchingly as I can, and to write about you. I think your work should be called to the attention of the poseurs of Helicon, for I believe above all that it is human, and that is what we need most. I shall be reading much more of your book as I have already marked many passages, and pray that you may at least find in my honest exceptions more chivalric esteem for your remarkable head than you receive from the latest reader, more guided by Lethe than Mnemosyne.

My dear Mumford, I believe I would relinquish writing altogether if the printing press could be destroyed, and people would stop publishing new books which are for lotus-eaters.

All this sounds very negative, and I must admit that it is the denying elenchus of Socrates that is today the source of my own thoughts.

However, I shall read your book with deep care.

Meanwhile, know how much I value your letter to me.

I am in the midst of a little book on whether man should have a phallus or not. Sophocles in his old age said that he was very glad to be rid of such a rioting and unruly member. I have used many ancient writers and have written it in a very mirthful manner, or so I think. Where, though, to send it? It is a short book. Could I send it to you to see what you think?

You have my deep respect and most earnest appreciation.

Both Rlene and I earnestly hope your wife Sophie has altogether recovered. It is said that the name, Artemis, comes from sound health, and your prose has that, and nothing in writing or thinking is more important than that. As you say elsewhere, what were Morris, Tolstoy, Melville, Gauguin seeking? "Plain animal self-respect." We hardly have a painter or poet in America who is good as any domestic beast!

Santa Monica, Cal.
June 16, 1953

My dear Mumford:

I have had no word from you in some time and hope you are again at the apex of your strength and that writing occupies you. I was rather troubled by my last epistle to you; I feared lest you unintentionally garble my entire attitude toward you as a person and an author. My own situation in our brutish world of letters is quite amorphous. I believe I am the most hated man in American literature. It is far too painful for me to defend my character. I would just as soon be the buckler of my own books which would also hurt my blood and my very soul. I do not think about what I have written because my sole purpose is to improve my spirit and to write better. Besides, it is too great a hazard to go back to earlier work or even to any book. No volume is quite ripe enough to slake the soul parched for infinite forms. Aside from all this, I have been plagued by a load of maladies; each day some new locust devours my health, or frets it, and often my days are a labor, and because I live in such congealed privacies my life, too, is a bleak mountain of satiety.

Now as for your own books, which I have only tasted in small part, and really much to my regret. I mentioned the other matters pertaining to my own plight so that you would not regard me too self-loving in not going at once to your printed pages. In one sense, it is not at all right for me to neglect you. It is contrary to my faith as a writer. I had hoped that my position would grow stronger either with Laughlin or Karl Shapiro on *Poetry* so that I could persuade one or the other to permit me to write about you. I imagine I told you I no longer write for the *Freeman,* and though I am deeply wounded by indigence, I do not mind this severance. I never had any inward connection with the magazine; like most periodicals the prose was a vulgar attack against language and worse against the intellect and the trembling bowels. I had no quarrel with these people. What occurred was that Chamberlain was cast out, and I was simply dropped. I detest politics; it has eaten up the living waters between people. Aristotle rightly remarks that energetic affections are the groundwork of a truthful commonwealth. I cannot endure the squeamish shibboleths of the wanton reactionaries whose aim is to kill the head of man, and I desire no part of any other political phalanx because each is a leveler belonging to one of the most wizened circles in Dante's *Purgatory.*

I hang on to destiny by Ariadne's thread, and, alas, my connections with people in the world are as uncertain. I had proposed to Laughlin that you edit one of the issues of *Perspectives USA*. I mentioned your unique talents and your considerable work with the *American Caravan*. Not least of all I spoke of your fervent probity, and had you no other gifts, that alone would entitle you to be ranked among the geniuses. Honesty in letters is well-nigh extinct. The Academy is the American bourse of literature. There is your friend Waldo Frank. Many years ago I had done a piece on Frank for the *American Spectator*; he was very discontented because he wanted the essay to appear in the *N.R.*; so I withdrew the article, and then it was not published anywhere. I remember at the time Waldo saying to me, "Edward, you know, writing about me is very hard." I wryly rejoined, "Writing is very hard." Had Waldo a more enduring heart he would have been a person of some standing in this country.

To return, *Perspectives USA* has the twelve editors, and I am not one of them! I had also told Laughlin that I had never received benefits from you so that my pleading was quite disinterested. What I was thinking, and this is such a roundabout suggestion as to appear bizarre to you, is that if you could do a small volume on writing I could get Shapiro to let me do a piece on you. I could then go to the other books. Right now, he has asked me to do an essay on D. H. Lawrence. I am no Lawrence acolyte; there was much of the feminine in him; his volume on Christ is really infamous, quite pederastic. However, cast aside all the erotic rubbish, and there are some very fine lines. He lacked any strength for masses; an unfinished foot by Michaelangelo has more power than an entire book by Lawrence. I would much prefer to do something on you, but I know I would not be successful no matter how much I entreated them to give me space for your books. I think you could do a little book on American Literature with unusual moral vigor and sense. There is as little sense in criticism as there are flowers in Tartarus. At the moment, making ready to do the Lawrence piece, I went back to some of Heine, and was so disenchanted that I could have wept. He was a rather shallow but most charming feuilletonist. Last night I looked at some essays by Voltaire and was pleased and replenished.

This may seem to be a rude suggestion, but, believe me, I am considering your own perplexity as an author. Whatever it is that stupid dust can know, I have some knowledge of the infamy of getting known in America. I am much too irascible to come into any easy reputation myself, and though I am dust I am not dirt, at least not filthy dirt.

My dear Mumford, you are likely to be bought and never read just as I will probably be neither purchased nor read. If you will forgive me for saying it, my own plight may be worse than yours, which cannot be a balm to you, nor do I mean it so. Do you know that Herbert Read in his last letter to me had the effrontery to tell me that he is famous? That is the end. I have not known a man in the world today who has sufficient intellectual marrow to survive success. My friendship with Read is very strained. I have told him repeatedly that he has elevated illiteracy in painting into a monstrance.

In reading many of your pages I saw that the book was brought out in 1931, I believe. You imagined that you were a journeyman when you knew Spingarn. I was a craven apprentice in 1931.

As for reading my own manuscript, if you are in the throes of labor, please do not bother. It can wait, only limbo beckons me to her arms. I have no publisher, anyway, and, frankly, it is such gall and hyssop to be in the wild, bestial hands of this publishing rabble that I send nothing out except to *Poetry* and to Laughlin, who every now and then asks me for a piece of writing, but not a book. Were he not surrounded by so many pathics, flâneurs, and grammar spados who cannot write, he would do some good things.

I earnestly hope that your wife, Sophie, has recovered; my own poor spouse is a typewriter drudge all day, leaving me here sometime in Elysian contentment when I can form one thought, and again in Stygian tedium when nothing, not grass, the sun, dogwood, or Paracelsus nurture me.

I send you affections and be sure of my genuine and civil regard for your nature. Try to consider, please, the little book on literature; it will be my pleasure to serve you.

My dear Mumford:

You have not replied to my two letters. I imagine I know the reason. I do not think your silence shows intellectual bravery or manliness. You know that when I had the occasion to review a book of yours I did so at once. Moreover, I got into a broil with Laughlin because he had not chosen editors like yourself, but had engaged flâneurs and pederasts. I had repeatedly urged him to ask you to edit one of the issues of *Perspectives*. In one of my epistles to you I suggested that you do a little book on American Literature. I thought you would do it with feeling and probity. Should you find that you desired to write about Literature, I could then try to help you acquire those readers who now turn to our false intelligentsia.

What doubtless hurt you were my words regarding one of your books written in 1931. They were obviously musings that came not from a complete reading of the book. The contrary is true. My eyes, Mumford, are as weak or nearly so as the evening in Isaac's pupils. To worsen matters I have no sight at all in one of my eyes. I had told you that could I entice the people on *Poetry* or Laughlin at New Directions, I would lay aside my own work to read your works with acute care and write about them. For me at the moment to wrench myself from the ancients and to go through your books, all of great length, would be another denial in my life. I do not mean that your books would dispirit me, but that however good they may be, I should be departing from my own living waters which sometimes ebb terribly. Moreover, I have so many maladies that it would be droll to recite them.

You have paid me some great compliments, and I was weak enough in affection to want in some way to laud you. I had some few conversations with you and saw that you had a most civil and discerning head. If, however, you think I am one to hide my inward thoughts regarding another person, you do me grave wrong. You then mistook what is fond and human in the blood for cant or something low.

Mumford, you complain you have no readers; and yet you can find your two gudgeons and loaves. Look, I worked ten weeks on revaluing Lawrence for *Poetry*. After the essay was read by the editor who gave me prodigal encomia for it, he advised me that he could use only about two thousand words of it. I had written about seventy-five hundred words. The essay on Lawrence is idol-breaking; what I thought he was in my shallow youth was quite different from what I saw in a recent perusal. The man had genius, but he had turned the stones into bread. He had regarded fame as a disgrace, but either penury, a severe deity and a great mentor, had pushed him from one novel to another. We live in a culture of waste, and Lawrence was a detritus of that folly. I had forgotten to mention that I shall very likely receive twenty dollars for my labor on Lawrence. Still, I would do the same for you, and will when the occasion comes, or when I can exact it.

Now my remarks about Waldo Frank may have offended you. Remember you never mentioned him to me. I do not know whether he is still your friend or not. We had been on the most intimate terms for seven years. Whatever you may think about him I have the imperial right to judge him as an author, and I repeat he is a very puling one. Whatever sensibility the man had he sold for the pottage of lentils. My faults may be grave, but I shall never relinquish my vision for the fields of Boaz or the grapes of Jericho.

You cannot know in what boreal solitude I live. You might not be able to endure it. Still, the fates advise us that no one has to bear more than his nature can sustain.

I had told you in a previous letter that I am more hated than Poe; my gifts are far greater, too; that does not mean that everything I write is Edenic. Far from it, I still do not know how to turn the gray water words into Cana wine. Besides, my rock of Peter is Doubt which sometimes heals the most Stygian wounds in the soul, and on other occasions is Golgotha.

You at least have no hardship in procuring publication. Each time I seek to print my words I must go out into the most fearsome combat. Pearce admires me greatly, but he won't print me. He is also vexed with me because I impugned a book of dross he had brought out. It is my moral duty to assail a bad book which is likely to pervade our miserable apprentices of the Muses.

When we first met again after many years you said with great and marvelous innocence that you were less a writer than a public figure. Remember that Hamlet had mentioned his own youth as a thoroughfare. We pay for every sin.

Meantime, I pray that you are at the top of your force again. Should you not answer this I shall have some rueful moments over it. The intellectual classes are very dishonest, and those who care more for the truth than for a pinchbeck reputation should be companions. Otherwise, the entire land is doomed; never in the history of man was lucre such a god, never was the church such a market place for Sunday mummers of the dearest parables in the two testaments.

I earnestly hope you will reconsider your ideas on the machine. Remember that it was Wilde who was the first to see the beauty of the machine. You are by nature opposed to all these pathics and Gadarene tombed perversions. I still think Ruskin was correct in desiring to cast away the inventions that have exhausted the Angels in men. New inventions can be looked upon as any other crime. Novelty is a wretched token of occidental ennui. What need has man of any more conveniences; he has so many now that soon he will either demolish the planet or be as weak as those Pygmies who were chased from the River Styrmon by the cranes. I had suggested that you read the ancients; for though I think that your style insofar as I know it has intellectual vigor, it is not yet potent enough in symbols.

I send you my good thoughts; it is futile to give men today your affections, for even our writers will in return send you the salutations of the business Philister. Do not take this remark as an offense, but I sicken in my most nether soul the American author.

Berkeley, Cal.
December 1, 1953

Dear Mumford:

Your most civil letter came to me some while ago; despondency, a nether god, prevented me from replying promptly. A

letter is an angel, and one should not avoid it or delay it. Besides, though, I have been in and out of the spital house, and
with no afflictions healed.

You have been in my mind often, and I have thought of your
work. For some reason, not inexplicable, both you and Herbert
Read have occupied my thoughts. He worships painting, and you
the machine. I do not mean that you sprinkle holy water on our
evil mechanical devices. But you see a great good in these inventions, and that troubles me sorely. Why a man of your noble
faculty can perceive that painting is a Moloch or a Baalpeor, and
not comprehend that the machine is another sin I cannot understand. You imagine, if this does not sound overweening, that
were inventions in the hands of savory people they would be our
Cherubim. Do you believe that Abel, which is the affectionate
blood and human conscience, can ever subdue Cain? Goodness is
so weak in this world that fable reports Abel was slain by a reed!
I mentioned to you in an earlier epistle that seeing beauty in
machinery is a great perversity unworthy of your nature. It is my
own feeling that you make the most earnest effort to be plain.
Paradox is the weapon of Gomorrah. No one unless he has the
mind of the Sodomite will deliberately mistake an isosceles tri-
angle for an octahedron, or look upon an alley as one of the
streets of Priam. I think you are an admirer of Tolstoy; did we
not once speak of his treatise, *What Is Art?* Here he speaks of
such wit as one gets in Baudelaire, Mallarmé, Verlaine, Rimbaud. He saw at once, with prescience, which is only sharp seeing, the grave faults of these gifted pederasts of Hippocrene. Do
not believe that I think I have avoided all the follies of our age. I
must struggle against every form of vice, one of which is aesthetics, really a subhuman use of the alphabet of Thoth. Suppose we
set aside the paradox which is the fox cunning of letters, and
consider the machine itself. I have a genuine respect for your
nature, and yet you are always busy. How much of this is the
result of the auto, meaning self or Narcissus or Ham, for the
automobile is self-love and always going, which is not troubling
overmuch with others. One has to have time for meditation,
friendship, an epistle, a poem, being tender Abel's blood crying
up out of the earth for men and even Cain. You do not see

people because you have too much to do; I don't see any one because I am afraid of Cain's reed.

But as for the matter of the auto, does it not damage the blood, hurry it so that it cannot be still and loving and brotherly? Who that goes everywhere in the land today says, "Am I my brother's keeper?" In this query lies the entire sin of our reflections, life, and books. What can you or I do with the airplane? What need have we of it? Will not one invention gender another and another until we are doomed?

I regard the airplane as a crime, just as I do a city of a million people. Inertia sires greed, and each novelty is another killer of the hands and the feet. Our hands are already very stupid and morose. What can we do with them? What do we do with them? Ordinary salutations are becoming feebler; people seldom shake hands. Have you noticed the new custom in trade; the shopkeeper no longer touches you, but drops the coins into your palm. The grubby news vendor is also ruled by this occidental Hygeia. But people require touch and caresses, even dirty ones are far better than none at all. We have these big, touchless markets, stores, cafeterias, machine food-places, which are the stores of Narcissus or Ham.

The more we look for beauty in a lathe or plumbing—and so many of our paintings today are abstract toilet thinking, and our sculpture the same—the more artful assassins we are of the yew tree, the poplar, begetting of children, and the love of the family lintel, threshold, and marriage house.

Even if a man of your gifts were to govern the use of the machine, it would not be a help. You could not escape the malefic effects of the mechanical demon.

I pray that you will reconsider all this. You say you are not read, and doubtless it is true; you have the fewest of intellectual readers because this tribe has well-nigh disappeared, as a result of radio, movies, television, these triune devils in the land. Believe me, I have been deeply bruised by the communists; they have hurt whatever I have written, and they are poltroon killers who do not overtly attack but bury what they oppose. However, these committees who are ransacking their thoughts are worse than the tombs of Gadarene. To begin with, to believe in our commonwealth is to affirm cupidity and the most infamous rites of money. Not once does this vile corpus of men see what injustice and greed have done to the earth. American democracy is a sham shibboleth that could arouse no Gideon. We are ruled by such skulkers that even the mention of their names offends the nostrils. Yet who speaks out against thievish prices? Who inveighs against our cities of Nimrod? The vices of Borsippa and Ur and the terracotta idols of Nippur are sweet moral air and pomegranates compared with London, New York, Los Angeles, the three cities of the debauched gullet. And all this, my dear Mumford, goes back to inventions. The radio is a wanton box more evil than Nubian voodooism or human sacrifice. For this box has immolated not only an entire nation but many races. All day long there is a recital of crimes that would nauseate Lucifer. The box has permeated education, a cutpurse hypocrite of the young. Can you tell why we need—sane and savory people who want to understand the Kosmos and all the rivers of the world and their children—this medium of filth? Do you imagine that the radio and television can be disciplined? The inventions themselves are for inertia, idiocy, being furtive, lying, and killing Abel wherever he is. What new inventions will these devils beget? When and where will it stop? And what man is so just as Seth or Noah who can govern and limit the machine? Not I? I cower before it, and flee it, for it is the Erinyes and the destroyer of noble fate.

My dear Mumford, I want to thank you very much for remarks about *The Flea of Sodom*. Your good words are nard and cassia to my soul. I work most of the day, putting the greater part of my labors in the drawer, the sarcophagus of the poet.

At the instant, I am at work on a long poem. Who will print it? I must write to oppose the Void, for in the beginning was Nothing, the enemy of God and human dust.

Maybe some day you might feel urged to do a small book on American Literature. Do not think my suggestion came out of a torpid moment.

Meanwhile, please take with these words my blessings which are much weaker today than evil. The tomb of Noah is forty Egyptian ells in length, which is supposed to be the size of the Patriarch's body. Of such stature is justice. You know the mean-

ing of the name Cain in Aramaic, regarded as the earliest of
languages, is nothing. I could spell my own name and efforts
so!

Berkeley, Cal.
December 11, 1952

My dear Mumford,

You say in your last letter to me that you were too callow to
discern Spingarn. I was more so than you when I knew him. The
growth of the American is very slow, if he unfolds at all. Remember Nietzsche telling that the book was ripe for him, but that he
was not ripe for the book? That, too, is always with us; we try to
seed friendship and fail because we are pushing Fate too far, or
because we are seldom ready in this sullen, uneasy hemisphere
to do anything that may illuminate our souls or whet our faculties. At least, I think, we were not invulnerable to grass or sun or
a moon in a human being; maybe we did not fix our own identities in such rich loam as we should, but we came away with some
extraordinary detritus, which is the leavings of another man or
generation upon which we must feed or perish of a low, pelting
destiny. Maybe we are lucky to have gone as far as we have,
which may be poor, considering what wild, characterless people
inhabit America. I have no sense of belonging to this land. As a
Jew I have no landmarks and no cave of Macpehlah to bury my
hopes and failures, and were I to own a small farm or hut I
would never possess it because the earth is not my heritage. Nor
can I look with any affection upon present-day Israel, a housing
project for all the miserable waifs of the world. Then as a writer
my bare table is a vast, naked Cordillera or treeless savannah, for
what fruits or gramen I plant here do not take root in this world
or feed a single soul. Birds fly into the grotto with stems, green,
or seeds to feed their young, which often fall between the crevices
of calcareous rock and spring up in abundance. A writer in the
occident is the urchin of the fowls, for whatever he brings to the
young is refused and if he drops it it never flourishes. We sow

always in stony places, but are more luckless than bird or cavern or rock.

I sent you the copy of *Poetry* magazine. Did you receive it? I sit here, gray rain weather on the window, but rejoicing in Pliny and in some Maya documents on herbals, and work. I trust that you have found the strength for your own labors. I feel as guilty as Cain because I have not gone to your books, which I intend to do soon as I imagine I have accomplished some reflections and written for awhile. I do not neglect books I have, but at times it takes me a season or so before I go to them. I had hoped to do some species of essay upon them, but there is upheaval at the *Freeman,* and I have no stomach for their quarrels, and at best derive some hard-earned pennies from them. If I do a long piece it does not get printed. I have a feeling that though you have found considerable attention in the world, our aesthetes pay little heed to you. I have a great distrust of aesthetics, which is not only the avoidance of morality, but leads people into the most foolish judgments and feral, jaguar paradoxes of Gide and Cocteau and his pathic acolytes. It may be that some time in the future I shall be able to write about you in a magazine that is interested in thought and in letters. At the moment, I know of no such periodical. The little magazines are tripods for homosexual cant and professorial buffoons.

Try sometimes, when you require new aliments, the elder Pliny or Theophrastus. I think that will not only be real viaticum for your head, but will give your prose a certain wild, rustic texture which we must acquire. Most of our modern writing is very metropolitan and that is a weakness. I find great pleasure in rereading Skeat on Chaucer or in Captain John Smith's *Travels,* which is full of strong idioms, and not vulgar like our own streetgamin patois.

I had been thinking of you, your health; my own has been quite faulty. I put one of your letters the other day on one of the learned pages of Humboldt, so that when I opened it, I would see it and then write. As you know, people don't say thanks anymore, don't write letters, and after a visit with them you feel as though the Harpies had just dropped their excrement upon you, which is exactly what they wish you to feel.

letters to
James Laughlin

Topanga, Cal.
September 25, 1952

Dear Laughlin,

I have your good words from Paris, and I am again very desponding. All these foundations seem to be set up to support drones and apostles of expediency. Out here I met a young woman, who considers herself no more than a mediocrity in my presence, but she has received a two years' fellowship from the Rockefeller Foundation to write plays. I went to the same institution two years ago and with the most bloat cant was turned away. Saint Paul once said, I praise myself since no one else lauds me. It is a sorry solace, and even if what one says is true, it is humbling hyssop in the mouth. Yet I am mindful of my long, though sporadic, knowledge of you, and I have seen you publish many volumes of men far less than I. I do not want you to feel that this is a churlish feeling about you. I have much affection for you, and have told you many times you have done a work that will be remembered. However, your task is by no means finished. You are still in the heyday of your physical vigor, and by now you have achieved some real force as an influence in America. It was once audacious to print Pound and Williams; it no longer is. You must, just as I must, fashion your whole life on Danton's gallant creed, "Audacity, more audacity, and always audacity."

Nor is it of fiery worth to print so many Italians who are just catching up with American naturalism of two decades ago. You know I found no fault in you whatsoever when you rejected *Bottom Dogs*. I thought your reasons ripe and fertile, and I rejoiced in your own perceptions. But, my dear Laughlin, it is not good to set aside *BD* and then print Nathanael West or the Italians. The late West, like so many of our little singing cicadas, was more than a three-fourth shut man. On a page he could chant and then as though he had plucked his honey, die altogether. Either we perish for the lack of inward reading, and the volition to continue until our honey is drained by fate, or we compromise. We had a few nineteenth-century men of epic width who would not do it. But then look at Melville, and I say that almost everyone who at present sings his belief would have forsaken him in his own day. Melville said, "If I wrote the gospel of my century I would die in the gutter." He wrote such a faith and perished unknown. His books, though our birthright, did not sell. What then happened? With bleak heart and a fissured resolve he wrote some poems which he published. But not getting printed killed both the spirit and the letter of the man. The letter killeth the spirit, and the spirit, rejected, killeth the letter. I have tried to bend fate, knowing I cannot alter it. It is a terrible tragedy to be born a writer in any country, but it is worse to be one in America. It is told that even in the golden age of Pericles that Anaxagoras was exiled, Phidias was banished, and Socrates took the hemlock. It is also related that Terence, glutted with the sufferings of disappointment, repaired to a small, pelting, coarse town and there died.

Now it seems that I cannot get help anywhere, and yet I have that little twilight prescience that tells me that two books I have written, and some poems, and maybe a few critical pieces, will become lustral waters for Helicon. It is alas the small comfort that is placed in the brazier without burning coals. For a writer cannot rest upon what he wrote, whether it be Prometheus or Lear or the sweet meditations of Thomas Traherne. I don't want to be slain lying in cold limbo, and I don't want you to consign me to this most evil of regions where no brother or sister or mother or friend touches you. For in America we hate the forgotten person, and I am, despite the greatest devotion and most penniless devotion to literature, a waif of the Muses. If one man can reach another and somehow touch and quicken him, I beg you to do for me what you have done for others, print me. For since evil penury is my fate, let not my load be unendurable by

also carrying in my soul the terrible burden of oblivion. "Alms
for oblivion," wrote Melville.

You are a rich man, and I am glad that you have this buckler
which protects you from insolence, and those chagrins which
make us stoop and give us such crooked ends. Every day I tremble for my bread and am made less by some mischance or chagrin
that weakens my living forces. The only shield I have is what I
can get onto the printed page. Otherwise I am doomed. You see,
Laughlin, should you think that I am a braggart, and that I
don't really hear Calliope and the naiads in their kelp and water
songs, know that I take small credit for my abilities. They have
only brought me the fattest shoal of enemies and poverty. Besides, what can dust know? My knowledge derives from guessing
and prayer, and those unexpected miracles of insight which no
one can order or anticipate or ever understand. I used to believe
that Socrates said he knew nothing because he was wily or very
vain, or because he had within his syllogistic spirit some cheating
Delphic oracle that gave him answers he already had. I know
now that this is not so, and that he had many quick, inward
reaches as sharp as the Pelion ash of Achilles, and that he was no
liar.

I remember that when some dunderhead of Hippocrene had
been praised far above Goethe the latter said very soberly that
this was foolish because he was very superior to the poetaster. He
also added that it was not his fault because he was not responsible for his gift. He wrote and something happened, something
was born. I write too, and an Angel of the other world appears;
another man writes, and he gets a reputation. You know that
among men of deep probity I am regarded as a writer of rare
faith. I have not been afraid to go about in the simpering world
as a man with windmills in his head as Don Quixote was said to
have. One of the terrible weights in Quixote's heart was that he
always had to prove that he was a knight of many truths which
the seraphs heard but which men mocked. Though it may sound
ridiculous, and I may seem to be senselessly blowing myself up, it
is madness to go everywhere proclaiming myself to be Edward
Dahlberg. It is an insane folly, and a murdering egotism, for I
shall never know who that man is for two reasons: one is that no

man can endure to know himself, and the other the world cannot bear it either.

Now, all this, my friend, is a preamble to a plain and humble and proud request, that you publish me, so that my fate shan't starve. I do not ask you to fatten my pockets, but I beg you not to cast my fate to impious dogs. Do what you can without hurt to your own person or principles, but do not be afraid to be vigorous in your belief in me. Remember, yesterday Pound was a name in the secondhand book dealers, and Williams not even a celebrated nonentity. You know that among my ardent defenders I have had good Ford Madox who once said to me when he had read the manuscript of *Can These Bones Live,* "I would consider it an honor to write a Foreword [which he was to have done] to your book, and let me, please, be your literary agent." You know what a chivalric nature he was. Among my defenders have been Ford, Aldington, Lawrence, Arnold Bennett, yourself, Williams, Herbert Read, Dreiser, Mumford, Stieglitz, Zukofsky, Basil Bunting, and many names you and I hold in esteem that I do not mention here.

I ask you, please, to reprint *Can These Bones Live* in your American Letters Series, for I am not at all represented there, and this is unjust. You know that you have just about exhausted your edition of the *Flea,* so that what with the arrangements you made with Nevill, you have incurred no loss. I have a letter from Peter Nevill saying that they would be interested in handling my new novel, "provided Laughlin should first give us his OK to publication, provided we do the printing for him and ourselves."

Mumford and Charles A. Pearce and Zukofsky have seen the manuscript, some thirty thousand words already written. Mumford has spoken of its prophetic design, and Zukofsky compared it with Swift in its satire and parable. Pearce wanted me to break it down into poetry, a long piece of which is to appear in *Poetry* magazine, Chicago. Pearce is acting as my literary agent, gratis, because of his belief in me. This book will be filled with Aztec and Mayan symbols, and with old rituals of the Asia-European and the occidental earth. You will not make any money out of me, nor will you lose any, because you have found a way of bringing out books that is not a road to bedlam and insanity.

More than this, I devoutly believe that if you stand by me, it will give you in later years that memory of frankincense and myrrh without which our sweetest Muse is clinkers and Hades.

I stopped working on the novel a year ago, having no bravery to go on piercing my spirit as the Aztecs did their tongues with maguey spines, for all writing is penance and bleeding, and I cannot let my own blood in caves and rheumy crannies.

Let me add, don't get bored with New Directions; it is of inestimable value to this hapless, torn land. Remember, being alive, too, is often a filthy, itching tedium which we must each day overcome or die in torpor.

You know, you have my deep affections. I have a letter from Herbert Read, saying that you had promised to see him, but have not done so. Another important matter for us is to give our closest attention to the men of immortal worth; think how much more we both should be at this instant had we seen Ford Madox Ford much more than we did. You know he used to ask me repeatedly to come and see him, and I was then too coarse to accept these plain, modest invitations, and now that, too, is a part of my deficit as a man, for we reckon our fate by our losses, more than we do by our victories. At least I have deep, sharp repining, for this, and remorse, though the Greeks did not deem it of such precious value as the Hebrews, is a great addition to the head, the lips, and our doleful ends.

Do let me hear from you; at this instant, I can only repeat to myself, "Is there no Balm in Gilead?"

Your friend,

_____

Berkeley, Cal.
January 12, 1953

My dear Laughlin,

Your letter has come, slowly forwarded from Topanga. I deeply regret I am not there to see you. Maybe you might be coming up this way. I am writing you at once to catch you if possible before you leave.

I have a high regard for both you and Pearce. As a matter of

fact, the leading poem in *Poetry* of the February issue was dedicated to him, and I shall send it to you.

Now I have some words from CAP* regarding his attitude
toward *Perspectives USA,* and I hope that I shall not be garbling
them. To begin with, he always spoke with admiration of you.
He does feel that you are doing too little for American authors
very expensively. I am of his mind in this. You are gathering
about you too many syntax flâneurs who have no vision and
whose influence upon writing is very noxious. I mentioned
Lionel Trilling to you, and you at the time may have thought
this was the result of some spleen. I assure you that most of my
foes are quondam admirers, but I distrust praise more than criticism. When Ford Madox Ford sent Pearce the manuscript of *Can
These Bones Live,* he wrote back with quaint candor that I was a
prophet but that he was too much of a poltroon to publish me.
When I was a young, celebrated author I received accolades from
many of the people you are now employing as editors, but who,
thinking I had dropped into limbo, extinguished me in each
volume on American Literature they published. What had happened was that I had decided I did not want a quick destiny and
a gimcrack fame that in the end would be hyssop and shame. I
mention myself here, because as you know I have been deeply
involved in advance-guard letters, and have influenced many
writers who have not only not thanked me, but have attempted
to maim me whenever possible. I do not think, Laughlin, you
should have that kind of editor. The periodical should represent
various points of view if it is to be plain and honest. It does not.
With the exception of yourself, and I regard you as a man of
great civility and honor and of real worth to a land sorely in
need of truth and gift, I feel that the editors are unjust, often
base, and regard American Letters as their private booty. Plato
has said that justice is not doing harm to one's friends or foes,
and you must print people who have that regard for the oracles,
if you are to render a service to this country. Now to return to
Pearce, with whom I never discussed *Perspectives USA,* he wrote
me in much this manner. I may be adding to it, but I think this
is the quiddity of his own feeling. Aside from yourself, I regard

* Charles A. Pearce

him as the only one who is a publisher today who deeply cares for
books that come out of the deeps of a man's soul.

I sicken as I see men working with words in absolute Sheol and
oblivion. I can only say to them that I regard Laughlin as my
friend, and that I have abundant affection for him, but I cannot
say to them, that here is a man who is ready at the moment to
quicken to what is new, and by that I mean, human, ECCE
HOMO, Flesh, Bone, Spirit. Look, pardon me for mentioning
myself, I am almost alone, if not so as a representative of a warm,
human literature, and I go begging as the wormiest Lazarus at
your threshold for some crumb. I understand you made Roditti
your European editor. Now, I never met this man, but he wrote a
scurrile and really foolish attack against *The Flea of Sodom*; I
took care of that, so I am not at all peevish about it. Karl Shapiro, who has been a friend of my muse, and whom I have never
met, let me do a lengthy reply in *Poetry* which I am told created
a good deal of attention. What I am saying is that I do not mind
a speculative difference; we have today a corpse sameness in letters throughout the land, and that is what is killing the Delphian
God. But what can such a man have as a seer, a Solon, to gather
up what is neglected in writing? That is the problem, that is your
Burden of Tyre, and mine, to see to it that some hidden poet is
not dead in the furrow to be honored by all the varlets who are
giving humbug homage to Melville in the most crass prose.

My dear Laughlin, it is no longer an audacity to print Williams. You were a man of prescience in reprinting *In the American Grain*. Believe, it is grounded in the smallest amount of
reading, still it is richly gifted, and has a poetic faculty almost
lacking in history, I mean, the native annals. He should have
gone on with it; he had no further ripening; whatever pushed
him toward his inward nature I cannot fathom, but he never
went to such candles or altars again. Pound, too, is a subtle
craftsman, but again he is not producing a human literature. He
never did. Loveless books gender Stygian barrenness, and that
is what ails the land at present. Not lack of talent, or brains, but
even a clever mind can produce something baleful and can be an
example for the apprentice-writer that will send him to Erebus.

Did it not occur to you, my dear Laughlin, that to set up

twelve editors, and to exclude the author of *Can These Bones Live* and *The Flea of Sodom,* a point of view absolutely extinct in writing now, is not only not just, but not good. Do not think for an instant this beggars my friendship for you. But what you are doing, and you are ploughing not the fallow but in Tartarus, is, quite without meaning to do it, to compound evils that have already given us Dead Sea glyphs. That is why a man of integrity, like Pearce, left, and not because of any disrelish whatsoever of your person. He feels that you have done some very admirable work, and who that is honest and loves the truth even more than friendship, will not say he is right in this? But he believes that your best work, for the most part is in the rear of your life, and you are much too young to be tired. Look, I have not your youth, or strength, and my penury is a constant ague, and I sit here at a table eight hours each day writing for whom? Do you know what it means to keep on writing with not a soul in the universe to see to it that your words drop into that tilth that will be the first sprouts in another's nature or book?

Use, Laughlin, your own gifts, for you are truly a humble nature, not feigning to be so, and I admire you when you say India is an enigma you cannot unfold. Who can? I have long laved my heart in those remote mineraled countries which the ancients loved. Ur and Erech, and the Ganges which is one of the four rivers passing through Paradise, in a word, Gihon, have been my deities.

I pray this will reach you before you leave. At the instant I am at work on a long poem seeded by Inca, Aztec, Maya legend, mingled with Plato, the Rig-Veda, Theophrastus. Does this sound showy? I mean it not so, but plainly as I send you my affections.

Santa Monica, Cal.
May 24, 1953

Dear Laughlin:

I hope you received my letter mailed to you a week ago. I have been plagued by an intestinal disorder which is accompanied by bouts of melancholy. Dispirited strength is the greatest ruin to one's life. I have to fight whatever tarnishes my force or diminishes it. Then I am in the middle at the moment, having left off writing the little book on the pudendum. The essay on the Southwest has taken hold of me. I had nothing of it eight days ago or so, though I had been going from early American *relacions* to Greeks or Sumerian cities. I thought of a title, "The Myth-Gatherers." Please let me know your will and mind. In my last letter I could only give you some uneasy remarks, a few rapid allusions, hardly any geography. The cartographers pierce me unto prayer. I take up Ptolemy as I do Psalms or Proverbs. Anyone who is concerned with the Kosmos has sufficient awe to write a poem or kneel before the humblest vetch or pulse. What astounding inceptions we have, and not even forgotten. In Ovid the earth is identified with Vesta. The Americas is a barbaric virgin with far greater hardihood than Colchian Medea. A river too is a marvelous, fierce damsel. Though the priest Marquette named the Mississippi Conception she is a very tigrish Mary. There are so many false ideas regarding our annals; the rudest facts are specious. I want to make some allusions to the Mississippi, to La Salle and Joutel. The ground, the great waters, we will never get back to the gods of energy until we have made peace with the ground and come to some worship of the rivers. It is as terrible a sin to use the soil, the water coursing through a ravine, as it is to look upon people for the advantages they will give us. Our fate has been so far from heroic because we no longer push back all limits and horizons as the discoverers did. There is enormous metaphysics in the lives of Cartier, Drake, Pigafetta, Behaim. For this reason one cannot reject as evil a Cortes or a de Soto; even their cruelties are Homeric, and I know when saying this that I am falling into the greatest danger of our times, our concern with aesthetics, which is the avoidance of human and moral judgments. One dare not make such a remark without realizing that Minos who weighs our acts and words has a crabbed visage. If he did not have men would kill all day long to employ a Pauline phrase.

My dear Laughlin, I don't think our pioneer wilderness men knew greater forest solitude than I. The problem of American loneliness was always very much in Anderson's mind. One day I told him I was writing about Melville and his implacable life, the great wastes of his bleak journey here. I believe he was literally parched by solitude so sorrowfully described in the Encantadas, that peopleless region and island of sand and tortoises. We are still a frontier culture, and the tangled mass and weight of inventions only hide the men of the sierras, the mesa, the mountains.

At the instant, I am out of the mood of the book, and so, waiting to hear from you, I am garnering the notes for the Myth Men.

You know, you have my true regard and warm affections. Could I give you a younger man's advice, I would say, read, read, and don't wear out your prostates. I was interested in Pound's passion for Tacitus. Pound had many intellectual Beatrices in his life, and that is very good for a poet. As Solomon might chant, There is a time for Pliny, and a season for Ovid, and a year for Theophrastus, and a moon for Erasmus, and a sun for the Pharaohs.

Well, I take my own counsel and return to the notes.

Again, affectionately,

Santa Monica, Cal.
June 26, 1953

Dear Laughlin:

Am I the bore in my epistles to you? It is easier for Sisyphus to roll the rock up the mountain than it is for me to draw a reply from you. You do not tell me whether you care for the essay. If you do not, I'll rewrite it. The damn'd lucre I need, but I work, as you do, that my name may be a precious ointment. You send me money, and I return you thanks, my sole exchequer, but where are the little gray words we try to turn into the Cana wine?

Now for the other matters about which you may feel I have

been too pertinacious. My dear Laughlin, I cannot afford to be a man of taste. I simply have not the money nor that much life left to be exquisitely silent and to wait upon limbo. I write and live by passion and then let what may happen judge me. It is hurtful to ask you many times to look at my manuscript. The Quiche Maya used worms to cure their eyes and also to paint their vases. My own work is of far less value than the worms. What then should I do? Shall I be politic with Laughlin? I might know how to grasp ever-changing Proteus, but how behave in this world? It seems to me that a shoal of writers who are chaff and stubble in the wind can get their books done, but after writing one I must be the most cringing beggar to get it seen. Do not imagine that I am vexed with you. You are a man of ample kindness, and I am one of preposterous inward necessities. Who really cares for the interior landscape of an alive but unsuccessful author? I do not know how thwarted you may be, but you have a great advantage, you are of the world, and I am not, and so I am against it, and it is against me. That cannot be helped. I cannot be Pilate and Christ makes me uneasy. I never knew a saint in my life, and though I have fought for morals in letters I have the lowest regard for my own dirt. Were I proud I would write and sepulcher every word on the Earth, for all that goes into the ground comes up sometime or other as Persephone. Unfortunately, I have not that sort of conceit or Spartan contentment. Would that I had so that I would not have to write wheedling letters. I have no dogmas although I write with composed fury. Still, could I make a wager with you, could one do so with fate, I would tell you that when the Angels beckon the poor writing dust to them that I will be among them. This is also foolish; it is no comfort to praise one's self. That is no good for one's soul; it is another man's remedy for his own low and mean dilemmas.

I know all this has not the easy fragrance of asphodels and maybe no human charm at all. I have heard of the whimsical poet, the congenial one, the sweet and honeyed chanter. I never knew myself to be any of these save for a fleeting instant, and maybe that was a pose of affectation in me.

Now to get to the very plain point: I've got this manuscript on the phallus. I think it might bait your faculties. In truth, I believe you have so much civil decency that you are afraid to see it because then you may have to publish it. I say that because I don't think you could be pierced by words originally felt and justly arranged without printing them. You would regard yourself a poltroon and think there was some mischief or skulking gap in your nature. As for the letters, I don't care whether you print them or not. It may not be right or seemly to do so, but whatever is right or comely, or however I should act, the truth is I am sickened by my own efforts to be better known. For years I didn't bother anybody and no one troubled me. For eight or nine years I lived in hermetic silence, and though I then had a reputation, a crass devil word, not a publisher in America offered to print me. At thirty-five I was a distinguished obscurian, and what am I now? You see there is no way to behave. If you are poor you must beg for bread, work, and friends, and I am very poor, a crawling poet. I say all this so that you won't be guided by taste, an infamous and lying word, which you can only employ when you are a money or a reputation author. If you are out of pocket you cannot be a man of taste. So then, please, understand my letters to you. It may be a great nuisance to you to hear the plaints of a man of many words. But ask yourself but once what would you do were you indigent; that is one curse, but had you two maledictions, to be poor and to be a writer, how would you behave? How then could Solomon or Aristotle advise you? You would be counseled, not wisely, which is cunningly for the most part, by your rent, your hard, bleak oblivion, and the desperado need to seize your life as you felt it scuddering. I feel my soul dying, before the ram's horn is sounded. Magellan asked the Portugal King to increase his little stipend by a miserable ducat a month. Having received a refusal he went out, for the Spanish monarch, to discover the earth and the islands of the Ten Thousand Virgins. The Straits are crabbed and windy, and the penguins are slattern and suety, but tell me what should a man do not to lose his life?

I send you my imperial affections, and though I be a dog in this earth I shall be a king in Hades.

My dear Laughlin:

I am sending the manuscript, *The Sorrows of Priapus,* as you suggested, to New Directions. The little book—unfinished—I think, is, I pray mirthful, for boredom is the pest of the Muses.

I am always interested in origins; without a knowledge of history we are barbarians and right now we are more rude than the Scythians. It is the visionary duty of the poet to acquaint the American with the past. Humboldt, a vast intellect, had remarked in the nineteenth century that climate had much less effect upon people than had been imagined. Compare the tribes of North America with the savage on the Orinoco or the Patagonians in the Sertao, and you will find the smallest differences between these Indians. All are nomads, or nearly so, and are the detritus of Asian hordes, Phoenicians, Basques; Cyclopes, himself, of a fierce race of giants, derives from the children of Ham and Cush.

History, history, teach the American the annals of the centuries that are gone, or he too will perish.

For me it has been a summer of affliction and the labor of words which are for the winds, the vain strivings of the soul for the constellations. I regard writing as a holy work of man, and yet as I consider the Pharaohs, and the unknown tombs in the valleys of Megiddo, I regard mortal labor in the alphabet as nothing.

I wish to God we were making sacred, albic towns. I have great awe by nature, but I cannot abide the American church. Would that we were Pelasgians worshiping a tree, a promontory, Ocean which is the skirt of God. We care for nothing; we are not even passionate nihilists. It is a bad time for a pulsing man in which to live; yet we must live if we can but to serve man who monsters his visage and ends.

I wrote you a letter many weeks ago, and I want to get this to the post office today, and return to the Promethean legends, and to the olden cities, Heliopolis, Magnesia, Erech.

You have, as you know, my affections and deep regard. Keep well, and work, for I swear by the tomb of Adam that is supposed to be near Damascus, that there is no other remedy in life. I see on the streets of this sterile, subhuman town old men and women, well monied, going about as though they were headless and without casting a shadow which is the reflection of the soul. What a malevolent purpose it is to have no other aim but to live for eighty-five years without an acquaintance with Epicharmus, Antisthenes, Porphyry. Do you know that one of the wives of Esau was a Canaanite, named Adah, the daughter of Elom the Hittite? Is that not in itself a marvelous fact? In Syria people still regard certain ancient cities as having been built by Nimrod. It is that sort of lore the American must acquire, and tremble for. Right now the most predacious Chichimeca is a just Minos compared with us.

New York
December 8, 1959

Dear James:

I want to give you my deep thanks for the tickets; we are going to the concert this evening.

I continue to work on the autobiography, rewriting and casting out the tares, and praying that what remains is the wheat of Demeter. You might imagine that I do not wish readers; I do, and very much, and am most grateful to you for all the efforts you have made for me, and are still making. But, my dear James, I don't want a vulgar fame; that phrase, best-seller, was coined in the slimy regions of Tartarus, and I have no desire to be a parcel of that sort of uncouth, sloughy inertia. You know how many brand-new geniuses we produce every season, only to forget who they are the next. At fifty-nine I don't want the pottage of lentils. Money I sorely need, but not at the cost of my life. My sole religion is literature; it is my only Petrine Rock. Alas, friends that are so important are far from me, and as the world is I prefer to be a city-eremite remaining in my room most of the days of my sun and moon, and there studying and reading. When I quit that one room my bones are in jeopardy and, who, I ask, will take my soul and trample upon it? Without any bom-

bast, I feel I wish to bequeath something to this sick commonwealth. You do it, believe me, and I honor you greatly for it. I
know, too, you want me to have the pecunia; what I could earn
would make the scantiest difference to you. At one time in ancient rustic Rome an ass sold for a penny; today you can purchase a man's probity for less. How many Nabals I have known
who went to Hollywood and are making more money in a shoal
of weeks than I could in my entire days? Do I envy them? I don't.
I have not the least desire to fall into the slime pits of Gomorrah.
Let others be shrewd; it will last for a day, an hour, and then
their dark night will come, and they will moan by the shores of
Cocytus because for all the money they have they did not compose one truth. One of the ante-Nicene Fathers, Tertullian, has
said: "That Truth and the Hatred of the Truth appeared in the
world at the same time."

Please do not imagine I am a fool, and want nothing more of
my days, whatever they be, than the dry crust and the crust of
water Abraham gave Hagar. I want more, but if wilderness is to
be my fate, let it be so. Better the desert than the fat, comfortable
heart.

I wanted to send you a few lines to express my deepest appreciation of all that you have done for me.

Meanwhile, I have asked Josephine Herbst and Stanley Burnshaw to review the book,* and will make the same request of
others whom I can ask without feeling base or morphewed.
Thanks again to Ann for her dear letter.

Look at these disordered and depraved children of the arts
today. They are sick, and who can help them. There is not
enough water in the Pool of Bethesda to wash the filth in their
spirits. Were I canny I would be a part of such a vile, hapless
sodality, and be Jack Kerouac (an admirer of mine). I have no ill-
feeling about these boys. But they are doing what was done
thirty years ago and they imagine they are avant-garde. You can
be scatological in any century; it is not new. Or a dung-eater
anytime; it is an old habit.

I wrote to Sir Herbert and told him that you would write him

* *Can These Bones Live*

and say that you are interested in our epistolary essays. In the meantime, the second part of *Because I Was Flesh* should be on the stands very shortly, five poems are to appear in *Poetry* this month, thanks to you, my Friend, and Yugen is publishing an essay. At the moment, I am making ready to lecture on *Moby-Dick*; the essay will be published by the New York University Press. I have gone to the very lees of this hapless tome on cetology. Poor Melville, he had not the least idea what he was doing; I don't read a novel to prepare to be a whaleman. If I want natural history, there are Buffon, Darwin, Bates, White, Parry, Drake, Esquemeling, the Hakluyt voyages. His book is a pathetic cento, the refuse of other men's knowledge, information, done for the most part by him in bombast which is supposed to be Elizabethan blank verse.

My warm love to you, dear James.

letters to
Robert McAlmon

Santa Monica, Cal.
November 3, 1953

Dear Robert McAlmon:

Thank you very much for your letter and for your very kind words about *Can These Bones Live.*

As I told you, I wrote two letters about you, but what will happen, I do not know. Whether I shall even receive a reply is also in doubt. We live, as you know, in the age of the big, the big inertia. People don't bother about the epistolary courtesies anymore. I always imagined that polite letters was the accurate title of literature. But most of the writers I know are boors of the Muses.

Our own plans are very vapory; we are thinking of settling, maybe, in the desert. I might as well dwell in one mastabah tomb as another. I have been thinking of coming down to the desert for several days to see how I relish the wind, the sand, and the mindless skulls about the place. Maybe, if it is not a great bother, you could ask Miss Knudsen where I could rent a room for five days or so, more or less. I don't want to put up at your adjacent room because I feel that I would be invading your privacy. Besides, everybody soon becomes the burden of Tyre. We are all too nervous to be together for any length of time. It is a desolate admission, but it is true. I used to think I could somehow shun my age only to see that I have all its maladies, or nearly all. I am as restless as the next man, and one of the most bored people in the Kosmos. I work, of course, but labor, too, for the most part is only the apotheosis of ennui.

Don't imagine anything about this is personal; I like you, and regard you as a fine man, and it would give me unusual elation to do something for your books. It is hard right now, but then it is always difficult for the gifted waifs in the earth, and that is all we are. It may be that Europe is the remedy for you; we want to go too, but I am already lacerated and fearful of alien thresholds and unkindly streets; not that the avenues I walk through now are my kindred or my nature. I hate the safe-deposit boxes they call thoroughfares in this country.

I should add, Rlene will drive me up and go back the following day, and I intend to stay.

I have not looked about for *Bottom Dogs*. The simple truth is that I no longer care for it. For that matter, I seldom risk looking at anything I write. If one is to ripen one has to forget every page which is a Gethsemane anyway.

Thanks again for your gracious words.

Santa Monica, Cal.
November 12, 1953

Dear Robert McAlmon:

I am troubled about my last letter to you. You may think it a fancy epistle, and I may have vexed you. I hope not. Do not imagine that I have a showy life out here. I live in the most congealed solitude. It is not my conception of a human Elysium. But the whole land is sick, and the earth is weary of men. At one time I rejoiced in knowing people, especially writers, and sought them out. A man who thinks is no stale gourd to me. I have the same fervor about poets and writing. I am afraid now; that is all. We spoke of Marsden Hartley; I knew him for about a dozen years, and when he was obscure and alone, as he was most of his life, he came to me. I was the friend of his painting and peddled some of his prose. He was a gifted nature, but after his death I learned that he had spoken evil of me. I don't know. I can tell you, Marsden never did me a kindness in his entire life. I introduced him to a woman whom he dearly valued, and it was to her that he reviled me. Many was the time that I railed at Stieglitz for giving attention to the little watercolor boy, Marin, and to the vulva painter, O'Keeffe while he set aside Hartley. He is one of many instances.

Do not be offended with me, or imagine that I have some skulking, proud feelings. I work very hard at writing each day, and when I manage a good line I thank chance and the Deity that sends clouds, rain, and misfortune.

We are both probably nervous people; at least I am, and people bore one another so easily in this poor season for affections and the Muses. Then, too, I did not know how to go about some plain matters. I want to be of help to you if I can. It requires time. I just received a most friendly letter from Laughlin. Unfortunately, our letters crossed, so that there was no mention of you. Anyway, he is slow to act, but he may, if I am pertinacious. I hate to see you sealed up out there in that jackal desert to which we may go also for seeming quiet and health! To go back to what I was saying, I could not ask you to rent your apartment while I was offering to be of help to your work. It would look too specious. I know you are a generous man, and that you are also poor. We too must husband our pelting means.

All this is plain, right out, and please accept it so, and also my regard for you. You did a great deal for people, and that knowledge pierces me.

Don't be irritated with Laughlin; he is doing the best job in the country; we may not always agree that what he prints is for Apollo or just the human kitchen, but he is the sole person in America who has a conscience. You may have hurt him; I would not know. I was so glutted with conceit myself. Today I hate self-love, for I do not see what there is in my mottled nature to be proud of.

As Chekov sometimes has his characters say, live long, try not to be bored, and don't think evil of me.

Santa Monica, Cal.
November 16, 1953

Dear McAlmon:

Thank you very much for the letter. I just took it out of the box and so have not had a chance to look at the poem. Will bring it when I come to the desert, maybe this weekend. I hope you don't imagine I have any greed about my own books; you certainly could not cull wisdom of style from *Bottom Dogs*. Once Swift said, "What genius I had when I wrote that!" I wish I had waited, because I can only say how stupid I was.

Don't think that I am greatly seared by Hartley's ingratitude; at the time I was stung, but I never mentioned it to Marsden. He seemed to want to see me often in his broken limbo, but he never made any overtures to me. However, I like a man to be as just as he is able; God knows the earth and trees have made us moist and unstable, and I dare not impute a sin to another man which is not in some cranny of my own nature. What seems very wrong in our modern congealed alphabet which is supposed to be litera-ture is the lack of feeling for the goddess Themis who goes every-where with her scales. What is most important is to be gulled; soon as one imagines one cannot be duped, the heart is a sherd.

But you and I weigh people whether we think we do or not. (William Carlos Williams is about as palatable to me as to you. I think he wrote one good book, *In the American Grain*. I said so in opulent words after our quarrel.) I believe that is right; never kill a book to maim a man. It is the poltroon's way. This is the season of the coward and the book-killer.

I shall continue to write to Laughlin. I have something of the same feeling for Laughlin as I have for you; both of you have printed works which no publishing merchant would have touched. I give you both the laurels of Apollo. I am not one of the flâneurs around him, but he has a real respect for me, and when I can move him to print you or Zukofsky or any human being who knows how to feel in well-arranged words that is my task and felicity. It may take time. I share your own misgivings regarding Rexroth and Miller. Rexroth has some ability, but he is too insincere to know himself at all. He misreads the ancients, and I am not making a pedantic observation. He simply does not know how to read; a great art, reading, without which there can be no imaginative letters.

I have no affectations about the artist. He is a very chameleon nature; at his best he is as searching as Plato, and at his worst a pickthank friend. Stieglitz used to say he liked a man even if he wrote. Well, it was a small epigram, and came as the result of many buffoons of writing he had known. As you know, without a Thucydides, or a Herodotus, a Strabo or an Erasmus, you won't have good cobblers or honest prices for mushrooms, or affections. What we need are not the dandies of the Muses, but people who toil to tell the truth. I believe Amiel did, and I like Flaubert better in his exhausted epistles, in his nether ennui and torn solitude than I do his Julian or Bovary. I think I care more for Baudelaire's *Journal* than for the prose poems. I am not sure. The life of the man is almost as stoic as Cato. The same is almost true of Tolstoy; who can read those tomes of boredom, the novels, save for *The Death of Ivan Ilych*, and again the letters, and the life. I like to see the hot human animal fight his passions, surrender to them, and continue the battle until he is dust.

We will certainly look for a place near you, so that when you are free, or feel like talking we can see you, or you see us or me, as Rlene will be going back on Sunday.

If you don't mind my saying so, I think you ought to turn to verse; when you employ symbols you are at your best which is the way of the poet; the Dunciads of naturalism cannot use a symbol, and have no understanding of your use of the gazelle or the horse. I am just glancing at your pages in *Pagany*. I had many things in *Pagany* too.

I am deeply sorry that your *Poems* were pulped; it is a dampness in the knees and arms and the head we so overestimate. I hope you will go back to poems. I think if you care to be a poet you could be one of the very few in the land. You may tell me to mind my own writing, and not bother about yours, but I feel that if you shunned the idiom, and went for the straight line, a very vague phrase, you could achieve some Pisgah for yourself. You are by nature an avid reader; Varro was the whetstone for Vergil, and Pliny made the most prodigal uses of Theophrastus. What I am trying to say is that the whole cult of originality is mostly humbug. If a man can make his daily Golgathas into a poem, like Verhaeren did, that is marvelous. Of course, Verhaeren relied on the whole Virgin Mary cult to express his massive tedium. Without that, and I am deeply pierced by all ancient religions, though I cannot endure the sight of a church, he would have failed.

What is this all about? I had a dear friend, F. S. Flint, whom you doubtless know. I once dedicated a poem to him which I never sent him. He gave up writing; he had learning, knew a great deal about Provençal literature, was a polyglot, but just quit. I don't think he had your force, nor did Joyce in his penny pomes, worth no more than they were titled. But man has to dig out his woe. Williams never did, and I have the smallest patience with his lubricious lines, and I think his *Paterson* in which he includes a letter I wrote to him, without my permission, and under somebody else's initials, is a fraud. The man is very spongy, and imagines by repeating the word rock about a hundred and thirty-five times that he can become hard or give the effect of having ophidian intellect.

My warm greetings to you, and I look forward to seeing you again.

I am sorry that you are a little annoyed because I said I did not like to see you lost in the American wastes of Beersheba; we are all Hagarene nomads, you and I; don't imagine I am being lofty or Sinaitic. My own fate hangs by the thread of Ariadne, and I have to hang on to it every day.

letters to
Josephine Herbst

Dear Josephine:

Thank you for your letter and for your kind words. I prize your friendship; Socrates says that men care more for a partridge or a quail than a friend; and one of the reasons we have such an impoverished intellect is that it is void of affections. I care not a tittle for a mind that is not as hot as the burning climate of Quito. I shall return to New York, and may be there in June, surely a little later. No Cain in the wilderness of Nod has been such a banished man as I have been in the past three years. I have had books and all the satisfactions of the tomb.

A manuscript of mine has been in the sepulchral files of Laughlin for well-nigh two years. He says that he wants to publish it, and is now looking for some painter to do drawings for the book. I have come to despise modern painting, regarding it as the lazy, sensual pleasure of the eyes. It is like music today, it makes the ears heavy and the mind sluggish. If you mention Bosch or Goya that is another matter. I read Vasari with the most zealous interest, and Ruskin's remarks on painters furnish my soul with all sorts of ideas and phantasms. Of late, I read that Picasso, at the fag end of his life, in order to secure privacy, has bought a large chalet in Nice! It is a quaint sort of retreat; as for myself, employing such logic I should go to the public stews of Toledo to be chaste.

Laughlin, of course, has given me no contract and no advance. At the time, I am still working at the book, so I do not sit and snivel at fate. Will empowers the spirit, and without it my day, unlike God's, is no creation, but the worst of temptations. Sir

Herbert says it is a great and profound meditation, beautifully written. It gathers epitaphs and rust in Laughlin's pockets, and in the meantime I study, write, and consider the lilies.

My dear Josephine, we are castaways of the Muses, unloved and vexed all day long. We are also a vanishing tribe, and I think we should hold fast to one another. I showed your letter to a very attractive woman here who has been in that debauched trade, the movies. She has a great deal of feeling, which is all that intelligence is, but has never been around one or two genuine males. I freely own there may not be more than that, and you may assert where are they? But at any rate, she has always been the prey of the artistic charlatans. It is very hard to comprehend the corrupt person with your mind. As animals we know what is fetid right away; as soon as we begin to think about ordinary liars we are confused; I regard no crime worse than that, for you can trust an assassin, a cheat, the worst wild ass of profligacy, but someone who prefers the falsehood to the truth, never. Anyway, poor dear, she is now pregnant, and the man who reads Blake, Rilke, and faints when he observes a lizard or an agate, has forsaken her. I have pondered the mystery of depravity, and I speak, not of the usual carnal weaknesses; some day, I pray, I shall either hew a mountain or write one line about this that may be true. I shall try; do you care for Pascal, a marvelous nature, a Christian now preempted by the Catholic Church which at best, as one natural historian said, serves as a good dovecot.

As for Europe, don't go; it is peremptory advice, and being good counsel you may not heed it, although I have never known you to have a froward nature.

I found Paris loathly, and all the bourgeois dithyrambs over this city is fit for the cloaca. Pederasts everywhere; witlings imagine they are avant-garde by reading de Sade, an unusual bore who knew very little about the exceptional sensations of Gomorrah. I met one little knave of Parnassus who behaved with great insolence toward me until I crippled him with a couple of cudgeling phrases. But these people lie in ambush for you, never being quelled, as their need to insult takes the place of talent. In the mornings when I came he saluted me with a banality from

Oscar Wilde. He had a peevish nose, what men care for in a woman often, but which shows weakness and a pallid phallus in the male. I don't know why I did not realize quite early that he was homosexual. The truth is that I only saw him three times. When I went to Spain he offered to take care of my books. I am a droll traveler, taking cartons of volumes with me which I never read. After coming back from Mallorca, which is the big bistro for English and American fairies, I called upon him, and asked him whether I could avail myself of his courteous offer which he had made several times. He gave me the most morose answer, but I did not know where to go, and so I left my books there. I asked him when he got up, as I wanted to return shortly for the books, and he said he was always up at ten in the morning. I came once after ten-thirty, and he met me with a waspish line he had taken not from Terence or Menander, altogether pardonable, but from a trite witticism by Lord Douglas or Norman Douglas, a man of some merit, though I confess I could never read *South Wind* without the most ample yawns. Then I heard through another fornication bore of Mount Ida that he was spreading gossip that I was knocking on his door continually. This was so untrue and I was so incensed that I ran over to his place and asked him why he was so base. He then demanded that I leave or he would beat me. I said that I had no intention of leaving until he had returned my books and I was entirely quit of such an unsavory person.

My books were in the cellar, he replied, and he did not have the key and I would have to return in the morning. I did not want another encounter with such a caitiff and told him to get the keys. He then rushed toward me, and as I pushed him aside, he was for the instant pacified. He again made the most clamorous threats, but I refused to move, and he gave me every grimace he had borrowed from de Sade. I would not go. Finally, he said that he would go down to the *épicerie* and see whether he could get a key. But in the hall he made some profane remark to me, and I threw him up against the wall, and he attempted to grapple with me, but it was an easy stalemate, and nothing in particular occurred. Downstairs in the bar he said to me as though I were his valet, "Shut the door"; this time I took hold of him and knocked him against the glass pane, and in rancor he said

to me, and I was altogether startled, "You cunt." The way down
to the cellar was a dark labyrinth; the stairs were very sinuous,
and there was no light or candle. This impudent churl went
down by himself into the depths of the darkness, and carried up
six heavy cartons of books, giving them to me with the courtesy
of Abraham to the three Angels who came to Mamre. I know
nothing about other people; the habits of a widgeon, a teal, a
dolphin I can comprehend, another person is as dark as the
enigma of a sphinx or the Kosmos. Let me hear from you, my
dear friend; meanwhile, as always, you have my affections.

New York
October 22, 1958

Dear Josephine:

I am deeply sorry that you did not see Sir Herbert. He is a
beautiful nature, but is involved in these absurd journeys, giving
awards to painters and sculptors (and never to writers; nobody
ever thinks of that), all of which does not kindle deep sympathies
in me. I have always said: A painter hangs his paintings, but a
writer can only hang himself. His real work is little known, and I
have been cudgeling him for three years to do a small book on
Ruskin, and now he says he will do it, and dedicate it to me. As
you know, I would never have a sleepy friendship with anybody,
and Herbert Read says that I am his conscience and Socratic
gadfly. May it please earth and heaven that I am, because it is
hard to convince anybody nowadays that someone gets himself
into difficulties for no other reason than to prevent another from
miring on his Holy Ghost. Last night I was at a dinner given by
an eminent cardiologist who was the teacher of Bill Williams'
son at the university. There was Edith Halpert of the Downtown
Gallery; also present were Mr. Abe Ratner, the artist, and
his wife, both very gifted natures. I tried very hard to explain
that you could not translate Bosch or Velasquez into one single,
valorous ideal or conception. On the contrary, whereas one looks
at Delacroix with a soporific intellect or none at all, it requires

intellectual attention to comprehend or even misread Plato's *Ion*.

To return to the cardiologist. He had several walls of very expensive paintings. Maybe some were good, perhaps not. I don't know. I long since resolved to destroy one art at a time. Ratner had a canvas which is an abstract Job. I don't know what that is, but I liked the man and his wife so very much that I refused to judge it, if I could. I decided to like what I saw in their faces.

I earnestly trust that you will write to Sir Herbert. Be sure that I will tell him repeatedly how much I admire *The Green World*.

It is a great delight to hear that Elizabeth is reading the books I suggested would be the ore for her feeling. After reading *The Compleat Angler* she wrote me a very fine letter, with lines that were granitic, and I am sure that this collision between other minds and herself will yield those values, and the apples of Haran which we would all pluck. I told her to be very cautious about this man in the English department. I never met a man in any English department that had a vertebra, and a woman of talent requires a strong man, that is one with a potent intellect. I know one woman who married a male weakling, and she is now homeless because she cowers each evening she has to return to him. Elizabeth said that what she wanted is love; yes, who doesn't? But this man loves this woman too, and she can no longer bear him or his passion. As for myself, I have long whispered to my heart the words of Nietzsche: "I no longer strive for my happiness; I strive for my work." I do not set aside the raptures of the flesh. The cost, alas, is often too dear and utterly dismembering. Let it be that I go to Gehenna with those privations that I cannot shed.

The finger is still inflamed. I have not one utensil in this apartment. My despondency has been too great for me to go out and buy these commodities. I sit here, however, with the memoirs of Saint-Simon, Herzen, the *Letters* of Coleridge, some remarkable passages from AE, and a good deal of John Ruskin. In the evenings I pore over the *Confessions of Saint Augustine,* and they heal the stinging asps in my heart. *The City of God,* too, has been a great ecstasy for me. I am religious, but altogether profane and unchurchly. Coleridge dropped to his knees twice a day, and Samuel Johnson said that he would as lief kneel on Fleet

Street with Kit Smart as not. But I too know what Ruskin meant when he said the gneiss in the Alps no longer moved him as it once did. God, devil, or minerals may be my First Cause; it matters not; worm that I am I shall expire in wrath against the Angels for no other cause than someday I shall be no more, and also without quiet because I also know I cannot be less.

I pray, Josephine, that my vehement credos will never be mistaken by you for inhumanities. I am very acerb, and I cannot help it, but I can be blown over by one soft word.

Again, I repeat, don't waste yourself on scribblers. I abhor all the nonsense about the times, the 'twenties, 'thirties, and the 'forties. My God, what do a thousand decades mean that we should neigh and sport over five lustra.

Let me know, please, when you come in, and I shall be happy to see you.

Bill Williams, you know, had another small stroke; I tremble for him, and also weep for him. He has done many things of which I disapprove, but how little I want to go on rebuking him. Poor, poor Bill, he is much too close to Nature. I would kill Nature could I save him.

New York
November 7, 1958

Dear Josephine:

I waited four hours for you, and feared that you were in trouble, but am grateful to learn that you are in good health again. I earnestly pray that you are. Please come to see me November 14, as you know there is no one I would rather see than you.

I talk to everybody about *The New Green World*. My former student at Boston University, and now a teacher at New York University where they do all within their power to prevent him from being a loving teacher, has bought your dear and tender book and read it with great feeling. Jonathan Williams, who publishes Jargon Books (a Medusa Gorgon title), is looking for your book. The other evening I strongly reprehended him for not buying your book and not knowing who you were except in some vague, misty way. Our whole literature is underground; no revolutionary party could lie hidden in the catacombs with as much secrecy as what is most important in belles lettres.

I wrote a most gracious letter to Mr. Richard Eberhart asking him, *please,* to write at once to Mr. White at Harcourt, Brace, and strongly urge him to publish Jean's poems.* At the party given to Bill Williams, Mr. Eberhart gave me the most prodigal encomia for *The Sorrows of Priapus,* and I thought that I could then write to him to be Jean's advocate. He had also invited me to come to Dartmouth, for what purpose I do not know. The truth is I do not know whether he is a good poet or not. Since he did not reply to me I suspect he is not. At the same party at J.L.'s apartment Selden Rodman told me he kept *The Sorrows of Priapus* at his bedside so that he could read some passages from it every night. God, protect us from this sort of bedside praise, for when I saw him at an opening of Mexican paintings, and had approached him (with the guileful purpose of asking him also to write to Mr. White about Jean), he did not recognize me! There are so few faces in the world now that people are so unaccustomed to a human physiognomy, they either do not see it or want to forget it at once. A face is as uncomfortable as a loving book. Of course, he then asked me to call him soon, and gave me his telephone number. What eccentric and wounded people we have in the land, and who hears the spring rains and the noise of the turtle?

I saw Robert M. Hutchins and we had a rather truculent talk. I am always alienating the people who could help me. What can I do? The Fund for the Republic, devoted to good motives, gets out booklets, chapbooks, and pamphlets done by eminent political nonentities in the most scrabbled, non-human style. Everybody today uses that academic factory vocabulary which is unsentient, utterly drab, and hopelessly lifeless. These people are determined not to feel anything, and are *eminently* successful. I like Hutchins very much; he has a Central Committee of Consultants, a bizarre and mirthful appellation. I asked him why he,

* Jean Garrigue

who had advocated the Great Books Courses, had not one imaginative writer on his committee? We are always getting corrupt people to clean out our Augean stables.

My finger is still swollen, and I have not done one line on the autobiography. If Hutchins is not absolutely put off by my waspish criticism I may do a booklet for him which would give me that nasty lucre hoarded in Tartarus. I asked him why he had such a fancy office. America, I said, is the Office, by the grace of the Bank. I told him I would rather walk into the jaws of Cerberus than step into one of our modern cinema palace vestibules of commerce. A most persuasive man, no doubt, and the quiddity of tact, but I can be as meek as Saint John the Baptist when I want to do something for another person.

As always, my dear Josephine, my love to you, and do not waste your strength. You need it for more lovely books with a woodland style which only Artemis or Persephone could have written.

Devotedly, your friend,

New York
November 17, 1958

Dear Josephine:

It was a joy to see you again, and I myself am strengthened to know that you have more vigor; guard it as closely as those who took care of the vestal fires.

We are to read sometime in March. I thought that might be easier for you; all arrangements are to be made to suit your convenience and not mine. Tell me, please, if that is all right with you. The people connected with the Living Theater seem clean and straight; I don't think they are flâneurs of Bohemia. Anyway, Josephine dear, I would not have consented to do the reading without you. Besides, I am no Narcissus who cares to pore over his past works. My early work I should prefer to forget.

I was angry with Sir Herbert; he is too charming, which is a great weakness. I don't like all this social efficacy which is the groundwork of a literary reputation. The sere truth is that he is best known for his least works. The Erynes will always pay us for those favors which we purchased too easily. Have you sent Sir Herbert *The New Green World*; please do so without fail, and I beg of you, forthwith. Herbert Read and I have been friends for many years. We had some altercation involving the epistolary essays. I replied that friendship, were it to be a benefit to both, had to be a soft as well as an acrimonious exchange. I am not Achilles or foul-mouthed Thersites, but I have no interest in a supine and facile relationship in which pragmatic adjustment and agreement rather than understanding is the basis. May the gods damn my soul and rifle me of peace in Orcus if I continue a friendship with anybody for bad or false reasons. The truth is that I was so perturbed this morning because he was prepared to *give* you one hour in Philadelphia that I could have written him the sharpest note. However, I have learned a little, not much, and were you to press me hard on this I should add that that is a lie too.

You did not write in the book for me, that is, *The New Green World*. I have asked you several times, and I am too vain to ask you again. Curse Absalom's locks and my arrogance.

Wherever you are, your fare will be paid, aside from the negligible fee, but there may be more. As you are our Lady Persephone you should read first, or if that is not good for you, maybe the audience will be relieved to hear you chant pages out of your most tender and dear *Boke* after I have been muttering for some while.

I am profoundly delighted to hear that your experimental novel has been a felicity to you. May it be a work of genius, not that I for one instant don't think you have it; what is genius but mountain striving, falling down every day, even seven times each day, and being preternaturally tender. Good grammar is an accident, and maybe even our guile with which we hide our nakedness. The trouble with the gray-haired syntax boys is that they write the most boring and hackneyed feelings in correct sentences, or what passes for that nowadays.

Do you care for Walter Savage Landor? He is very close to my heart. Swinburne wrote a fine tribute to him; he also did a lovely homage to the neglected Blake.

Well, as Waldo Frank used to say, I must now begin my great masterpiece; whenever I called him he was either commencing a bad book, or was in the middle of it, or trying to finish it. I care as much about masterpieces as I do about posterity, though I own that tombstone fame is far cleaner than what is known as reputation. I write because my life would be too wretched and dirty if I didn't. I awaken in the humid morning in this foul city utterly joyless and defeated. Each morning should be a miracle of the awakened heart. But I fear each new daybreak as I go to my four-dollar oak table to compose one line, which if it is good, is as small as the cummin seed, and of far less worth than that to the Universe.

Will I see you before you go to Yaddo, and how long will you be there?

At this writing I intend to return to Spain either in May or June.

Hoard your energies as others do their self-love.

Again I love your BOOK and your nature.

Herbert told me that he looked at your face for a long while admiring the contemplative vitality he saw there. He is such a generous-hearted boy, really a man, of course, and I must needs stand idly by and watch an exsanguious brach of these dead states demolish him.

Devotedly,

New York
May 23, 1959

Dear Josephine:

I have your very fine letter and deeply prize it. Our disagreements are trifling; they do not matter since I love your brave spirit, and admire what you are doing in our nihilistic wilderness. When I hear from you I know I am not alone. Nobody exists, even physically, save by the miracle of other loving eyes.

Of course, please use any letters of mine you wish. I am proud to have you write about me. It is not only my good fortune that I do not care for my early work; it is my soul's relief and the hope of my life, should it not be any coarser than it must be because I am flesh, that I do not have to think of a book I wrote so many years ago.

You promised, my dear, to send one of your novels; if you still want to, I should be most grateful if you would.

I am so glad to hear that they cared for you, as they obviously would, at Michigan Central College. You know that if I can get that lucre you need, since you know how to live and survive in all human deserts, be sure that I will do so. You know I am not babbling, and that it is my privilege to be of use to you, pray heaven I can.

In a few days I shall be writing to Sir Herbert; he has been in Italy, and that is the reason you have not heard from him. Stanley Burnshaw and I spoke of you very warmly. He would be a very good person for you to see again when you come down to New York. He is tender and most generous, and you can also reach him at Henry Holt; he would be very delighted if you would call him. I am a close friend of Stanley's, and again I am thinking, Josephine, of people who will want to help you. I cannot bear to think of you in this brutish country without the feeling and merciful eyes of others seeking you, and wishing to comfort you. Forgive me if I speak so. All of us are visionary waifs of the arts, poor, hapless children of the Muses, and yet it is we who can eat the miracle gudgeons and the barley loaves. Oh well, I explain too much, fearing you might misunderstand, and even imagine that my own concern for you might seem lofty or craven. How could I be the former? Pascal says that man is so stupid he cannot invent a worm.

I abhor, as you so rightly say, all this nonsense about the 'thirties, the 'forties, and so on; my God, do they think that we come to anything in ideas, further wisdom, or more ikons, in a meager few lustra? Why it takes at least three thousand years for the human race to rest long enough to produce a number of pyramids, a pylon, a pair of sphinxes, and one wise pharaoh.

Your book deeply moves me; may all the energy in the Universe be your guide. We have to be so lucky to write one good thought. Can you imagine, my very dear Friend and most Gifted Josephine, either you or I talking about the next great masterpiece we are going to write.

I have the wondrously loving *The New Green World,* and I wanted, by your leave and grace, one of the novels, for I am now halfway through the autobiography, so that I could cull from them those feelings, meanings, and comprehension of our wretched, dismembered country which we both love without being stupid and refusing to see what we see.

Now should you later want to appear in *Big Table,* please let me know. How about *New Directions Annual*; Laughlin is now gathering together his material, and is going to make his selections this summer. You hardly need any introduction to him from me. If you are interested, though, and want to send him any of your work, please tell him that I suggested it as I am an ardent admirer of yours, and positively and devoutly believe in the principles of your style and spirit, the same thing as we both know. Ultimately, there are no good thoughts in a bad style, and a man who writes poorly is only expressing his miserable and weak nature.

I could write you much more and still not thank you enough for your most thoughtful and marvelous epistle. Who can thank another enough, and how can I be sufficiently grateful because Nature allows you to live.

I go to Spain June 4 on which day I sail. My address there will be: Viajes Marsans, Palma de Mallorca. I come back to do some teaching, and to give a lecture on Herman Melville which is to appear in an anthology to be published by Henry Holt. I hope you garner my meaning when I ask you to see Stanley Burnshaw!

The other day I saw a raw and ambitious obscurian whom I have been helping in the past two years. Do you know what he did to me, and worse, to himself? He picked up a magazine in which he had an article, and stamped it, With the compliments of. . . . I got up, saying that in thirty-two years or so of writing, and myriads of follies, ineptitudes, and tormenting stupidities, I had never done such a foul thing to anybody, the alleged celebrities or even the pariah in the gutter. Does not Cervantes say that all affectation is evil? Oh my God, won't people learn that man, the wondrous, pensive animal who would love if he were just the angelical beast that he is, is nothing if he is not plain?

Josephine, this is no good answer to your own letter, and it shows so clearly that you are in a high-blowing vigor.

As always, my admiration and love.

Forgive me when I am testy. I say I am vain, irascible, thought-less, lewd, and have withal a few faults. My vanity is not alto-gether incurable because I am sure to have at least one chagrin before the sundown of any day. I am safe here in this one room, but am in total jeopardy as soon as I step across this threshold.

Enjoy your most lovely house, be well, and give all of us that truthful and most tender book which only the affectionate and the truthful can give.

O my heaven, what a beggarly letter, and I wanted so much to write one with many fine thoughts in it; what an ass at the lyre is man. I speak of myself, of course.

Again, your devoted friend,

New York
May 30, 1959

Dear Josephine:

I have your lovely epistle of sorrows. When I heard that John Hermann had died I was quite shaken; you had come to my apartment at 36 Grove Street with John, both of you such virile and handsome persons. Then I met him again in New Orleans, he was broken, but not sniveling, selling Venetian blinds for Marc Antony! My God, Bob McAlmon, too, as you know, sold trusses for his brother in El Paso. All fallen, they and us; what is our whole history; we asked for bread and we were given a stone. I liked him very much, even his defects which were amiable. Of course, I do not feign to have known him. But I do not pretend to know anybody. Could I say that I understood one human being in the earth I would then know who commenced the Uni-verse.

How grateful I am to you for sending the books; I shall take them to Spain with me, and read them there. I know what you do will be infinitely human, and what else matters in a book? Give me a tender book or let me live *bokeless*.

I wrote to Paul Carroll, a very living person on *Big Table,* about you, and the book you were doing, really two; I have not forgotten, and told him it would be wonderful if he would write to you, and more remarkable if they would print some parcel of your feeling and vision.

Even among the best of them the Stygian cult of youth obtains; what else has one for his decay but maybe a little more knowledge about one's stupidity? But I like many of them; you are right, of course, about the humbug idiom they imagine is the language of our locality. It is really the diction of dementia praecox.

I saw James Laughlin, and he said, "Edward, I am sure you are going to be a success." "Oh," I said, "please, you depress me; I may be utterly vain, but I am not coarse."

I leave Thursday, and return for some courses and a lecture. I never last at any college for more than a semester. Some people say, who have not seen me in years, that I have mellowed, but I only smile or laugh at this. I am just as furious about injustice, our crazy land, and the fatiguing varlets in Washington as I ever was. What am I mellow about? I shall always be suffering flesh, and know unto the last that if ever I write one good line it will be an accident. Does not that ancient pedantic grammarian, Demetrius, say that a good line falls out by chance, and that one has to be lucky with the Muses?

This is Decoration Day, one of those ghastly, obituary holidays in America; the whole city is shut, just to emphasize that the faces are shut too. I abhor Sunday, Father's Day, Mother's Day, the Fourth of July, and every tombstone day we set aside as a false memorial for some person, event, or parent which has behind it the malefic purposes of the state or the merchant or both.

Well, I can't be too mirthful today, Josephine; it's Memorial Day, and John Hermann is dead, and whatever he meant to us, little or much, with his extinction, some part of us has died. Did you hear—and forgive the profane allusion—Elliot Cohen, editor of *Commentary,* died of a heart attack? He was a man of unusual bile, and had little else to live for save spite, revenge, and to hide the works of others. I never knew why he hated me. I cannot recollect the reasons for some altercation or other a generation ago. Why should I? I called Nathan Asch when I was in Berkeley, and he said that I had once spoken harshly to him. He also used the tritest of phrases, calling me a highbrow, adding that he was a pulp scribbler. In concluding, he said, "Why don't you call me sometime, and we will get together," and I replied, "You fool, what do you think I am doing now?" When he was young he had the undefined idealism of the callow; but there are no ideals which are not absolutely clear, just as there are no thoughts that are not uttered.

How urgently we need thorny truths in literary criticism, and your book should give us the light and the warmth of the head; let the mind always trail the heart. Does not Cervantes say that it's the hams that uphold the mind, and not the mind the hams?

Well, my dear, gifted Friend, I have gabbled too much, and I fear in a desolate vein.

I think the books arrived, for I have a notice for insured mail, but I will have to wait for Monday to go to the post office and get them.

My love to you, and always my faith in your powers too.

Your devoted friend,

New York
December 5, 1959

Dear Josephine:

I have your marvelous letter. I wanted to reply to you at once, but got so involved in ten tomes of the ante-Nicene Fathers that I was so weary and vexed by the time I had finished I had not enough force to send you enough thanks for your most prodigal encomium. Of course, I am grateful to you for caring for *Because I Was Flesh*. One has to have a good and a charitable heart to be a good reader; heaven knows one has to have all of that to compose one human line.

Now, Josephine dear, I think it would be very good if you would review *Can These Bones Live* in *Commentary*. I don't read it; the truth is I find all magazines undigestible, and if it does not offend your gracious and feminine heart I should rather chew offal than spend my time finding out what is up to date in our jackal letters in the last issue of some American periodical.

How right you are about Saint Anthony Adding Machine Burroughs; people are always angry with me because I don't read what is very scurvy, and even impugn it without troubling to find out what my nose tells me beforehand. Do I have to have every experience to know the scantiest truths? I appear where I can, and let it go at that, making no concessions to anybody. The other day I saw Laughlin, and he said to me: "Edward, this book (referring to the autobiography) might be a best seller." I was utterly crestfallen, and the blood ran out of my cheeks. "I don't want to do a book like that; that phrase, best seller, was coined in the Valley of Hinnom." I should be mortally ashamed to have so much beastliness in my skin; one can only do what one is. If I have a rabble of foul longings in my bowels, it will show itself, and rather than commit such a felony I should turn to that poignant line, and give up the ghost: "Thou fool, this night shall thy soul be required of thee."

Now, don't forget to go to Carnegie Fund—I know, as Pantagruel says, that you suffer uninterruptedly from that disease, the want of money—and get what you can. Go to the Author's League again; you are a very brave and distinguished author, and should not have to suffer from the worst of all fluxes, penury. If you can get a little reserve for yourself, do. You know that if Stanley is able to continue the lectures next year, I shall do my utmost to get you one, and for an evening you will receive at least two hundred dollars, an El Dorado for us. I won't be seeing him until the 11th of this month, and I shall make some arrangements so that either you and he can meet, or the three of us can gather together.

I know by now that you laugh at me when I tell you that one of our American Epics is a bad novel, but I tell you there is not enough narrative in *Moby-Dick* to fill Hagar's cruse. And as for wisdom, too, since I don't care how a man makes a book so long as it fetches me, there isn't too much of that either. Well, what can I do? I break old idols; I eat, sleep, and awaken in the morning looking for the Aurora Borealis.

I enjoyed seeing you very much.

And I want to say again I am very proud to be in your *Boke*. You are a rare and brave spirit in our Wilderness, and I intend saying so. We have both fought through all the darkness, eating our limbo quietly while the cormorant churls had their hoaxing and whorish fame. Let it be that way; I don't think I would change it. Character is fate and that's what writes the books, not grammar, nor being clever, or imagining that one is the lion or the fox; we are all doves—thinking of your wondrous piece of narrative—roasted on the spit, but singed or broiled, we at least come out hot; and I would rather be cold or extinct lava than indifferent.

With my warm love and deep thanks.

New York
May 16, 1960

Dear Josephine:

I have your very fine letter, and am grateful for it. What else have we but a few morsels of words from those we love and admire; do I need a telephone to bring a human being to me? What did people do when there were not such malefic instruments? They were far better, as you know. Now that we have all these hideous machines which make the most sloughy Calibans of us, there is no need for one person to see another.

Well, I know you are a wondrous nature, filled with the same passionate despair as I, fumbling from one book to another as we do, praying for affections, flowers, and even tombs, human closeness, vegetation which makes us smile and rejoice, and for that rest from people who tire us because we are no longer accustomed to see them. How weary we are with people with whom we are so little associated. I saw Sir Herbert a few hours before he returned to London by plane, and went away with the most oppressive and doleful feelings, in some sense sorry that I saw him, because I realized that we were more impermeable from each other than two stars in the same galaxy. How to cross those frontiers of another soul; we cannot, and we cry out for plants, gneiss, and for laughing flowers because we cannot touch any one or thing, ultimately. So I sit here in this crypt of a room, called a city apartment, and when people come I am depleted by them, and when they do not I am starved. Yet I would be very near to my own kin, to you, and a few others, very few indeed.

Speaking of the vernal equinox, and what springs up because of Persephone, the best piece of writing in *Paterson 5* is your lovely, leafy epistle.

Yes, dear Josephine, I should be most beholden to you, if you would do a piece on *Can These Bones Live* in *Poetry*. You might suggest, if you deem it necessary, that the volume was never reviewed there when it was published in 1941. As you know, the gutter papers pay no heed to reprints though they were not reviewed when they appeared the first time. So you get two burials; the dour truth is that books would have some hope of a life were there no newspapers at all in the land. They are police and burlesque gazettes, and it is no longer possible to garner from them any real news whatsoever. I never thought it possible for an American newspaper to deteriorate.

I earnestly pray that you will do other *portraits*; the one I read is marvelous, strong, sinewy prose, and coming from a nature that could only be as thewy and hard (not inhuman, God no) as the words she employs. I shall myself be alluding to the very tender Bartram book, and to you as the Woman in the American Wilderness, not charred and wasted, but somehow despite all denials, penury, a fierce Sisyphean struggle, able to nourish others because she is not a desert herself.

Of course, cite anything I say in whatever letters I have sent you, with or without using my name, and use, as you said you wanted to, the correspondence with Sherwood Anderson, or anything else, as you desire to do, and as it seems to be suitable to the Form of your Book.

Stanley Burnshaw was exceedingly pleased with your feelings about *The Poem Itself*. Let us somehow be together, not a sodality of fools and trimmers, but as fellow-palmers who pass by the Cave of Mammon, and tell our truths as best we can. Be sure, we will never get the young self-loving saints of ordure and pederastia to do anything for us, even to feign that we exist.

I always detested the monks of literature, the pecuniary purists on Mount Ida; now that those shrewd basilisks of letters, Pound, Eliot, and the late Wyndham Lewis, who had every foul blemish, and who was at best a few vascular phrases and never a person, have blown their stony breaths upon a whole generation, it is our task to bring back even the weeds. How we yearn even for the tares in this asphaltic land!

Well, my very dear and most gifted Friend, I thank you first for being alive, and for being able to send you my own Atalean sorrows, which are your own too, and for your imperial kindness.

I shall look today for the magazine, *The Noble Savage,* as I am most eager to read your essay or memoir on Spain. I have lived there at least two years, but do not pretend to know it as you do. Even were I so bold as to feign this, I should want to read what you have to say, because there are always perceptions in the heart of another which are not even intimations in my own. Besides, reading your thoughts is an act of love, and I must love or be more starved granite than I am. I am sure that rocks have feelings too, and express themselves more and better than our decayed scribblers.

It is deeply good to hear that Jean received a Guggenheim award. I do not try to get money from these people. I have detested all those legal pimps of letters too long to receive anything from them but the nettles and a nosegay of silence and contempt.

So please do, dear Josephine, whatever you want with any work of mine.

I sometime think of that poor, afflicted man, Williams, and I wish I could say that I had a tumultuary heart for him; alas, I have not; he has been too perfidious, and though I think he did a wondrous book, in *In the American Grain,* he has had no development. One book, maybe one chapter, that is the history of American writing; each one chisels his epitaph in as few words as he wrote, that is, wrote well, no more in length than an hexameter.

As for myself, my life is my disgrace, and any book I do, if it be any good, is only the effort to record it with the passion of Prometheus. Pausanias says that he saw in one of the fanes he entered the clay which Prometheus had molded when he created the first man. Jesus took the clay and moistened it with a little spittle to heal the man fashioned by Prometheus, and still we are blind.

Part of my desponding feelings I owe to Pound's depraved and scurrile prose and verse; what a gallimaufry of nonsense there is in speaking about his metrical skill, as though one could not be a caitiff, a worm, and a liar in a well-formed canto too. Eliot errs a little less blatantly because he is a colder sharper; but none of these men have the least amount of blood circulating through their verse or prose. The salt marshes near Cadiz taste sweeter than their technical rot.

I shall get the periodical today, or order it at once, and write you, my dear; be sure of my great appetite for it.

I send you my steadfast love and admiration, for I would have every syllable in my soul be an homage to you.

Your devoted friend,

Soller de Mallorca
August 18, 1960

Dear Josephine:

How delighted I was to find your epistle; I asked for mail when I went to Palma, not expecting any, but there were two for me. We live so much in seclusion, being hermits of letters, that word from the world seems like seeds or pollen dropped by some Cherub, one of those great contemplative birds of the Old Testament.

I cannot tell you, Josephine dear, how grateful I am to you for doing the review for *Commentary*. As for being detached, who but a churl who has no attachment to a single human being in the earth feigns to be so. Of course, detachment is praised in the Bhagavad-Gita, and it is the true vision of Confucius, but we are Western, and though I am deeply pierced by the Rig-Vedas, and other such sayings from old India, I have never had that kind of nature. I love, I err, I am dust, and that is what I hope to be, and alas, am. God save both of us while we vibrate, think, and imagine we have one conception worthy of the Universe or even of the smallest gnat.

Now the Mallorcan house is finished; there are details to be taken care of; but we are living in it. The house is about forty degrees cooler than it is outdoors, and I am not being mawkish or giving you foolish remarks. The old peasant rock dwelling is surrounded on three sides by those great mountains which Atlas must have cast up out of the sea, for does not each person, dwarf or giant, make his own burdens so that he will not have a niggard fate. At dusk we beat the branches filled with almonds, and we have eight such nut-bearing trees, and two fig trees, tender citrus saplings, plum-bearing ones which should yield their fruit in a year or two, and a well, about fifteen meters when the bucket first pierces it, and I delight in drawing up the cold water furnished by some small rivulet or current that comes from these sere prophetic mountain ranges. For I love what is dry and what is wet, the orchards and Oceanus, as well as the sweet-limbed Nereids which preside over minute brooks, wells, or even a puddle of rain water.

I selected the furniture, all antique, tables from Aragon, Catalan, Estremadura, and Madrid, Castile, all your Spanish earth, for nothing is ours save we give our hearts to it, a wizened truth, very old, and even trite, and so little understood by occidental peoples. But you know it, and that is why I am a devoted admirer of yours.

I feared that I might have vexed you by suggesting that you be wary of employing the vernacular; I tried it in the second fragment from *Because I Was Flesh*, and it has been a thorn in my flesh ever since, and I cannot wait to mend that, and, of course, I did not have the effrontery to send it to you. Thinking of you, as I often do, I could not refrain from feeling that the only good thing in Williams' last poem is your letter, and all those winged and almost bird-like delights in the honey of flowers. I should, perhaps, not praise you, while I set aside another, but poor, sick Williams, for whom I have so much compassion, although he has erred against both of us, never had any real development. That is the tragedy of the writer in tierra incognita, not yours, and I pray not mine; let my sins come not from weakness or from being a poltroon of letters; the honey comes from the lion's carcass. The weak hurt us most, and it may be that though earth, clay, marl, are as we know utterly perishable, they are far more stable than that other mighty element, water, regarded by Vergil as deceitful.

You know, or I tell you again, you have a refuge in the house here when you want it. Should you desire to go to Europe, all you have to do is to tell me, and I shall give you the key. You know how much I care for your own marvelous home in Bucks County, and I hope you will not think I am overweening when I risk asserting that you would enjoy this Mallorcan house, built of rock quarried from the mountains, and by some peasant family in the very beginning of the eighteenth century. Soon as you talk about architecture you make an entire nation homeless.

I have done a first rough epistle on Eliot and Pound, two basilisks of literature; believe me, please, if you can, that I am not throwing down what is good, human, or tender. I go to genius kneeling; the worst and most horrid fault of our century is the fetish of originality. I am sure that when you composed your most tender gospel of love in our American wilderness—I am, of course, referring to *The New Green World*—you did not care a straw about being new, different, or up to date, those horrible shibboleths of a sham Gideon. I am Woman, or I am Man, naked in my sins, always fallen, though I am not Christian, but how can we be jubilant unless we rise each day from the dust.

If I have any money left at all after paying the bills on the house, it will be my delight to bring you something from España Mystica; you know I want to, for I do not think anything can fall out, save what should have been kept for the mole, the kite, and ossifrage, from a skinflint soul.

You know what we get from scribblers, even their encomia sicken us, and again, you must know with what joy I shall read whatever you have to say about my own work, and be sure I am no disinterested admirer of yours either. The books we are indifferent to, or do not teach us something, are the volumes we should not trouble our spirits about.

Please guard your health, your lovely and rare Muse, for I bless both.

Your loving and admiring friend,

We leave Palma, or I should say from Palma, on the Israeli liner on September 6, and will return to the Horatio Street apartment.

Allen Tate is doing a lengthy piece on *Can These Bones Live*, and so I regard myself as very lucky in having both of you pay heed to me. I only live, or think I do, because I have a few friends who remind me that I do. I heard that Lowell, the poet, thinks that *Because I Was Flesh* is a classic (usually a stale word from pithless professors of literature who make fifteen thousand dollars a year from anthologies). I am still rancorous when I think of that uglified and damned professor who did a long piece of word-garbage on Bartram without even mentioning you. But I said to Rlene before I commenced reading Bartram, and the introduction: I'll wager with you that he will never breathe one word about Josephine.

How goes your own *Boke*; how very few books on American Literature there are that are not grammar manuals for Polonius.

New York
January 25, 1961

Dear Josephine:

I have your very thoughtful epistle and thank you very much for it. You are indeed no pauper; I am the beggar, asking those poorest of alms, an hour or two of a friend. It is in bad taste to remind you of anything I have ever done for you; and had I not been hurt by you I would never have done so. I felt that once in thirty years I could turn to you when I was dejected. My life has been mountain conglomerate; hunger and penury have been my raiment often. But, alas, for reasons you know best, I cannot come to you even on so rare an occasion.

Do not think that I am not deeply mindful of your battle, and do not honor you for waging it. I could no longer be a communist after I realized that we gave ourselves to that scorpion, the Cause, and had no time after that for a friend. I write to understand myself a little better and to have friends. Otherwise, it is an ugly passion. We know enough of the sepulcher without making our lives one. What good will we be to each other later? Yes, there is the book, but what of that pang, life, and are we to relinquish it utterly to make books? There is a strong ascetic strain in me; I too cannot give too much to life if I am to possess those precious seeds of Zeus for a book. But at some point I must save my forces for human love, not physical affection, but that ideal love we have for those whom we care for, those who compose the only volumes that matter. If that too is to be denied, then I do not know why we are prose stylists or poets. The books for the life, and not the life for the cloistral and congealed trade, the making of more essays, testaments, and poems.

Can we not somehow hoard our strength for our very few friends? For those whose angelic faculties are essential to our own darkness and lights?

These are accursed days for both of us, Josephine; you, sick and torn and brave, and I too sealed up in a room, depleted by any crowd which is always untruthful and bestial, hankering for companionship which does not exist in our country.

I have known perverse writers, ugly to you and to me, who imagine that solitude is an ecstasy. Yes, it can be one, but I am as solitary as I need be for what I have to be and do; I require no more. Delacroix once said: "I write for myself alone." I say: "I write, and am alone." I know people in America never say that they are lonely; if I am not as ragged and as penned in as I was, it is that it has become my habit not to be. Wrong it is, and I am sometimes defiant, even when I do not need another, simply because I know we cannot have a Vision without at least five people who are bread and wine to share it.

Yesterday I wrote to you, and I pray that nothing in my letter offended you. It was not my thought to do so. Say, Josephine, what you will, I was thrown down, after I had called you and thereafter never had one word from you. Well, let it be now.

Nothing, alas, is ever won, and all is lost; make a very remarkable book. You know what fervor I have for the Bartram book, and for *The Hunter of Doves.*

I shall be referring to you and to your work in the autobiography; Laughlin is anxious to have it, very, and I have had two other publishers, besides, who want it, but I have the contract with N.D., and am deeply satisfied that I have.

There is no good time in which to rebuke a friend; at noon, no, at four o'clock, and at dusk, when one's energies are flagging, or when the Pleiades appear, we are too nervous or shaking.

Take with this my love and admiration for what it is worth, and each of us will crawl back into that crevice, and write, and may God pardon both of us.

Soller de Mallorca
March 13, 1961

Dear Josephine:

Your postcard came several days ago, and now your deeply perceptive essay or a fragment of it which you have sent me. Aside from many thoughtful observations, one remark that I am very grateful for is that you recognize I never lost connection with the European mind. Of course, everything American is in my marrow, a tree, a ravine, sumac, the Rockies, but unless I know the experience of Attica and of Rome, what else can I be except a provincial scribbler?

There is a slight pedestrian error, Josephine; I was twenty-eight when I completed *Bottom Dogs* in Brussels.

No; I had never read Brecht; it is, however, very good and just to acknowledge one's influences, and you know there is a good deal of cant about such matters today. But I have heard of Brecht for a long while, and your point is exceedingly fine. It is a book of radical nihilism, and in spite of much heartbreak and reading I continue to be a nihilist always in search of form. I hate evil, an ingredient of any good in man, and I loathe anybody who imagines that he is any good at all.

There are acrid phrases that I relish a great deal: ". . . the

underbelly of what we like to call the American dream. . . ,"
"cinder-hardened, work-grimed, flayed," "that civilian warfare of
nerves and exhausted energies," "the sulphurous fumes of a
nether world." But I will not go on as I could easily cite many
more words put together with so much justice and wisdom.

I cannot refrain from quoting you again: "What he experiences is a simple and frightening 'being there.' It is a presence, a
deposit, an inertia. It is the heavy weight of things." The con-
summation of this insight is marvelous. What a book yours will
be. Please get it done so that I can refer to it in *Because I Was
Flesh*; and, of course, Josephine, I shall quote you in *Bottom
Dogs* to be republished in fall.

I wish I could read the whole of it. Laughlin wishes me to do
the autobiography in two volumes. You can be sure that I shall
not indulge in such pachydermatous follies as Williams did in
that unfortunate volume of his about you, your late husband,
John Hermann, and even torn Robert McAlmon. No; he never
had much talent; but I could not bear to see him sorrow in one
of those back alleys of Palm Springs, and withal to be kicked into
the dust. Whatever my large defects may be I don't hurt people
who are maimed, or who, to use the vulgar words of Williams,
"have slipped." Well, you are right, we need a great vocal wilderness, the vast forests crying out our needs and denials, for we
have never gotten out of the terrible darkness of our beginnings.

I was exceedingly lucky; within a few days I received two
remarkable essays on my work, one coming before yours by Allen
Tate, which is a great tribute and to appear in the *Sewanee
Review*, and now yours, and let me assert again that I am most
grateful to you for your perceptions. It is never really a question
of disagreement when two minds collide; you comprehend my
rejection, and there is no doubt that you know what you are
seeing. I have always believed in Nietzsche's "transvaluation of
values." Break the idols, and make other ones. I don't disavow
Nietzsche, as you see, but Melville was too half-formed himself to
know what he was doing. Not that we ever know. We write we
know not how or what, and pray to the energies that it may come
out right. Some people who write never have any luck, because
they have no strength; others do not fail only because they have

the force. That is about all there is to it. You can worship evil
(which I don't—and come out of it with a rare poem, as Lautréa-
mont does), or even virtue if there is some satanic fire in your
blood as there was in Milton. I am deeply sorry that my own
words on Melville upset you; believe me, I was overthrown myself. I had, to be truthful to myself, to acknowledge a great
and vast error that I had passed on to others in a book. Besides,
look at the sort of epicene boys of letters who have used him as a
venal larder. You might say, you can tell me, the same of Shakespeare; but Melville is not Saint Shakespeare. But still this does
not take care of the argument. No matter, I had to do it, and
that is the way I have had to write and live; maybe it has been
wrong, but one can compose a book so too. Being in the right,
alas, is no touchstone. Look how many bores have been correct.

Have I thanked you enough, Josephine? How can I? I will
make use of your book on Bartram and the long masterly narrative, *The Hunter of Doves*, which has not gotten the attention
that it should. But here I should be useful to your work, which is
my duty as a writer and which I shall most gladly do. How many
people are there in our century worth bothering about; yes, writing about, that is another question, since scribblers reveal the
nonsense, the idiocy, and the famine of our age.

Again, I wish to salute your book which I am sure is a work of
genius, and I do not use that word wantonly.

We are underground writers and thinkers; that you know, but
someday we will take our revenge against the imbecilic politicians who imagine that they are the history of America. But we
are.

I earnestly pray that you are in good health. I had to leave the
big ditch, New York.

Please let me hear that you have gotten my epistle, my thanks,
and my profoundest appreciation. When will it come out, I mean
the whole part, in *Commentary*? I say let me hear from you,
Josephine, because you may by now have wondered why I was so
churlish as not to reply to you before. But as I am in Spain that
is the lucid reply.

Soller de Mallorca
April 23, 1961

Dear Josephine:

I wrote you above a week ago; a few days before I had word from Ferlinghetti of City Lights Books that he thought my introduction "beautiful," and I was particularly glad because of the quotation from you. That I mean literally; I am never at all sure whether what I do will be any good or how somebody else will respond to it, and I wanted your statement to appear in the republication of *Bottom Dogs*. It is good and the prophetic truth.

Laughlin now proposes to do *Because I Was Flesh*, first volume, in '62, and I shall have a chance to say something about you that is deeply good, I pray. In a short introduction to *Bottom Dogs* I had some difficulty; how should I refer to you and not seem trite. I used the word in alluding to you, eminent writer; is that all right? The whole piece is no more than a thousand words long.

As for Robert Coates, he passed out of my mind in Paris where I remembered him as the author of *Eater of Darkness,* Contact Edition. I also mentioned John Hermann in the introduction, suggesting what we had attempted to do, and that I believed that all of us failed. I did it, I hope, simply, and without patronizing the deceased or the living.

Did you see Granville Hicks' review of the book by Herbert Read and me; he has been lying in ambush for me for twenty-eight years. You do not know, dear Josephine, the stories that pass about regarding me. Somebody, the name is not important, retailed the story that I had stood over Lawrence when he was dying, and made him do the introduction to *Bottom Dogs!* A communist once said that I had hired a ghost writer to do *From Flushing to Calvary*; if so, I should have hired one who could have avoided all the defects in my work. O God, character takes care of everything, and nobody can hide behind a good or a bad style.

Will *Commentary* do the essay, I mean, yours, on my work; I hope so. Hicks accuses me of envy; why should I attack Lawrence who praised me; would it not make far better sense for me to say that a man who lauds me has extraordinary genius? If he is that gifted and gives me an encomium, imagine what a giant I must be! You know they are even stupid and lack shrewdness when they are trying to knock down a man.

My warm love to you, Josephine, guard your health; my nerves are sick these days, and not even the sun, that balm of Gilead to my whole soul, is any help.

Your constant and admiring friend,

Soller de Mallorca
December 19, 1962

Dear Josephine:

Your letter just came, and I am replying at once as you asked me to do. Of course, I *want* you and Jean to come; there is plenty of room, and as you have a marvelous house in Bucks County, this place may appeal to you. I hope so.

But, my dear Josephine, there are no people except ourselves, and we are disappearing; we are in a peopleless wilderness, and Hagar could not have been more solitary or thirsty for the angelic fountains of perception than we are. Would to heaven, not caring a mite for that region, that I could say there is one human being in Soller who has reaches beyond mammon, comfort, or greedy ambition. There are the usual arts and letters tramps in Soller; I know a couple of translators in Palma, who should translate themselves into some other shape.

The autobiography is done, and should be published sometime in spring. I just got a letter from Faber that they were really impressed with the Ms. but could not see how they could take it! I would not change one word in it to please Eliot or his anthill scribbler, Pound. What do we do? I have no morals, no deity, and don't require one; and yet some things disgust my entrails, shake my pulses, and make me feel more rotten and depraved than I am, if that is possible. Even in the past year I have undergone another change, and don't even care for the measure of stability that was Kyd's or Webster's. If somebody asked me why I was writing, I could only answer that man is monstrous where there are no truthful writers, and maybe just as bestial when there are a few; the only difference there is, is that one poet or novelist feels less solitary, even if he knows that somebody else inhabits the globe whom he never sees.

However, none of this makes me too grum. Along with my enormous defects is an enormous interest in anything that lives, and that is not the result of any virtue I have, but is the consequence of a nervous disorder. If my mother had not had robustious thighs, and great laughter in her bowels, until she no longer had the force to struggle against too many maladies, I should be a stupid noddle. She is my only saving grace, and had she not been such a remarkable character, I should be the typical misogynist, quite neutral and disemboweled.

The address you have is my post office box; I live about two kilometers from the town; so if you and Jean can let me know when you are coming I could meet you at the train; by the way, there is a little train, really an electric tramvia that takes less than an hour from Palma to Soller (the train ride from Palma to Soller will cost you about twenty-five pesetas each). If it is too complicated for you to do that, you could get a taxi for twenty-five pesetas in Soller to here, C'an Peretons, Son Salas. Tell him that we are about a half a kilometer después de la Bar Frontera.

Since I last saw you a large university has offered to buy all my papers, notes, and letters (there are some very good ones from you), and to start an Edward Dahlberg Collection. When I first heard this I thought I was reading my obituary notice; then, I thought, by Zeus, someone wants to buy my sacerdotal trash, and a university at that! I won't tell you which one until the negotiations are completed. Jonathan Williams and his friend Ronald might come down. He is a great admirer of yours (I introduced him to *The New Green World*). Jonathan is a very gallant person, and he reads, imagine a young writer who reads. I still think you composed a very tender book on Bartram; if you would heed me, and nobody will, so why should you, you would use *The Hunter of Doves* as your paradigm. I told you some years ago that you had discovered a form that was amazing. That's your

style, and at the risk of offending you, and I don't want to do
that, but I know what is good (and that form for me was perfect), you ought to return to that. I know nothing about literary
canons, and rather imagine that taste depends upon your body,
which is the only mind we have; when people babble about the
will, the intellect, the instinct, I look for the arms, the legs, the
torso, the neck, and the nose. I feel so strongly about this, and
have, if nothing else, such an immense love for literature that I
would beg you to work in that manner.

Have I gabbled too long? Doubtless.

Meanwhile, my love to you and Jean.

Soller de Mallorca
May 24, 1963

Dear Josephine:

I have your letter which harrows up my soul; so much bad
luck, sickness, and nobody to care for you. You could have come
here; I had told you there was a room for you if you wanted it.
But I suppose you had your reasons for not coming. Besides, I do
not at this juncture in my life pretend to know what people do,
why they do it, or even who they are. If it is not tedious to hear a
short recital of my own woes, I must say that I had a stomach
hemorrhage, and high blood pressure which affected my eyesight.
I had five blood transfusions, and now can read a little, but am
feeble and useless. But so much for that.

Laughlin tells me that he has been hearing from you; so far I
do not know whether the Ms. has gone to the printers. Besides
the autobiography, I have another book which is being published
by the University of Minnesota Press, a volume of essays and
memoirs. I think I told you that the University of Texas will
publish a book of my verse later.

Forgive this brief but trite note, Josephine dear. I am incapable of one meditative phrase.

You know that I am very happy that you are going to do a
piece on my work, including the autobiography.

Poor Bill Williams died; he wrote, as far as I am concerned, one remarkable book, *In the American Grain*, which the young fools know nothing about. Had he continued in that vein, I think he would have been a great writer, more, a wise man. I should not use the word, great; it is odious, everybody today is either a painter, a writer, a poet, and all great, and positively inhuman, and disemboweled. When people ask me what I do, I stammer, and then manage to get out the creeping words: I write. Do I? How do I know? Is this humility, I distrust a humble man. It is. And there is nothing more to do.

What else, my dear friend. I wish you were here so that I could be of use to you, and then I would know that at least there would not be the infernal struggle for sun and bread.

Aristotle says that words perish as leaves do, and I remember how unnerved you were when I used the word *arriba*, speaking to the dog, Mala. Of course, I understood your feeling at once, and the word has since become odious to me also.

Would that I could persuade you to do more portraits, flinty, and yet for all the prose flints there are the buds of May strewn over them. It is one of the few pieces in modern writing that I care about, and I don't have much feeling for what is being done at present. Did you ever see a photograph of the demented adding machine scribbler, Burroughs, and see how the Mary McCarthy's drop their ecstatic spittle on that kind of satanic ink? It is really horrible, not only the lack of sense and taste, but honesty, my God, is there none?

Sick or not, when you and I get together, by letter or otherwise, we always talk, and I have begun to speak again, having been mute for two months. The other month Edmund Wilson's book on Swinburne was reviewed; he revels in those decayed nineteenth-century parties, including "quiet homosexuality." How do you like that for venal cynicism, and an attempt to drag in the pederastic trade. I don't care anymore what people do, or how they exercise or entertain their bodies, but I don't like commercial Hellenism.

Your devoted and loving friend,

Dear Josephine:

I have your marvelous words and am so grateful for them. What am I to do about the noddles who review the book, or who don't? Nothing. There is much prattling about freedom of the press, this print vermin I abhor very deeply. We talk about the RAPP; we've got it in the newspapers. Who more rigorously censors books; that they do it mainly for venal rather than political reasons, does not matter. The result is our U.S.A.

How often I think of that autocrat of our novel, Dreiser. When he lived I had the most urgent desire to know what I could about him. There was a time when I was unable to read his books. I am really ashamed to say this, because I admire the man so much. He had a strong physical prose style. Now we have the epicene, or just the neutral sort of syntax, very nauseating, and boring. It takes a man to create a woman, maybe a banal remark; nevertheless Dreiser was such a person. Do you know Ford's *Portraits from Life*; there is a fine piece on Dreiser. Of course, there was a good deal of Street and Smith in him, but after you have condemned the man for all the Gargantuan stupidities in writing, you cannot eradicate Dreiser. In a way, I liked Dorothy Dudley's book on him, not a good one at all, but still far better than the exsanguious academic tomes about him.

My despair is that I get to learn so little about other persons. If I knew something about you, all my fault, I should do a portrait of you. This is not flattery, or nonsense, I would do it.

Of course, I shall be most eager to see your statement on *Because I Was Flesh,* and then your essay. What the boobs will say is another matter. You can't kill them; you get rid of them, and they sprout up more quickly than those stones known as the Cadmean men, for stones they are, little writing rocks of unfeeling.

Before I had commenced this letter I had all sorts of thoughts I wanted to send to you in appreciation of your consoling epistle.

Now what I have said amounts to nothing, and it troubles me. Imagine, for one thing, trying to be profound, a buffoon's intention.

It is most heartening to hear that you have company, your energetic niece and Jean; we need companions, for who is so much of an orphan as a writer? I still think *Call Me Ishmael* is the most prophetic opening of a novel in the whole history of fiction. I know you get piqued with me when I underrate Melville; of course, he had genius; it is my simple and perhaps obtuse feeling that he wasted it because he had no friends to guide him, or even misguide him. Can you compose an epic of over five hundred pages and not know, say, Euripides or even Frank Norris? When Upton Sinclair had some vigor, and he was never a seer of letters, and I hope that is not a bombastic phrase, he had companions. They gave him that force that later passed from him. Look how many people received strength from Randolph Bourne.

Julia was deeply pleased to know that you remember her, and both Julia and Rlene send their affections to you. You can see I would not be alive a week without the healing companionship of sympathetic women. Maybe the best of men are only counterfeit women. No matter how I have tried, I have never been able to draw from a male friend the love I need to see, hear, speak, and write.

Write when you are able to, Josephine dear, and please know how much I prize your Mind and Feeling, there is no dualism meant here, for intelligence is nothing but clear feelings, or emotions lucidly understood. All that humbug about reason, intellect, and emotion is all right for the academic boys who are doing bursar grammar manuals on aesthetics.

Your admiring and steadfast friend,

Soller de Mallorca
November 2, 1963

Dear Josephine:

Your very good and thoughtful letter has just come, and I feel strongly about replying at once. Of course, you are right, a statement from you should come from your essay; for it is the language that always counts as we know; praise in the usual blurb style is bad because the diction is poor. I am not referring to your statement which I since have seen and for which I thank you very much—and again thanks.

Now I am very fond of Jonathan, but he seldom takes my advice although he dedicated a very fine poem to me, and called me his mentor and teacher. At the moment, he is vexed with me because he sent me a piece of verse, some genre of lullaby done in an uncouth idiom (and which he thought was a divulgation of Southern sensibilities) that I considered tawdry and coarse. It was a little pamphlet in defense of the Negro. But the bottom of the misery is not the Negro, it is America; and if we (we is nonsensical, it is not I, indeed, no) liberate him, what do we offer him, America? In short, he'll have the same sort of liberty he had during the so-called period of Reconstruction. He will have the right to be hungry, or if better fed than he is, the freedom to be as depraved and as worthless as the ordinary white American. It is a pitiless tragedy. To be short, if one is to compose a poem to persuade the American to liberate the Negro, he has to compose it in a language of symbols and myths that will free the white American who is ready to emancipate the black one.

Anyway, I wrote Jonathan a very sharp letter, telling him to sit somewhere and be quiet in a room and work. After I wrote him, I reread his essay on me, and only then saw his reference to you, which I greatly misliked. It was I who sent Jonathan to you, telling him how much I admired *Hunter of Doves* and *New Green World,* and I urged him to read them. Did he? I don't know; I should be quite willing to doubt it. You might wonder why I am saying all this; do I have any of Cain's guilt on my hands; no, none. But I did send him to you and that troubles me sorely. Jonathan is a very gifted young poet, full of fine whimsies and trash. His publishing misadventures have been the cause of many admonitory conversations I have had with him. At the Living or the Dead Theater, Jonathan had arranged to have Kenneth Patchen read his verse to the accompaniment of a Dixieland band! There is the whole fable, and the real secret to all the useless obscenities, the pederasty (often premeditated and bloodless rather than inevitable) of our young Beat rebels. I never found out what they were opposed to; they seemed to take up all the gravel and clinkers of America, the filthy music, the morose and morbid misconception of an idiomatic tongue (not as Congreve or Swift so marvelously understood it) as though she were a tender bride.

Should there be any doubt as to my own feelings about your work, no one can misconceive that after looking at the allusions to you in *Truth Is More Sacred* and in the various references to you in *Alms for Oblivion* which the University of Minnesota is publishing. Few in the latter book do I praise; and those I loathe will know that also, particularly the tradesmen of our venal literati.

Of course what you say about *Bottom Dogs* is right; I would not have minded at all your references to me in your piece which was essentially on Nathanael West had I not felt that it is unjust to talk about a writer's imagination as if he only had written one book. There is no need on my part to differ with you and I freely admit that the two books by N. West are superior to *Bottom Dogs*. I have had the feeling that no matter how many books a man writes in the United States he is always the author of one volume, that is the last one he wrote. The others are automatically expunged, because nobody bothers to think about them, except to praise them when they were published, and having fulfilled that obligation to forget them entirely. One of the very few good things Eliot ever said was that Europeans study a writer as a whole, whereas the American is concerned with fragments, or to repeat, the last book—and there has always got to be a last new book or else the author is as good as dead. Now, don't misunderstand me, I accept your estimate of *Bottom Dogs* entirely.

Also, you will write what you must; I do believe that if you are at your top when you do dissect and then put me together, I will then be lucky, because if the language is good it will be a tribute to me. I suppose that if you happen to compose a remarkable essay on a scribbler he then becomes a memorable figure.

Doubtless, every man deemed his own age a miserable one; if you recall in *Can These Bones Live,* I said, quoting another man, that in the golden age of Pericles Aeschylus was banished, Phidias was exiled, and Socrates took the hemlock. But are not some centuries worse than others? Spite of the credo of dirt that

obtains in all American life today, the result of hygiene, no
doubt, and the other vile cult of vulgarity, I confess that I would
rather be alive now than say at the time poor, torn Melville
existed, though it may be that the nineteenth century produced
better writers.

I had hoped you would never see Jonathan's essay, not that I
imagine you have nothing better to do than to fret about that. It
was I who was doing the fretting.

You wrote a very fine letter, Josephine dear, and I have kept
all of your epistles, and deeply prize them.

Julia is exceedingly pleased to have your affectionate greetings,
and she sends her own warm affections to you. *Alms for Oblivion*
is dedicated to her. It is true, as you say, that I have often had a
Mary or a Martha at my side, but when I did not, and that too
was often, my life was worthless. I am hopeless, erring flesh without a woman, am the same one with one, but at least I can abide
myself then, somewhat.

You have, Josephine dear, my love and gratitude, and please
let me see a copy of your essay on me as soon as you can. This
letter too may be full of those contradictions and paradoxes you
perceive in me, but I am an uneasy man, never sure, for I have
no Petrine rock, and walk on water because I am unstable.

Your devoted friend,

Soller de Mallorca
November 9, 1963

Dear Josephine:

I lay awake many hours last night thinking about your letter.
Of course, Jonathan, who is gifted, can write rubbish. I would
rather write a truthful book which might fall into the hands of
two Negroes than pass another law giving this unfortunate people the right to vote in savage Mississippi. If you can find an
American Negro who comprehends the Logos, you have freed
him, and translated him into an Epictetus; no matter how much
bread you give a man, he is, as you know, a swine only fit for the

masts and acorns Circe will allow him. But then America is a
hopeless land ruled by clowns who cannot speak or write the
simplest words simply. What are we to do? You must write a
marvelous book, and I must do my utmost to tell what truths I
imagine I know in words that are just and properly associated
with one another. What ails Jonathan is hankering for novelties.
Neologisms make cowards of us all.

Otherwise, I sit here, or lie in bed, doing my best to regain
strength. What I have in mind is a book of adages. Who will buy
or read it is of no matter to me. That reminds me of a problem
you present: you say that you must write your essay so that
Dunciads can read *Because I Was Flesh*. Of course, this is a
paraphrasis. But my feeling, and this is against my immediate
interests, is that you must needs compose an essay that has all the
speculative ore of Eden in it, and if nobody can understand it
save you and I, that has to be. Only the best writing can cure any
of us. Fame purchased at a bargain price is the whore that sits
upon the waters of Babylon. Naturally, I know you wish to do
what will be a great benefit to me, and of course, I need that
advantage. However, if I read the essay with pulsing joy because you are writing at your peak, then I must accept it too as
alms for oblivion for you and me. All this, and so much more was
I musing upon as I went to and fro in my bed thinking about
your own very fine epistle and considering the lilies, the Andes,
and sterile Calloa which is often far better than the tender olive
yards of Bethlehem. What seems to be bad for our days is so often
a benison for our books.

However, by the time this letter reaches you you will have
already completed the essay, and what I say is only aliment for
our vagaries anyway. I hardly wish to meddle with your task, and
am only deeply grateful to you for performing it as you wish.

I wish there were a few more of us so that we could go into
Gaza and be triumphant. But by now I know there are no victories, and that only our defeats replenish us.

Julia always reads your letters with much pleasure. I told her
what sweet words there were in them and she quickly if not
instantly agreed.

Tedium often lies as heavy on my head as the Andes. But like you I rejoice in a day of sun and zephyrs and imagine I am happy though I know that cannot be.

When I wanted Jonathan to meet you telling him of my high regard for you, and my long friendship with you, I hardly expected him to ground his silly judgment upon your early work. Suppose he did the same with me what would I be? Just another nobody. It is marvelous that before Homer's hero was called Ulysses, and he had performed his astounding exploits he was called Nobody. That is what Lucian says. But here we have a foolish boy. This is the American way; they are all boys, and though I have been Jonathan's advocate for some years, admonishing him for publishing such elite trash, I have always wondered whether he would ever be anything but a talented youth. I deeply hope I am wrong. But our whole century has been a chronicle of boyism.

Well, Josephine dear, you have my deepest thanks and, of course, my love; Julia sends her affections to you. Later when you are finished with your book, and want a change, and I have some money in my pockets, you can stay here for a long while; what I always fear is that I may be a bore, and have nothing to say to you from one day to the next. But Julia and Rlene will be here too.

letters to
William Carlos Williams

Dear Williams:

I don't mind being rebuked by you for a fault. But my dear gifted man, how was I to know where to reach you? The only communication I had from you was a postcard with four bare lines saying that you expected to be in California sometime in the spring. I wrote you two letters after that asking you and your wife to come out and have dinner with us. Had you no quarters we would have bought a bed for you and Mrs. Williams. It is true, I could have written to Thirlwall and asked him where you were. But since you had not told me I had some real misgivings about doing this. You had not accepted my invitation, nor was there any word from you at all. I do not go about wooing chagrins, and had unusual hesitation about trying to find out where you were since you were so silent about it.

Should I tell you the real truth about my feelings toward you? It has been my one desire to repair any differences between us. Then I say with some embarrassment, because Americans hate you or flee from you when you send them affections or express some tender feeling about them, you are the only poet in this land I feel close to. I am very dual, Williams, but I try not to tell lies. If a gnat scratches me I howl as much as Achilles, and so I live here in congealed privacy.

My wife, an ardent admirer of *In the American Grain,* wanted very much to meet you, which is another reason why I should have desired to avoid you!

I find talk very healing. You know I am plain with you, for you recall our letters to one another when I lived on the Cape.

My former wife has your epistles; otherwise I should have sent them to Thirlwall. But that is not the point: you reprehended me at the time, and I wrote you the letter you printed in *Paterson*. You told me to use my hands; of course you were right. No writer should depend upon literature for his life, bread, and the aliment of the spirit. Eric Gill in a fine little book, posthumously published, and called *Last Essays*, did lettering on headstones; he said that every author should have some manual experience. Do you know that Gill had to cut the marble for Maillol? It is too late for me to find the ease the hands give us; it is hard enough for me to make one good sentence.

Now if you don't think I would be such a knave as to ask a real kindness of you while shunning you, or that I am such a sloth as not to telephone a man for whom I have always had a profound regard and affection (the quarrels were only a part of my feeling and involvement with you), then I wish you would read the Ms. Now should you deeply care for it, I want to make acknowledgments to you. I say it this way for what pleasure could you have receiving homage either from a bad writer or a rotten book? Despite my arrogance, I am also the timorous dove about my work, and I do not want to be more of a fool than nature has made me by saying what you will feel. I have all the faults of flesh; all flesh is grass, says Isaiah, and also weeds, guile, the droppings of thrushes, skulking, ambition, cheating.

I have never been behindhand in doing you honor, Williams. You doubtless forgot that Ford and I started the group called the Friends of William Carlos Williams. You know, I asked Waldo Frank to join us, and he refused because he did not like the name! I must now tell you one more thing; you recall that three dinners were given, the first to you, the second to Cummings who did not appear, and the third for me. You were sitting next to me, and I was poring over my novels to find some pages to read. You were very testy, and turning to me, said: "For Christ's sake, Dahlberg, how much are you going to read?" The truth was that by that time I had come to have such uneasy feelings about my first three novels I was looking with some anguish for something that did not cause me to wince. Far from wanting to read aloud a great deal, I did not think there was anything in the three books worth reading at all. Tolstoy once said, "Many people write books, but very few are ashamed of them afterwards."

Meanwhile, you have my genuine affections.

Santa Monica, Cal.
August 25, 1955

Dear Bill:

Your letter has just come, and I must reply at once. First, it was a rare grace in you to read the Ms., and you have my full thanks for that. Some of the very good things you say are, for me, at least, marred by certain pragmatic considerations. You want me to cast away the first part of the book which Laughlin cares for most. He said to me, "Let's face it, who's interested in the Aztecs!" altogether unmindful of *In the American Grain*. Have you ever had a success with a book? What happened to *The Flea of Sodom!* Almost nothing; abroad one review appeared in *The Statesman*, which I never saw, and in the United States there were seven reviews of the book. What hope had Baudelaire? The most he looked for was a *succès d'estime*. There is the mysticism of print; people canonize garbage if it is published.

Suppose I had suggested that you throw out "Jacataqua," a wonderful, acrimonious essay on our epicene dames, or tell you, as Laughlin had intimated, "Who cares about Montezuma or Champlain?"

In 1925, when *In the American Grain* came out, who read it?

It's an accursed perplexity to turn to another writer and ask him for help, and then oppose him. Could I advise Burton that his *Anatomy of Melancholy* was too long? Or tell Izaak Walton to expunge half of his book, for though it is short it is too long for those who have no interest in natural history.

I am on the wheel; I have to stand by my book; too much has gone into it, a lustrum of agony, reading, hindrances, boreal silence, all the harsh strokes of a sick century. I have bent fate wherever I could, or imagined that I did, without avail. It had been my penultimate expectation that you would deeply care for the book; there are, despite differences in nature, great similarities in temperament. We go with our identities, the Holy Ghost that ever guides us, to the same rivers, to sea salt and the old god of the alphabet, Thoth, for our source. Our veins are surcharged with old fables, annals.

You once called me pigheaded for making some criticism of *Paterson*. The truth is I have great sympathy with the intention of the book; I had perceived that you had mentioned the word, rock, seventy to eighty times. It is a very odd repetition, and authors, poets, have no more than one or two themes in their lives, and may write no more than a single book though they publish two dozen. Rock is your Peter, your image for volition in which the American is very weak. Ice, too, is your lodestar, for in your own broken obscurity as a poet, this was your will; your niggard denials were the chant of the ice and the rock which pained you no less than the "nails in the wound."

Had you said to me, eradicate this page or even ten or twenty, I would have heeded you; but when you ask a very experienced prose writer to throw away half of his inward ore, I cannot heed this. Have you forgotten your own travail, and what so many advised you to do, to speak so to my own nature? How many pages are there in any volume that will content Hamlet as well as Polonius? Do I require many readers, or can I ever gather them up? When I do a brief book, I am too sententious, or a wise one too profound, or a gay one, prolix.

The truth is that as much as I care for you as a writer and a person, I should not have risked my trembling pulses. I should have waited for publication, and then sent the volume to you.

I see before me words you should not have written, and I have to be repetitious; let me quote you: "I don't think the book has a chance with a publisher, not the chance your former books enjoyed and of that you know better than I." Pardon me for saying it once more to a very gifted nature who once could not get his own poems and prose published. My books were always interred by venal scribblers. What was the fortune of *Can These Bones Live*? The book was sent to the gallows by the papers, and they are worse than a famine of locusts or an invading army, or given not even the bloody field, Potter's Grave, by the Marxists. The book sold less than three hundred and seventy-five copies; that, too, was a writer's book, and it made a strong mark upon authors, but who mentions it? Lethe is our water, and not the lake of Memory. Laughlin would have published this book long ago had not *The Flea of Sodom* had such a niggling success. Where then is my Patagonian mineral; no matter which way I turn, or how I write, there has never been any El Dorado for me. Even you, my good friend and admirer of *Can These Bones Live* and *The Flea of Sodom* kicked me into limbo in your own *Autobiography*. Still, I have real affection for you, and don't imagine I am your little Sermon-on-the-Mount acolyte. No one kicks me—as fat Jeshurun was said to do, for he had a fat heart—and goes unscathed if I can help it. Bill, it may be that I am doomed in Erebus. Do you know *Rejoice in the Lamb,* a marvelous poem? What happened to it? The author wrote it in Bedlam, and it remained in a drawer for two hundred years, and when it was published by Henry Holt one hundred and seventy-eight copies were sold in a period of thirteen years, and there were no reviews.

Either we stand by each other, and I guess we must somehow endure one another's foibles since every book is a monstrous fault, or American Literature is doomed. It is close to that now, but I'll hang on rolling the rock up the peak as Sisyphus did, knowing beforehand that it will come down again. That is laboring for one's destiny, and that is the way a book is made, and I know no way of writing a book that can deeply fetch more than a half dozen poets. I had prayed to God that it would draw you, as ice or fire or rock does.

You may be right about expunging your name because it interferes with the text. However, it has been in my mind to write something as homage to you at the head of the part on America. I would never have gone to Cortes, and to Montezuma, and to myriads of other sources, monks, friars, conquistadores, whom Prescott drew from, had it not been for that visionary book, which had no success in this world, and the fewest of readers, *In the American Grain!* How many noddles today tell you about the success of your books; what a wry smile it must wring from your face. As for success, the worst devil in the American language, I would rather bow my neck to Astarte, or to Moloch or to Baalim, than to that uglified beast which has killed the letter and the spirit.

Now what to do. Do you feel strongly enough about the book to write to Laughlin; he is printing a covey of empurpled pathics and punctuation boys of the Muses. Give him any misgivings, and I might as well return to my charnel house, my books, some of which are too long (Garcilaso de la Vega's *Royal Commentaries* is over six hundred pages, old-style pagination), but it is a part of our haste; we want compendia, the epitome of a tome; make it fast, void in a hurry, read at gamy, racer's gait; but thinking is slow, and Buddha has enough patience to remain seated for thousands of years.

Please thank your good wife, Flossie, for reading the Ms. to you; let me hear further from you, if you have a mind to. I'll break the voiceless ramparts myself somehow, if you don't care to come to my aid. Let nature break my life and will first and pour it on the ground; that is being alive on the quick of my soul. All else is getting a reputation, and being a little infamous; maybe darkness, and not light, is the only hope of a writer who will tell the truth even if it takes him over three hundred pages to do it.

Meanwhile, my affections to you, and I pray, miserable nihilist that I am, for your health.

————————————

Palma de Mallorca
September 20, 1957

Dear Bill:

I am told by a dear friend in Paris, who is married to Henri Matisse's daughter, and who is the one vibrant head I have met in Europe, that France today is ruled by the gendarme and the concierge. In socialist Denmark I knew a highly intelligent author, a woman, who had come to America and there had a child by a wretched scribbler. Poor and forsaken she had to return to

Copenhagen, where she earned her niggard indigence doing reviews for the Politiken, and giving occasional lectures on Middle English and Early Danish. She lived in the slummy part of that beautiful city, trying to support a wonderful boy, sturdy, loving, and very masculine. It was my joy to bring him oranges, chocolate, and those precious morsels which his mother could not afford. She told me that the socialist police had called on her one night, asking why she had not paid her taxes to the government. Poverty was her reply. Do you recall the epitaph on Thomas Churchyard's tombstone, "Poverty and Obscurity doth this tomb enclose." A week later they returned, threatening to remove her furniture and have it impounded by the government. When she again pleaded that if she gave what kroners she had her little boy would starve, the police said: "We went to the Vin Handel last evening and learned from the proprietor that you had bought a bottle of wine; if you can afford to drink wine you certainly can pay your taxes." She then said, "I am so poor, and so driven to despair by it that I had to have a bottle of wine to relieve me of my melancholia."

I am quite sure, too, that people only have the kind of government that their bellies crave. Furthermore, I cannot cure one soul in the earth. Plato took three journeys to Dionysius, the Tyrant of Syracuse, and once was almost killed and on another occasion was nearly sold into slavery because he imagined that he could influence a devil to model his tyranny upon the *Republic*. Seneca was the teacher of Nero, and Aristotle tutored Alexander of Macedon. What did they teach?

We are content here because it is cheap; my wife can eat châteaubriand for seven pesetas, about fifteen or sixteen cents. Going to the shops in the morning is a ritual; there is the greeting from the woman who runs the *panadería,* and the salutation (courtesy always eases the spirit and relieves the nervous system) from the man or his wife at the *lecheria* (where you get milk), and an expansive smile from the humble woman who sells you three pesetas worth of helio (ice). This is worth more to me than living in the states and earning those grum dollars which entitle you to trundle a trap-like wire cage through the massive, gloomy halls of a supermarket, and after a half hour of self-service (for what else can you get out of a mechanical nation) going to the cashier who mutely drops your change from her grubby hand into yours, for fear that she may touch you, unmindful that it is she who is full of worms.

I am no expatriate by nature, for I have been in exile in my own land since I was a boy, first in the wanton streets of Kansas City, then in an orphanage, and then a waif of letters in New York. I no longer have the gullet for it.

Not only well-to-do tourists come down here; there are girls from the Midlands, and young sturdy lasses from the factories of Birmingham and Manchester, and their soft English civilities are far better than the coarse diction or the manners of some fungused professor who is misteaching thousands of lost students in our colleges of lower learning. Yesterday Paul Leek, the secretary of the Friends of William Carlos Williams, came to lunch; he heard I was here, and we talked a great deal about you, and I told him how much I cared for you.

An English publisher and his wife and Rlene and I went to Alcudia the other day, and we looked with great reverence at a marvelously preserved Roman Gate. Nearby was the remains of a wall, and the bricks drew from me that sigh and prayer that one has in handling a Babylonian cylinder of baked clay. Now, I hear that the American Air Force is going to establish itself at Alcudia, an ancient, handmade town and as finely wrought and honest as any Utopia Ruskin or Thomas More ever conceived. What happens when the American Military moves in! In Seville you could get two years ago a whole house for four hundred pesetas a month, about eight or nine dollars. Then came the American Air Force, and some noddy in Washington, totally unfamiliar with economic conditions in Spain, gave hillbillies from Kentucky and Arkansas (I wouldn't live in the South if they gave it to me), who were earning twenty or twenty-five dollars a week, a rental allowance of one hundred and twenty-five dollars a month! Immediately all the dwellings that had rented for nine to ten dollars were let for one hundred and twenty-five dollars.

A year ago we were in Toledo, and when we went to the house of El Greco, I touched the table where he sat and ate, and trembled, and that is art and literature, which no emboweled grammarian can ever understand. For writing books is a form of love, and if it is anything else it is a lie and a curse brewed in Tartarus.

Now, my dear Bill, keep well, that is important to me, very, and I say the same of Flossie because she is so important to you.

Both Rlene and I send you our love; we live on the Calle de la Salud, and when you think of that street, remember that it is on that Street of Health that we offer you our salutation. Myself, I am damnably plagued by the ulcer, but I shan't show such poor taste or shabbiness by complaining of my maladies to you!

Palma de Mallorca
September 1, 1957

Dear Bill:

I never had any reply to my last letter and would not have known you had received it had not Jack Thirlwall sent me a kind word or two on a postcard. I hope you will convey my affections to him and explain that I have not written him because of a kind of wormy lassitude from which I have suffered after completing my book.

Southern Spain was too sterile for us; all traces of the Carthaginians and the Romans have well-nigh disappeared; though there are some fine littoral hamlets twenty-five kilometers from Malaga there are too many former Nazis there to suit my palate. I have no interest anymore in endeavoring to cure the sick commonwealth, but I am still politically squeamish. There is Goering's widow in Marbella. I heard one trashy writer, altogether venal, and a Jew at that, tell me how charming he found Madame Goering! When I read that Poppaea was seeded by Nero I am ready to go to the vomitory.

I told you of the Anglo-American group we had in Torremolinos, all more or less indigent. Most of them lived by hitchhiking into Gibraltar where they bought Scotch and then smuggled it into Spain where they sold it at a fairly good profit to the saloons. There were two English frumps, vastly buxom, one a teacher and the other a social worker from the Midlands, who used to wear massy skirts, beneath which they hid the Scotch. When the Spanish officials came to inspect the car they were riding in, these women would give them such an ample smile that they were always allowed to pass the frontier without any difficulty. There was Dominic, an Irishman, who had been in Sadler's-Wells ballet; he too was a smuggler, and was living when he had the pesetas in a room with a girl, half Irish and half German, who had the blue eyes of a well-bred Siamese cat. The cockney nurse who took care of all of us when we were sick finally became quite ill herself. The Spanish doctors in the south are worthless, and when she was very sick, and the physician came, she had to tell him what to prescribe for her. Without any examination whatever or a urine analysis, he at once gave sulphur or penicillin to the patient. If the patient recovers that's his fault. Her mother came down to join all of us; she had been a police sergeant who took whores to jail. Whenever the daughter and the mother quarreled, which was very often, the nurse would say, "Lovey—shut up."

They were a bizarre lot; when the nurse was broke and had to return to London to seek a job in a hospital there, Joe, the Alaskan who read all day with a kind of cloistral insanity, took her to Gibraltar. She found there that she did not have enough money for her passage back, and all day at Gibraltar they cudgeled their heads to see how they could find money for a ticket. Weeping, she searched for a handkerchief which was deposited in an immense satchel-like purse, and rummaging for it she found eighty dollars, or its equivalent in pounds.

Here, which is far less impoverished than Cadiz or southern Iberian towns, almost every peasant, no matter how humble, has a patio. We, too, have a kitchen garden and raise tomatoes, parsley, cauliflower, celery, endives, spices, and have, besides, several orange trees and a lemon tree. We have to buy little for our table, and as I do not eat meat, we manage.

There is a large English colony here, and quite a number of American residents. The women are monied brachs, and if there is so much homosexuality in the world now, one look at these pecuniary female savages divulges one of the real reasons.

My dear Bill, you can be sure that I think of you often; the other day I picked up *In the American Grain,* and I feared to look at the pages lest they would not seem as strong and remarkably molded as I once thought. It's a classic of our country, Bill; make no mistake about it! Smollett, very good when he is acrimonious, has not your gifted style; ultimately we read a man because he knows how to write, and it is form rather than matter that startles us.

Let me hear from you, Bill; the truth is I worry about you a great deal, and the reason I don't write you so often is that I don't care to burden you with correspondence. You have your own trials which you bear like Cato.

I pray that both you and Flossie are in good health; you have my love and admiration, Bill.

Palma de Mallorca
February 10, 1958

Dear Bill:

I sent you two letters to express my strong feelings for the wonderful little memoir in *The American Scholar,* but have had no word from you. I have read *The Farmer's Daughter,* and if one can separate art from nature, this is nature. All these people live and they are all dead, no less so than the same figures in Gogol's marvelous fable. After some critic had read *Dead Souls* he said, "I never knew how tragic Russia is."

Your women live in a galled economic matriarchy in which they are beaten to death by the men. Most of them are boys, never ripening into men, sometimes charming boys, but always boys. The women, their mothers, support them, as you narrate. Of course, you can't have a couple of generations or more of masculine children without a Margaret, Solomon's little sister who has no breasts. Often skinny women have astonishing passions which do not kindle us, and bring us not their beds but return us to unsatisfied lust. All your flower lines, if I may so speak of them, are again so natural and never false poesy. You write of them as easily as you do the loving canary or the sunflower seeds. All these people, lonely and broken, the women working in obscene factories which kills their hair and their softness—Good God, what is there to be done! When I was a boy I saw such fine buxom lasses from Saint Joseph, Wichita, and Joplin, a joy to behold and a marvel to caress, but now the hoyden, the machine-shop harridan, is three-fourths boy too. The whole American spectacle is nihilism and Dada suicide. That is why I went away.

The sickness of course, is everywhere. The Mallorquin women are often very pretty, good cask-like bodies, but alas, stupid. Ignorance is another matter, quite venial. Once Tolstoy said that when it was not accompanied by malice it had a kind of genius. Montesquieu was no fool when he said that were it not for the Venuses he met at court he would never have written a line. I think you are like that, and I know I am. I have a few men friends whom I greatly care for, one of them yourself, but otherwise the only people who have added one cubit to my life, or taken me from the middens and the piggeries, are women. As you say: "If she'd only had a BODY! She looked more like a boy than a girl." I think the American is going crazy; of course, his appetite for sickly, emaciated women, almost hipless, is homosexual. Put a woman in slacks, and you can't undress her without feeling like a Sodomite. There's puling Margaret, utterly thin, with nothing of the Shulamite in her but "the savage fistful of black hair sticking out prominently at the bottom of her belly."

There is one woman here, a quondam ballerina whom I am very fond of, and she of me. She had studied with Pavlova. Then she met a very delightful young man from Connecticut, with soft hair, very intelligent, an amiable boy. Georges Duthuit, the French writer, and husband of Henri Matisse's daughter, said to me: "What shall I do with my son; he has an agile mind, a friendly aimless character; he reads Stendhal and Flaubert like any charming girl of nineteen."

One day the ballerina complained to me, "I teach Mallorquin girls all day at the academy, and when we get back to our ten-dollar-a-month flat, I'm numb; Russ won't get a stove, he says it's an extravagance." Poor darling, she married someone at least twelve years younger than herself although she is still quite attractive. From that moment I began to tell Russ what a joy a stove would be, he could read more, and the flat would be a solace, even a Balm of Gilead. One day I went with her to the *ferreteria*, the hardware store, to see how much a stove would cost. She looked absolutely distraught. "I can't pay that much, Russ will be infuriated." I paid half of it though I could ill-afford to do so. Then the modern nonsense about getting a workman to install it, to puncture a hole through the ceiling and wall, and to cement it. I told the *tendero* that he had to get one of his men to install the stove, otherwise she wouldn't buy it. He said he wouldn't do it. I took her by the arm and turning about said with great emphasis, *"Buenos tardes."* When we were outside the door he called us back to say he would have it done. "When?" I asked. He said, right now. She bought the stove. A week later Russ came to see me, his charming face radiant, "I'm so glad I asked G. to buy the stove; what a blessing; I'm painting and reading more."

A zipper salesman came to Palma with a wife, and two daughters of a Jewish orthodox background whom he at once put into the Catholic school here. He blamed his wife for many wasted years, about twenty-three of them, and locked himself up all day, painting until nightfall. He ate his meals grumly, hardly talked to his wife, and with the exception of his older daughter, a blooming biblical Judith, cared for nobody. He had resolved that to be an artist he had to be a kind of ghetto Spartan. They lived here a whole winter without a fireplace, a stove, or any kind of heat or fuel. The wife used to come to see me often. She was more than half-mad, and spent her whole time cursing her husband. She was taking, at the doctor's orders, enormous doses of thorazine. Sometimes she came at seven in the morning and spoiled many a working day for me, but I had not the heart to admonish her. I have always hated artistic preciosity, and have always said that the adjective I lost one day I would recall the next. I don't think we forget anything except what we cannot digest or that is hostile to our nature. I counseled her as best I

could, saying that she could not live with a man and revile him
so without injuring her own health. I had promised myself that I
would never get involved in her malignity, but she poured so
much foulness into my ear that one day, without thinking, I
blurted out: "Why if he is such a monster, tell him not to come
and see me." From that time on I never saw her again. If you
damn the most miserable villain because his wife says he is that,
you do nothing but condemn her appetite and her habits which
she loves.

Well, Bill, my dear, gifted friend, thanks very much for sending me the good, seminal story, very good.

I am at work on a novel modeled on the Elizabethan comedy
and the picaresque tradition. For ten days of February there has
been warm-smelling sun, and I sit on the patio with lemon and
orange trees, and in my shirt-sleeves, writing. I earnestly hope
your marvelous tribute to Ben Shahn and to me is printed. Aside
from the *Nation* not a single newspaper or magazine in New
York has printed a review. So you see, I have been no melancholy
Saul about my book, and no whinling. I can write a book, and
hew it as one does granite; I can quarry my identity, but I am
helpless here. Dreiser, whom I was very fond of, once said as we
were walking together: "What we need is not freedom of the
press, but freedom from it." He was a very reflective man, and I
cared for him more than he knew.

Long life to a vigorous artist's brain, and my love.

Palma de Mallorca
March 7, 1958

Dear Bill:

Your very good letter came yesterday. My reply is tardy because your epistle came here by regular mail, and that is very
slow.

I walked about six miles yesterday, looking at the old Mallorquin sandstone houses in the native quarter. I like ordinary

Spanish dirt, it is so much more savory than the money streets of the tourists. What you tell me about your wonderful Memoir that appeared in *The American Scholar* interests me greatly. Women know a great deal about our strivings; are we not mountains, hills, and rivers because of them. Besides, good prose is an alive body. I don't care a straw, Bill, for learning. I read to pass the time, and to find out whether what I am saying is stale or foolish, or good because it has been said before by somebody else in another century. If we didn't have any brains at all we might be as intelligent as a pismire, if we were lucky. There's a marvelous remark in Webster's *The Duchess of Malfi* on humbug erudition, and I'll see whether I can find it because I believe it will make you smile or laugh: "I knew him in Padua—a fantastical scholar, like such who study to know how many knots was in Hercules' club, of what colour Achilles' beard was, or whether Hector were not troubled with the toothache. He hath studied himself half-blear-ey'd to know the true symmetry of Caesar's nose by a shoeing-horn; and this he did to gain the name of a speculative man."

Are you going on, Bill, with your Memoir? I cannot repeat too often how very, very fine I think it is. There's the spermaceti of Leviathan in it. We've had so little of warm human wisdom in our literature that we cannot afford to lose this. The highest compliment I can pay you is that I wish I had written it.

The other day a Spaniard came here to interview me for the Palma papers. Palma itself has a year-round population of about one hundred and fifty thousand; John Calvin has not crept into this town; the evenings on the Borne and the Rambla (really the *paseo*) are a soft murmurous mirth. There is none of that loud, hysterical noise of the American. A holiday in the States has become an obituary notice. Nobody with any sense wants to be in the streets. Anyway, the Spaniard wanted to know what I was doing, and so on, and instead of talking about myself, I spent the whole time on Miguel Unamuno, Pio Baroja, Ortega y Gasset. Every now and then I break into a fit of modesty, for all that he got out of me was that I was born in Boston.

You remember the British nurse and the American surveyor I wrote to you about, the one who had gone to Alaska? Well, the

nurse was in love with him, and he was chasing every piece of
beef he could find at the bars. I'm a marriage broker by temperament. I thought that if I could influence this man to read (and
he sat in his small cottage reading Grote's *History of Greece* or
Budge's *History of Egypt* for at least eight hours a day), that
maybe I could get him to marry Katie. He was living in a white
stucco house with a worthless painter and I got him out of there.
I did not lose an occasion to tell him how good Katie was. She
was a rather skinny sloven with lovely red hair, and was so
meager because the only life she had was to help sick Englishmen
and Americans. When she fell sick herself she had to tell the
doctor at Torremolinas what to prescribe for her. The only reason they don't saw off your legs is that Spain, thank heavens, is
not yet the land of the machine. Well, three weeks ago I saw
Katie in Palma. She and the young American were married, and
very happy. Katie was well-attired, her flesh blooming, and most
affectionate. He has a fine-paying job at an air base in the mountains outside of Puerto de Pollensa which is at the other end of
this isle of Prospero.

When will *Paterson 5* be out, Bill? I am very anxious to read
it.

The diaries of John Ruskin have been published, a great deal
of dross along with some pure ore of feeling. It pierces one to
know that Ruskin's faith was greatly shaken in his later years,
and that when he saw again Alpine gneiss he looked at it without
the rapture that he had formerly had. He was a great man. Do
you know his father was the partner of the Spaniard who made
Fundador Cognac here. He had left Ruskin a fortune of five
hundred thousand pounds which Ruskin dissipated in great
kindnesses to artists and friends. His life was one great wound;
he had fallen madly in love with a ten-year-old child, and had
continued to carry her in his heart until she was a woman, when
the parents, for what reasons I know not, forbade him to see her.
He was a wonderful prose writer, but whenever a book of his
came out, those locusts, the newspaper critics, ate up the book.

You speak, Bill, of melancholia. I know obsidian despondency,
and the knife of doubts. Would that I were there when you gave
your talk to those craven boobs of the arts. Do you remember

what Chekov said when he saw two painters pass him: "There go a pair of artists." A very simple remark, but right.

Every now and then I get an admiring letter from someone or other, but of a very droll sort. When we were in New York two fops of literature arrived and said to me: "*The Flea of Sodom* is the greatest book of our century." I thought: "Oh, oh, what do they want?" They wanted all sorts of things, none of which I could oblige them with because what they wrote was avant-garde refuse. The other day I received a letter from the two, saying that they would give me something of theirs for a copy of *The Sorrows of Priapus* which they regarded as the best book that has appeared in twenty to thirty years! These entrepreneurs are now appearing in *New World Writing*; what a barbarous title. What's new save that which is old differently expressed?

Speaking of the mind, I remember when I was on the executive committee founded for the release of the Scottsboro boys. We met at Dreiser's manorial apartment on Fifty-seventh Street. One of the communists began to talk about the need for an intellectual approach, and Dreiser said: "Oh, if it's brains you want, that lets me out." He was a very fine man, who taught me how to read Shakespeare. He was a very reflective man, and I was proud to know him, and he took great delight in my wild heterodoxies. When charlatans came to see him he received them sitting on a regal chair which was on a dais; but if he liked a man, and thought he was plain, he was most friendly. Why he could not write better I cannot understand though he did a fine piece on Randolph Bourne, and in a poignant style. He had a strong, physical style, but like so many of our savants was interested in spiritualism, table-rapping of one sort or another. You know his genius is glutted with Christian Science. I understood his motives for going into the communist party. He thought America was a hopeless country. Alas, what is our government but a canonized life insurance company. For me, there's no place to go to except into another book. I can't cure a commonwealth, and am fortunate if I can find that resin of Gilead to heal myself. I find, Bill, that a letter from you is a medicine, and a very good one.

My prayers, Bill, for your health and for Flossie's.

Also my love and admiration. You've got a mine in that

Memoir; I'd give more for that than I would for a claim in
California in '49.

Palma de Mallorca
March 17, 1958

Dear Bill:

I have your very fine letter. Your other epistle that came by
ordinary mail took seventeen days to get here; your last one, by
air mail, arrived in four days. Thanks very much for sending it
so, for the earlier I get word from you the more delighted I am.
We cannot be too judicious when we praise a younger person.
Suppose we are wrong, our hearts are still not pinched and
parsimonious. Besides, the whole of life is a mistake, and I intend
to commit it as valiantly as I can.

You and Flossie know Isabella Gardner; she is a rare human
being. I know her almost entirely through correspondence, having seen her once for less than five minutes. She wrote two very
fine poems in her first book where she employed with much inly
skill Linnaeus and Thoreau. I have been urging her to go to
natural history for her symbols and ritual. I have this day a good
epistle from her, and surely there is much fine judgment in the
following remark: "I cannot feel that a reference (no matter how
deeply felt) to Linnaeus or Bartram or the Minotaur redeems a
poem or *makes* it a poem any more than I feel the absence of any
such root or reference makes the poem *not* a poem."

I read because I fear risking a line without the help of some
savant or other, or I go to a volume because I am bored or empty
and want to be filled again. Moreover, I do not think I can be
anything much more than the vessel of thousands of years of
human experience. Somehow, by the use of myth you get away
from private heartache into universal art. The other day a
painter asked me whether I was not greatly impressed with El
Greco's painting, "The Death of Count Orgaz," which I saw in
Toledo but could not recollect. We remember what is useful to
us, and forget what we are not ripe for. I readily owned that I

could not recall it at all, and cited Nietzsche who once said: "The book was ripe for me but I was not ripe for the book."

I deeply hope you will help Isabella in any way you can. She has great admiration for you, and she tells me she is going to visit you and Flossie. She is first in my mind because she has the most tender heart. There is another writer whom I have never met, who reviews books for his bitter bread. He is accursed three times: he is an honest writer, absolutely deaf, and indigent. He has done an essay which was published in one of the small magazines on Dadaism and Nihilism, very acute. The first half or maybe two-thirds of it is very penetrating analysis of this period of violent nonsense, and devout hatred of the burgher in literature. The last part of the article falls apart, but that he could remedy by rewriting. There are stylistic difficulties; many of his words he derives from that humdrum and specious language that has come out of psychology, economics, Freud. Did you ever meet a psychologist who knew anything at all about another human being? It is not a long piece, and I took the liberty of suggesting that he send it to you. Should you find the value in it that I do and have some good and heartening word for him, it would give him copious felicity. I have also asked Herbert Read to help him in the same manner. These Ishmaels of the art are our responsibility. Give me, O heaven, some moiety of luck, and I'll hand it out to other writers as though it were my purse.

Would it be too grievous a request, Bill, to ask you to write a letter to the Institute of Arts and Letters asking them to give him some money? He has just been evicted, and lives in a slummy room on Avenue A, and that's the bottom of our Fleet Street.

His name is Jack Jones (could he be more anonymous).

I am delighted to hear that Jo Herbst and I are to appear in *Paterson 5.* I wrote to her a good many months ago, longer than that, but I did not hear from her, nor knew what had happened to her. As I haven't her address, would you please, when you write to her, thank her deeply for reviewing *The Sorrows of Priapus.* I knew dear Jo when she was an exuberant young woman married to John Hermann. I met John in New Orleans, and had not seen him I guess in at least ten years. He was selling Venetian blinds for an interior decorator in New Orleans by the name of Marc Antony! The latter's wife was the sister of Alma Gottschalk, now dead, and one of the heiresses of many sugar mills outside of the old Creole city. I had had a letter to her from Sherwood Anderson which went something like this: "Dahlberg has a brilliant mind, but is down on the world." I thought it a quaint introduction, but of course was very glad to meet all of his friends and ardent admirers. There was only one flaw; his warmest advocates began by denouncing Sherwood's books, each one saying that he wrote better than Anderson did. I soon found myself his sole defender amidst all of his friends.

In New Orleans I came across a protégé of Alma's, the daughter of a sea captain who plied up and down the Mississippi, and was a devotee of Herman Melville. The daughter, I can tell you, was a beauty, half Irish and half Swedish. I was so enticed by her that I drove with her to Baton Rouge, home of Huey Long's college, the University of Louisiana.

Like all fascists he was a great moral prig, and had established myriads of ordinances to prevent the coeds from sleeping with the college boys. One statute was that no two students, male and female, were allowed to stand in the shadow. Of course, there was no shrubbery or bushes on the campuses. She drove me about through the countryside glutted with charming lakes, and when I asked her to stop so that I could kiss her, she said that she couldn't. I thought she was teasing me, and became rather annoyed with her, until she told me to look behind me. We were being followed by Huey Long's motorcycle cops who patrolled the campus and the environs to guard against sin and conception. I was so thwarted by these police-duennas that I returned to New Orleans, and when I went back to New York I heard that I was engaged to her. Alma had spread this report to increase her girl's prestige, which was quite a laurel for me. I think I would have gladly married her. She was in some ways the perfect Mater Dolorosa, with the body of a dairymaid and the features of one of the disguised page boys in a Shakespeare comedy.

Jo Herbst and I were going to do some articles together attacking the scurrile cant in newspaper book-reviewing. We couldn't get anyone to print it, and Jo was frightfully ill at the time, and all her quondam health so miserably impaired. I always enjoyed her vast exuberance. Aristotle says: A poet is an enthusiastic nature. It's the best definition I know, and describes Jo Herbst better than I can do it.

Do you mind this rambling letter? I am thinking of another very fetching woman, a painter whom I met when she was eighteen. She had married a well-known communist, and was the youngest person ever to get a Guggenheim award, which she well deserved. Sometimes a foundation makes a mistake and gives a talented person money. She left her husband to study under Diego Rivera; the communist in a fury wrote a very objective article attacking Rivera as a Trotskyist. She passed out of my life although I had never known any of her favors which I had desperately craved when I first met her.

Some years later I met her living in penury at Carmel, and, of course, divorced from the communist. She was earning twenty-five dollars a month giving swimming lessons to children, and asked me to help her. She was easily beautiful enough to be in pictures, and I told her that I would talk to Upton Sinclair about her, and he said he would aid her. Then she said one day to me, "Edward, let's go away together." I hesitated, not because she was direct and simple with me, but for the following reason. This, in brief, was her narrative: when she had gotten the Guggenheim award she went straight to Mexico City. One day she noticed a rash on her face, and within a week it spread. She went to a Mexican doctor who told her at once that she had syphilis. To make sure of his evidence, he began to prick the acne on her face with a needle, until she looked horrible. After a few weeks of this treatment which cost her a great part of the Guggenheim money, she kept to her room, and disappeared. One day some while later, a Dutch chemist came to see her, and asked her why she had vanished. After a long turmoil of silence she began to weep, and said "I have syphilis." He looked at her, and said, "I don't believe it." He took her to a laboratory and gave her the usual six hundred and six tests, and found them absolutely negative. However, she was such a fantastical liar that I feared to risk it, and besides this was long before the grace of our god, penicillin. She disappeared again. Several years later she had married someone in the Social Register on Park Avenue. I met her one day when I was collecting money to bring out Kenneth Fearing's poems. She told me of her riches, adding that they had a large yacht. When she mentioned this, I asked her whether she couldn't give some money to help publish a book of verse by Kenneth Fearing. At that the yacht was reduced to a rowboat.

Again she vanished from my life for another lustrum. When I saw her again she had had another misfortune. She had returned to Mexico, and there met the Spanish Minister of Justice of the Loyalist government. He was then in exile. They were soon married, but tardily she found out that he had a wife and three children in a Spanish prison. She had by that wedlock lost her alimony, and fallen once again into poverty though she was living in a fancy atelier on Sixty-seventh Street. She gave a party, inviting among others, Tamayo and myself. I told him to stop doing skyscraper murals and to go back to the Mexican Cordilleras and the peons. Tamayo had a very cruel face, or so I thought, something of the mestizo brigand. I saw her a few days later and she said, "Edward, I'm terribly impoverished, I don't know what to do." I listened with compassion, and then suddenly midst this doleful narrative she rose and went to the telephone and called Air France, asking for first-class reservations for Paris!

The last I heard about her was through a bookseller in Hollywood. She was then forty-five, and to be sure never without a man, but still melancholy, thinking of her lost beauty and of the time when she could have walked beside Helen of Troy or Aspasia, and be sure that she could inflame as readily as they. To see a woman go down is worse than the destruction of seven-gated Thebes. When a man decays he tries to console himself by believing that his mind will make amends for the demolition of his youth. A woman has a more perfect intellect which is her body, and when she thinks with it she seldom makes a mistake, and when that dwindles, what happens to her mind?

Will you be sure, Bill, to send me an inscribed copy of *Paterson 5*? Have the book charged to me at New Directions.

My love to you, Bill.

                                        Your admiring friend,

Palma de Mallorca
April 23, 1958

Dear Bill:

Within the past month I sent you two letters, and as I have not heard from you, I hope the reason is that you are very much occupied writing and in fine health.

I will not dwell long on the fate of *The Sorrows of Priapus* save to assert that it was reviewed in one paper in New York. I wrote to the newspapers even entreating them to give some attention to the volume. They did not even deign to reply. The greatest hoax is all the nonsense about the freedom of the press. Tolstoy could not tolerate a newspaper, and Arthur Symons regarded it as worse than the locusts that preyed upon the vegetation in Egypt. Since my demands are rather modest, not looking for Patagonian ore from literature, or hankering after a cheap fame, such a suppression of my book, and I can call it by no other name, has thrown me down. I received a letter from a communist, with some genuine talent as a poet, who told me that he could not get his work reviewed or printed because he is an avowed Marxist. Doubtless there is real truth to it, though I cannot get my books to readers because I am opposed to communism. It is therefore taken for granted that I must be a political blackguard or a reactionary. Now, to go on with another volume, which will in turn be hidden. I must say that Laughlin has been very kind about the whole matter. People talk about his faults, unmindful of their own, without speaking of his immense graces.

Forgive me, Bill, for prattling about this. In Proverbs it is said that a wise man will fall down seven times a day, and rise up again. Have I ever gotten up? And as for wisdom, who has it?

I continue to marvel at Spain. There is considerable misunderstanding about the position of the authors who have not quit their own homeland. There is a great pro-Jewish feeling here in Franco's Spain. The late Bishop of Seville, a Jew, an overt friend of Israel, was a Catholic bigot. There is a viscount here, a Carlist, whose family goes back to Isabella, and who is a warm adherent of Franco, who said recently that there is nothing left that is

important to be except a Jew! One of Miguel de Unamuno's
contemporaries has demanded that modern Spanish history be
rewritten, and that the Chronicles cannot be honestly recorded
without mentioning the immense role played by the Jew. Aside
from this, most authors, Catholic, left, right, or center, are
avowed opponents of the present regime. They are a marvelous
lot, these Spanish natures. What a difference, for example, between old men in the United States, and the aged here. One so
often associates those hapless codgers in America, who are so useless, with latrines and our wretched public parks which have
become vast areas of Sodom. I find it a great pleasure to look at
the older generation of Spaniards. Whatever they do or don't do,
they are above all human. Ecce Homo. The face is a fine, wise
book.

There is Anthony Kerrigan, his wife, and family, who are our
neighbors. He is Irish, obviously, and married to a charming
Jewish woman from Chicago who is a very good musician, and
has great familiarity with old Mallorquin songs which one publisher of music has just printed. Kerrigan did a wonderful translation of Barcia's *Chronicles* brought out by the University of
Florida Press, and has just finished in very fine English a rendering of Pio Baroja for the University of Michigan Press. Baroja,
like yourself, was trained to be a doctor, and was a Christian
anarchist until he died about a year ago. Like Unamuno, he was,
I think, a Basque; these people have extraordinarily broad faces,
very broad foreheads, and pointed chins, making almost perfect
triangles. They are obstinately independent, very intelligent,
and their origins obscure. Unamuno, himself, whose *Tragic Sense
of Life* was the manual of my soul when I was twenty-three, was
always being appointed rector-for-life of the University of Sala-
manca, and always being expelled from the country.

I read recently a fine little essay on Judas by Borges. He is or
was from the Argentine, was in Spain for many years; it was then
rumored that he was dead, and then there was a report that he
was alive in South America. These intellectuals and visionaries,
heretical Christians, and new Logos makers, lead lives as obscure
as Christ's or the Ebionites'. They are in permanent trouble;
their rooms and apartments are often searched by the gendarmes,

but nothing very much occurs, and they go on denouncing whatever happens to come into their minds. Speaking of the newspaper, it is somewhat different from an occidental paper. They print almost anything a writer has to say.

The Americans here don't want to return to the States. Nobody who is serious wants to be in Paris. This land, still a marvel to behold, will, alas, be the prey of the machine in a decade. The Spaniard now, or at least the Mallorquin, has no fear of his emotions. He will meet you, embrace you, weep before you, and they are always having some tragedy or other. The families are large, and they have little money and, if one can say so, big courtesies. Today Rlene went to the cobbler's, and there were tears on the cheeks of the shoemaker; the other day I spoke to another Mallorquin, and he was shaking with grief. It is a sweet vale of tears. There is a lovely white flower called the Tears of the Virgin, you could call it Spain. Outside of Seville I too was convulsed; there was a heavy forest of cork trees all bleeding, the bark stripped, and trunk crimson, and high cairns of wafer-like cork delicate enough to eat as the Monstrance, food for the Catholic. There are rows and rows of olive yards planted in terracotta-colored clay upon which the porkers and the brown goats browse.

Let me know, Bill, that you are all right, and that Flossie is too. Please know that I think of you very often and worry about you a great deal. Rlene and I talk of you almost every day.

Your loving and admiring friend,

Soller de Mallorca
July 1, 1958

Dear Bill:

It was very kind of Flossie to call to your attention the review in the *New Leader*. Of course, I was very pleased, and both Rlene and I send Flossie our affectionate thanks.

What is the date of publication for *Paterson 5,* and have you had page proofs yet? Both Tolstoy and Balzac spoke of the consolation of print. Addison and Steele were so utterly tired and bored with their work that they had not the appetite to correct it. I earnestly hope your Poem will be a tonic for you, and look forward to seeing it with the greatest interest.

We were in Soller, a Spanish hamlet almost unspoiled by tourists and the disease of trade. We met there two brothers, one ninety-one and the other eighty-five, retired English businessmen who had more sense and sane judgment than the bogus youths of the present day. They had lived in India, South Africa; the older had spent seventeen years in Russia and had met Tolstoy in Moscow. What a celestial privilege. He has the most genial face, with faculties altogether vibrant and clear, and is married to a German woman many years younger than he. We did not know them, and came in to make inquiries. Rlene and I were accorded the most exquisite civility. Thirty-three years ago the older brother had bought a simple peasant house for less than five hundred dollars, which included a marvelous orchard of lemon and orange trees and a profusion of flowers that could have drawn envy from Adam before he was cast out of Eden for being lubricious or discontented.

The visit was a remedy for a previous one we had made. There was an English or Scotch man who had houses and rooms to rent. He was about seventy or so, an inveterate pederast, and more avaricious than Tantalus. He had deviscerated an old Spanish house which looked like a rectangle of virgin rock and clay, absolutely unaffected architecture. He had replaced the original entrails of the dwelling with toy fixtures and modern technical gloom. Rlene went upstairs and I hovered about the door making ready to quit the place when an old Spanish woman entered. She was weeping, and at first I thought she wanted to see the owner of the house. Then she went outside to talk to the proprietor of a small *tienda* (store), and I followed her. She turned to me and said the home had been hers, and that her mother was born there, and she was so wretched that I could only repeat with what distress you can imagine how deeply sorry I was. And I was and still am. I am sure that knave cheated her, found a way of appropriating her birthplace, that of her mother's, and other ancestors she venerated. The politeness of these humble peasants is in itself a kind of rapture for one accustomed to the rudeness of busy occidental people.

You know, Bill, I can't help but worry about you. I don't care to burden you with a correspondence; well, write when you have the inclination, and if I have anything to say that can in any way entertain you or interest you, that is my deepest pleasure.

Be sure, again to give my deep thanks to Flossie. I hear that the *Prairie Schooner* is going to publish your piece on Shahn and me. Is that so? Karl Shapiro is one of the very few people, and poets, editing a magazine who is not vindictive or revengeful, but, on the contrary, is very kind, and even merciful to those who labor for wind, and the vanity of vanities we call poems.

I wish that you would go on with that personal Memoir (in *The American Scholar*) and don't be vexed because I am pertinacious.

As always, my love and admiration.

Palma de Mallorca
July 20, 1958

Dear Bill:

I have your thoughtful and good letter and thank you for all you say about my own words to you. What you say about your age saddens me though there is no reason whatever to feel that your powers are dwindling. Maybe they are different; I thought so when I read your autobiographical piece in *The American Scholar,* which was wise and European.

Longinus wrote that when Homer composed the *Odyssey* he was nodding; if that is true, my God, let us all then write in our sleep. Plato did the *Laws* when he was seventy-five; they lack the animal energy of the *Dialogues,* but how poor we would be without them. Would that the epistles received from young people ached with the intellectual passion that yours do.

Suppose *Paterson 5* is a failure. Modern man never pardons a genius for not being successful. Why should a poet have to compete with himself, and why has he not the right to fail? Think how much one can learn from what is unfinished or has flaws provided the hand is Michaelangelo's or Melville's or Whitman's. Melville was a failure almost continuously after *Moby-Dick.*

How instructive is *Pierre* when Melville was very old, about thirty-two or thirty-three! What a tragic, burning mind there is in *Clarel* or the *Wilderness*! Is it poetry? Maybe not, but who cares?

What you say about Woman is poetry too. You comprehended her importance in literature in *In the American Grain*. In a line or two on Emily Dickinson you introduced me to this magical failure, and she is imperfect, and a nature as white as the sepulcher or as Melville's Whiteness. You refer to that marvelous whore, the Virgin Mary. The other evening there was a cavalcade of fishing boats going into the harbor at Palma and celebrating their patron, the Virgin of Carmel. At Burgos there is a painting of Mary Magdalene; she has breasts to pillow a Christ. All the women in the pagan medieval Christian church are sensual and were conceived by their artists to delight and bless men. Mariolatry is absolutely essential to any literature, legend or religion, and the greatest lack in American books is a Phryne, a Magdalene, or a Leda. Also at Burgos there is a skirted Christ; he is the symbol of the feminine and the male in creative energy. In the Jewish cabala the female, the genetrix, is known as the Shekinah.

When you spoke of your friends who were giving you so much counsel I thought of Job on his muck heap, and how his friends reproached and advised him, which lacerated him as much as God's goodness and Satan's malice.

I am most anxious to see *Paterson 5*. I have not had a page proof of my letter you included; there may be some errors in grammar I want to correct, but won't do anything without your permission. I have a great pride in my very humble contribution to *Paterson 5*, and thank you again for the honor.

Rlene and I went to Soller again to see the two English brothers, and remained there till almost midnight. Both, the ninety-one-year-old Charlie and the younger, eighty-five, wanted us to remain longer and talk. Charlie was sprightly, and still a great devotee of Aphrodite, or else I should say his remembrance of pleasure is very sharp. While we chatted a German woman from Cologne was caressing the nape of his neck, and he was tenderly stroking her thigh. His wife, Carlotta, a Prussian, who has lived in Spain for thirty years, said later to us, "I want Charlie to be happy," and he was.

To get to their house we have to pass a row of low Mallorquin homes, all with their doors ajar; the families sit on the patio, and no one fails to say: *"Buenos tardes"* to the passer-by. The civility of the Mallorquin is very moving; their voices press your hand.

The prices are as interesting as the cost of pennyroyal, rosemary or garlic was in the Greek agora. Tomatoes sell at six cents a kilo, which are two pounds; melons in season are four cents, a kilo of black cherries, eight pesetas, about fifteen cents. These tender, human prices make me homesick for my boyhood in Kansas City. Enough of the best liver to be had anywhere and sufficient for two meals for a couple costs about forty-five cents. A liter of *vino blanco corriente* (good ordinary table wine) is around seven cents, and in the interior cheaper. In the earthen hill towns, still untarnished by tourists or the automobile, one can live on very little. At Murcia two years ago we were told of a Swedish writer, his wife, and three children whose total expenses were about thirty-five dollars a month.

Spain too is falling; the Western world has crept in; the intellectual classes are about as bad as they are elsewhere. No one has replaced Unamuno, Ortega y Gasset, or Pio Baroja. There is no one today of your stature in Spain.

Your garbage crowd is at Palma, and at the Calas, the coves and beaches surrounded by tawdry hotels, and fancy-monied tramps. Travel and Thomas Cooks have killed almost every virgin land. A bad tourist season, which they are now having in Spain because of the political situation in France, and upheaval everywhere, may save the country.

We see two Spaniards, a man from Alicante, and his wife, a Mallorquin. They pay fifty-eight pesetas a month for their apartment, that is about one dollar and fifteen cents. There is rent control, and those who occupy flats or houses whose rents are determined by the housing commission are able to survive.

The old Spain is always a wonder; there is no architecture in the United States to compare with a humble home in Mallorca, Estremadura, or in the Pyrenees. As soon as you have architecture anyway today you have foolish opinionated buildings, dogmatic functionalism, and all the depravity of an up-to-date, inhuman city. Nobody is educated enough anymore to build a simple, unaffected home which is as good, and has as much feeling, as an ancient proverb. When I look at a motorcycle or a taxi there are tears in my heart. For all the earth is ours, our habitation and sepulcher, and every country that falls under the infamy of money is a terrible wound to every other people.

The degradation is everywhere. At Soller we met an English woman who has a daughter at Oxford and who told us that the education there was indifferent and bad.

There is a droll, retired major in the same town. He rents a modernized sixteenth-century house; it is deviscerated, all the entrails removed, the hearth, the granite floors, and he pointed to the fixtures and the gloomy ornaments which he said made it look like a water closet. He had been in Spain in the first days of the civil war, and had to leave on a British warship because of the danger and bloodshed. At Ibiza, he said, a lovely island several hours by sea from here, the communists murdered thirty-three out of thirty-six padres, and machine-gunned over two hundred people, women, children, and men. He is a brave man, lost his arm in the First World War, and has no reason not to tell the truth. The oppression was everywhere and on all sides. The Spanish people have the greatest dread of any more bloodshed.

The other day I walked down the Calle Calvo Sotelo and saw a nun who was picking her nose, which I suppose is pious.

Rlene and I send Flossie our affections.

My love and admiration, Bill; I am happy I had sense enough to dedicate the second part of *The Sorrows of Priapus* to you. I am always amazed when I do anything intelligent.

lettres to
Isabella Gardner

Santa Monica, Cal.
January 23, 1956

Dear Miss Gardner:

Understanding, friendship, a poem—all these hang by the thread of Ariadne. Now my plans are still amorphous; even the teaching. I may go to Denmark, but then each day is a wintry defeat, a new river source, and the renewal of some god long forgotten.

I should quit this town in a few weeks, but I am not sure. Baudelaire took a year before he could resolve to leave Paris to go to a town nineteen miles distant.

Your own dilemma is upon my mind: what you read; have you found that viaticum in the books I suggested to you? One cannot ripen without the Vedas, other sages, or making every effort to approach the Tree of Life guarded by the Cherubim.

I by no means scorn Rilke; it is my feeling that you must now go elsewhere. Few writers today are pursuing the quest for Buddha, or even wooing the clean suffering of Job. We produce many books but few men. This cannot happen without a decline in the gentleness and the character of women too. I freely own that I have known more women who were a blade of grass, a pensive arbute, a nature, than men. It is necessary, though, to recall Stendhal's remark: "The reason that Turkish literature is so mediocre is that the women are so brutish."

I shall continue to write to you if you wish. Should I stop over at Chicago, perhaps no more than to wait for another coach to take me to New York, please have lunch with me. I may not be able to let you know in advance, but I shall try. It may be that I shall leave on the sudden.

Ripeness is all, says the Poet; and the tragedy of American Literature is that no one writes more than one book. Each one then goes to his silence and his life thereafter is a tomb.

What I would say to you is very simple: shun modern books. Go back to Beginnings. Ritual will heal a line, a stanza, your whole head; you need symbols, Isis, Hathor, Typhon, the Cabala for your image and vision. Go to school with some master, Ovid, Plutarch, Livy, Tacitus, and you will then find the river back to your own identity.

Do not read Plutarch except in the Sir Thomas North translation; again eschew contemporary renderings of ancient savants and works. Do I sound dogmatic, too sure; underneath my Rock of Peter sings the Great Worm, DOUBT.

I send you my appreciation of your own nature, and pray that you will ravel out in some way that will draw the strength of the Kosmos to you.

Santa Monica, Cal.
February 12, 1956

Dear Miss Gardner:

You will get nothing out of a reading except the "expense of spirit in the waste of shame."

Whether I shall be in New York by spring I do not know. If I have coarse students I shall throw over the teaching and go to Bornholm, the ancient site of barrows, and then Copenhagen.

You must heed me: don't be busy. That's the national disease; people are always avoiding one another because they are doing what only depletes them. Only the herd are together. We have such a miserable literature today because those who could ripen are not sharpened by one another.

Read, read, read; dying, writing, and friendship are private, and people are much too public to have the time to die as Cato did, or be Plato, or to nourish a friendship.

If you know anybody in New York who is a human being, please let me know.

Palma de Mallorca
September 27, 1957

Dear Isabella:

I am troubled about you and fear that my reply to your good epistle was not what might heal your despondency. Perhaps I babbled too much about my own book, which is foolish. I cannot, as you know, offer you canons for good writing. There are no laws; there is only the energy of the soul and the mind. What with the help of Plato, Chapman's *Iliad,* and the *Georgics* and *Bucolics* by Vergil, who can say what may not be the bourne of your identity? I believe we are producing throughout the world a cold and morose literature which is wilder and more of a bog than some marsh in Scotland.

Why does one write? It is a very hard question to reply to; yet there are some simple replies which the blood offers. One, for affection. When I served my apprenticeship, as though one ever did anything else throughout life, I imagined that after writing books, and divulging my own trembling pulses, I should have many friends. The opposite was the truth. When I wrote badly, and received the cheap applause of the press, I had those herd acquaintances, which one had better eschew in this earth as well as in Tartarus. When I wrote better, it seemed as each good book, if I do not seem arrogant to you, were a dagger in the head of those who could not write. Little by little I found myself more and more cloistered. Now, most, if not all of my friendships, are of an epistolary sort. I fear to see people lest it should be a querulous encounter. Everywhere there is such a distrust of the head, not worth very much, true, because there is so little love. If I cannot write or compose in some way or another the hymn to Demeter or the cry of the tender Shulamite, I reckon my life as all dross and no Helen.

This is a note and an entreaty; please read those books which I suggested, and do not be too impatient. I cannot tell you how they will affect you; but is it possible for Homer, Horace, Lucian, and Vergil not to dilate the spirit? You must find the source for yourself, not directly in private experience; it is curious that though one has felt acutely, and that all as Keats says, presses down upon one's identity, the approach to one's woe and travail

is through ritual and myth. One has to tread lightly upon one's
veins or blast them into a great darkness. Art is not straight and
plain; were it so, then all that is chaff on the palate could easily
be translated into a Golgotha or into the Cana marriage wine.
Quicksilver is most useful in an ass's skin, for everything must in
some way be covered if the naked truth is to be found and deeply
felt.

This is a reverie.

My love to you, Isabella.

Palma de Mallorca
October 27, 1957

Dear Isabella:

It is very sweet of you to be so concerned, and I thank you for
it very much. For the most part, I never trouble to read a review,
for if I bothered I would not have the soul to write. If Mr. Rago
wants to do the book, good, if not, so be. If one lacks spirit one
seeks power, often of the most dreary sort. I don't care about
being influential, or having any power in this world. The world
is not for me and I have never been for it. One should do all one
can to find out where the ore of El Dorado is in one's spirit, and
there do one's mining until the end. It is said that in Potosi, in
Bolivia, where there was more gold than elsewhere on the earth,
no grass grew. And I love grass far more than the metal of Pilate.

Now, I try the best I can to advise you, hinting and persuad-
ing, if I can, but not to meddle too much with your own Muse. I
liked the poem, "The Widow's Yard," very much, and, Isabella, I
want to be of use to you, and to tell you, without good manners
or guile, what is very good, and what is not.

I live more or less as a recluse, not by choice, but because I find
I cannot endure the cant of the lying literary world. I was asked
to do a long piece on Randolph Bourne, for the *New Mexico
Quarterly,* one of those dried-up oracles of our colleges, and so
being a spark of tact, I forthwith attacked the academic rabble
and the universities! I told the woman, of some charm and

human goodness, I imagine (I never met her), but who will be intolerably frightened by my plainness, not to use it, as I did not care a straw one way or the other. I had spent about a week on it, but who can be wise or good or not even imbecilic in a book review? In the early days when I was a close friend of Waldo Frank, he took out his book reviews and showed them to me, and though I was then too incoherent to make a clear reply to such nonsensical vanity, my flesh withered.

Now after two years of reading I am making ready to do a novel going back to Le Sage and Boccaccio, Aristophanes, Plato, as my models. I won't risk a line without first consulting some savant or other. The ritual in Aristophanes is really quite marvelous, some of the passages on the festival of Demeter; the jesting is often scatological, and it is quite amazing how much of that kind of feeling there is in great men, in Swift, which often makes Gulliver so odious. With your wondrous compassions read sometimes *The Miscellanies* by Isaac D'Israeli, the father of the Prime Minister, really learned.

My next task in the novel is to impugn pederasty, for you cannot have a great literature when men cease loving women. Without Dido or Helen, or even a criminal Clytemnestra, there can be no Homer or Vergil or Aeschylus. Aside from Chapman, I don't know a creditable translation of the *Iliad*. Golding's translation of Ovid has had a long fame, but picking it up some weeks ago, I was dismayed by the preposterous English, not archaic. But I have no great hankering after the modern illiterate tongue used in the gutters and in the colleges.

There is perhaps no victory against fate; the five acts of tragedy is in the Private Act; Hamlet's resolve is in his intellect although the end must be death and carnage. But I believe in impossibilism and in the most devout anger against falsehood, perfidy, and the loveless books and nations that exist everywhere. When I receive a letter from someone who sends me his best wishes, or good luck, or very truly yours, I wince, and find my whole day a vast emptiness and a Promethean desolation.

If I am not a more comprehensive identity after someone has dissembled or committed some unreasonable act toward me that is not direct, simple, and plain, then I was born for no good reason. To be a writer is to learn how to be fleeced, cheated, tread upon. Don't imagine that I make any cult of pain. I can howl just as loudly as Achilles when my skin is scratched, but I would rather have died at Ilium than be a liar today. I would rather be the object of the ruse and the snare than be pusillanimous.

My relations with Williams have always been bizarre. I think he is going to defend the book, or he says so, but who knows? He has been an admirer, shall I say behind closed doors, of mine, for twenty years or more. But he is incapable of being straight; he can be sweet and even generous, but he cannot be direct. There is some flaw in his nature which makes him either lie or commit an injury rather than be truthful.

When I was on Cape Cod with my former wife, and I did not care whether I pulsed or not, Williams and I got into an altercation. I don't remember what it was about, save that I always thought he was rather nonhuman, for I don't care about mind, genius, skill, art, if it is cold or neutral. When Paterson appeared there was a letter signed by T.J. printed along with the poem. I heard about it two years after publication. The letter was mine! Well, I hardly cared whether he did it without my leave, as I have no legal character, but I was enormously piqued that he should do so without even making acknowledgments to me. When I called this to his attention (it was at the time when I had fallen into limbo because I refused to write any more naturalistic or noxious realistic fiction) he answered, "Your prose is your signature!"

At that time I tried my best to help Louis Zukofsky who could not get a line printed. We were teaching at the same college, and little by little I grew sympathetic to his hard portion, and began to write to Bill Williams who was then vice president of the Institute of Arts and Letters, composed of the canny businessmen of Parnassus, and asked him, first why had he consented to join such a grubby lot, and secondly, why, since Louis had helped him when he was obscure, did he not come to the rescue of Louis, and see to it that he got one of those awards they invariably give to some witling or nonentity. Our correspondence became more vitriolic and so by the time his Autobiography appeared, I was excluded from that although we had been friends since 1929. There is, ironically, one mention of me in the Autobiography made by Charles Olson who said that I had done one thing for him, knocked into his head that the only path from one sentence to another is perception, that all else is miserable hiatus. Meanwhile, after getting Zukofsky published in England through Sir Herbert, I found magazines, including the *New Direction Annual,* to print him. He did a very fine essay called "Bottom: On Shakespeare," which no one would have, and so I called up Laughlin and said that Zukofsky had done a wonderful essay and would he publish it, and he replied, much to my surprise, "If you think it that good I'll do it without looking at it."

To Williams' credit, he did go far out of his way to get *The Sorrows of Priapus* published. Don't ask by what logic this man moves, or by what unreason. I am deeply fond of him, and never know when he will tell me a gross lie or a truth. I don't like weathervane relationships; there ought to be a sufficient quantum of memory in man so that you can abide him and he you. Perversity is one of the greatest sins in our age; do you know Paul's Seventh Epistle to the Romans? Quite remarkable, and wondrously revealing a man's defects. For we, alas, live more by our blemishes than by our virtues, which are the result of our dismal and meanest faults. Or so I believe, and regard myself, thinking as Pascal did, that no man fears himself enough.

I tell you these things, Isabella, not as gossip or to be unkind to Williams; there is a very prodigal dedication to him in *The Sorrows of Priapus* (for which he has the greatest admiration), and in one letter to me he said, "Edward, you do not realize your importance to the corpus of American Literature." And now that his own letters are published, there is not one of his to me included; if you can resolve that, you know God or understand the Kosmos. Let no man, unless he be absolutely insane, imagine that he knows anybody at all, or does this sound too darksome; I am jocular too, and please regard all this as the mirth of Solomon when he is sad, and pining that all is vanity of vanities, but still smells the spikenard and the fragrant pillow of the Shulamite.

I close this, Isabella, and thank you for your kindness. For since I am not Cressida, I must needs be betrayed Troilus, for that I think is the role the gods have destined for me, and it does not in the end matter if I can say it in a strong style; for it is form that matters most.

My love to you, Isabella.

Palma de Mallorca
May 30, 1958

Dear Isabella:

Your good, tender words sweeten my methaphysical royalties. Thank you very much for them. I devoutly wish you could have been with me, but then all our talks and communications have more to do with First Causes, and are therefore ether, vapor, and primordial beginnings. By now, I am almost resigned to epistolary friendships and aetiological love.

Now, I am exceedingly sorry that I have failed to secure the books for you that you urgently need for your verse. I should have taken care of that myself. I feared, however, that some books might cost more than you expected, and I don't like to be responsible for other people's money. Even when I go to a bank and cash a check I feel like a forger. Then I am as guilty about everything that I do as Cain. However, if you wish me to write to Quaritch, or to Miss Christina Foyle who has always shown me the utmost civility, I will be glad to do so, and have them send the books to you to wherever you will summer. I do want you to compose some very fine poems. Meanwhile, you should, Isabella, write at once to Barnes and Noble in New York to see what you can procure there. Did I mention Xenophon's *Anabasis* or Arrian's *Anabasis,* either in the Bohn Library or in the Loeb Classical Library? I don't recall what sort of list I made for you. Your daughter might be very taken with either of these books. You speak of your son who was thirteen; one of mine will be the same age in October, but if I met either of them on the street, I should not recognize them. You know, if I saw you, I might not know you, for we spoke no more than three minutes. You can say that my deep feeling for you is as pure as a man can make it.

I don't think Rago has printed a review of *The Sorrows of Priapus*. Why I can't tell, since Mr. Duncan wrote that he had read the book three times, and that Rago had asked him to do a short book review! That after Rago's letter warmly extolling my work. I am not a squalid commodity, and my vision cannot be hired! I had had a wondrous epistle from Archibald MacLeish saying that he was anxious to write about the book in the *New Republic,* but nothing happened, although he has always been very charming and kind to me. Josephine Herbst wrote to New Directions, asking for a copy of the book, saying that she wanted to do a piece on it, and nothing came of that! Williams' piece never appeared, nor has his twelve-page essay on *The Flea of Sodom* ever been printed. How grateful was Flaubert when Baudelaire came to his rescue. Baudelaire, himself, waiting to see what a debacle his *Les Fleurs du Mal* would be, could hope for no more than a *succès d'estime,* and who paid any attention to Corbière?

It is worse in the States because the country is too big; all great civilizations were born in small lands. The Elysian fields were no larger than a bull's hide which had been stretched out, and was as much territory as Menelaus required. Carthage was said to be of the same size. When Euripides was played in Athens, a city of sixty thousand inhabitants, half of them attended the performance, and I don't believe that London, when it was muck and mire, in the days of the real, though ravening Elizabeth, had any more people in it than that.

Have you never seen the great bull, Zeus astride Europa? To live out one's life in American Suburbia is, at least for me, a wizened portion. To go into starved, eyeless streets each day, void of antique buildings, and without having a single shop or edifice or ancient monument to appease the heart and to placate the blood is too hard. Every time the American sets about to improve a city or town he destroys whatever is good in it. The most characterless city in the world is Los Angeles, the visionary spa for purple-haired dowagers who are rich. I cannot stomach the entire brutality of the American economy in which men and women are apart all day in order to get their miserable bread and debility. There is neither the Mater Dolorosa in an Ameri-

can hamlet or thoroughfare which has been dunged upon by tin
and rubber. I sometimes wonder whether anybody genders or
feeds any longer except the automobile? Did you ever see any of
the pistachio or meringue-pie bungalows in Los Angeles, or look
at a picture window? The houses or *sets* are all façades, without
entrails or interiors, and the pecuniary lawns are too desolate to
be a homely and simple burial site.

Did I mention Sir Thomas Browne's *Urne-Buriall;* if you have
read it, do so many times; also do not fail to read the *Religio
Medici,* and his *Garden of Cyrus,* as well as his *Common Faults
and Errors.* You must find a language for your feelings, warm
and good, to transfigure them. What is known as the American
tongue is stylized sloth. It requires great activity of the soul to
speak coherently, and then how much more to compose one's
emotions as Pindar or Propertius did.

Did you ever get Christopher Smart's *Rejoice in the Lamb?* Or,
again, your daughter might care a great deal for William Gilchrist's *Life of William Blake.* His widow read the *Leaves of
Grass* and fell in love with the giant baby of our Muses, and he
was also a baby homosexual, nonpracticing of course, and when
Mrs. Gilchrist proposed to come up to Camden, New Jersey, to
visit him, Whitman was terrified. What would he do with a
woman, and a fine one at that. Imagine any woman nowadays
falling in love with a man because he wrote a remarkable book.
Take a look at American women, and you will see what is the
matter with American Literature. You can't have a visionary
civilization unless women and men love each other. I can't bear
the cinema anymore because it sickens me to watch a pansy make
love to a Lesbian on the screen.

When I was a boy, growing up in the wild, leafy streets of
Kansas City, men and women sat on porches in the summer
evenings; fine, fleshed damsels ran off with men to Joplin or
Topeka or to Tulsa, Oklahoma. Pederasty was an underground
vice, and few ever mentioned it, because no one could image that
a man would seek another male to express his lusts when he
could mingle with some wanton or chippy or girl with a carnal
heart. I knew cattle ranchers, livery stable proprietors, locomo-
tive engineers, and corrugated Johnnies who were employed in
the roundhouses or in the West Bottoms where all the factories

were located, and the field of asphodels for them was a woman. Of course, I can't get my books reviewed because I believe in the old orthodoxies of sex. I am afraid of using the word, Homo Sapiens, anymore, which was so fashionable and erudite when I was at college.

The American tragedy is the tragedy of separation. People have to be together to make a Golgotha legend or to be the neatherd as the prophet Amos was. Have you ever asked, Why don't we write amorous verse anymore? Once Gorky came to America, and, naturally, he was taken to Coney Island. He looked about, and said, "My God, think what a mournful people the Americans must be to get their recreation out of mechanical amusements." When Gorky came to New York with his mistress, and at the hotel did not indulge in the usual American sex cant, by writing in the hotel register, Mr. and Mrs. Maxim Gorky, the United States Government almost collapsed. That little socialist prig and sere eunuch who perpetrated the *Rise of Silas Lapham* sent a strong protest demanding that Gorky be deported. William Dean Howells' friend, Mark Twain, did the same. Do you know that when Margaret Fuller, a brach of Concord, heard that Elizabeth Osgood was a friend of Edgar Poe, she organized a delegation of women who came to see her and to demand that she relinquish his friendship. The mournful, obituary truth is that I don't think poor Ishmael or Israfael Poe derived any real manly advantage from this charming and consolatory attachment.

You, poor darling, must do the best you can, and as I recollect you, you are a splendid, robust woman, and can survive anything.

Much love to you, Isabella.

Palma de Mallorca
June 11, 1958

Isabella dear:

Your letter makes me very despondent. Melancholia is a raging fever as evil as nightshade or white hellebore. I am very troubled

about your mood. Summer is in your blood, but February in
your head, but this is always so, at anytime. You speak of aging
which deeply saddens me. I have a strong impression of you
rather than a delicate knowledge of your face, and I remember
you as vibrant and a woman in all your powers.

I should have gotten the books to you, if only as a simple to
heal the tentative night in your feelings. It was not much for me
to do. Maggs had always taken care of me promptly, but I don't
know what has happened there. Were I in London I could have
spent two days looking for volumes for you on Charing Cross
Road and in Cecil Court. You are very honest, though you have
no need to overestimate the intellect. At the instant I have Sir
Herbert Read's letter which came this morning, and I cite it
because it should disclose to you what you can do, not by becoming a she-scholar, a Gorgonian pedant, which I had never had in
mind, when I thought you should be, shall we say, a savant of a
few rare books. Read says: "There was a wonderful letter of
Emily Dickinson's quoted in the *Times Literary Supplement* a
week ago [May 30] which reminded me of you: 'You inquire my
books. For poets I have Keats and Mr. and Mrs. Browning; for
prose, Mr. Ruskin, Sir Thomas Browne, and Revelations. I went
to school but in your manner of the phrase had no education.
When a little girl I had a friend who taught me immortality. . . .'
But you probably know it. What a pure if imperfect genius she
was; and how she reveals the limitations of those critics who
condemn her, Blackmur and Yvor Winters."

The letters of lovely, injured Emily, starving in a New England backyard for thirty years, particularly those from about
1861 and on, if I recollect rightly, have suns, moons, rivers, and
planetary thoughts. Of course, I agree with Read; I could never
stomach Blackmur or Winters.

I have felt since I first corresponded with you that there was
darkness in your life; as Keats once said, it pressed down upon
my identity. Now as though you were wooing troublous waters
you are going to Wellfleet, the charnel house of so many heavy
woes of mine. I remained aloof from everyone there though that
did not protect me from libel and wormy slander. It was there
that I wrote "The Rational Tree," the tree of death and the
famine of the soul in Orcus.

I had suggested, and still without any empiric knowledge of your life, that you quit your environs that lie like Atlas upon you. You have not come into the heyday of your own spirit. Even today Tony Kerrigan spoke of you as a gifted woman, and I have so written about you to William Carlos Williams, and desire, as I told you, to get your poems when they are ripe, or as you think they must be, into Sir Herbert's hands.

You know I am your friend, and wish above all to help you in any way that I can. Would that I had the purse of John Ruskin, so wondrously generous, every hurt person was his kin; I should send you money and advise you to go away for awhile. The will is the source and the river of all our thoughts; without volition we cannot go to Golgotha or to Apollo which are suffering and sun. Do not think I speak of physical pain, yea, it has been my portion all the days of my life, and I comprehend your fears and am stricken by your forebodings. What I pray is that I am somehow reaching you; the greatest tragedy is that no one ever crosses his own boundary into the territory of another identity. Could we do that we would know who commenced the Universe, and why we are here. Those little white stones which separate one person's earth, water, and soul from another, and which the ancients regarded as gods, make mock of all that we feign to be understanding.

I do not know, Isabella, how old you are, and have not the least interest since I detest the American cult of youth. Is there anybody so senile today as a young man or vacant woman just out of one of our academic dumps? In Europe, and this is as true among the peasant classes as well as people with minds, women with many more years in their flesh than you have are thought of as exceedingly desirable, particularly if they have hearts and minds. You are a child waking compared with those women who, because they had a waking and pulsing nature, were a balm of Gilead to a Nietzsche. When I was in Berlin, two days after the Reichstag fire, I met a marvelous lady deep in her fifties, who had had a salon there before the criminal Nazis came to power. She was Jewish, beautiful, and with four daughters. It took me twenty-four hours to discover what this cultivated Madonna failed to see. She knew Porto-Riche, Rolland, had translated Zola when she was sixteen. What she could not believe was that Hitler would exterminate her and her daughters. I begged her to leave at once, which she could have done then. Almost her entire family was liquidated. You, too, are the prey of some impalpable nemesis, and you must extricate yourself.

I earnestly hope you will heed me; go off somewhere, for awhile, anyway, to perceive what it is that is diminishing the lights you need, and quenching the hearth, which is a Vesta in every tender woman.

Your devoted and very loving

————————————————

New York
September 22, 1958

Dear Isabella:

Your letter came this morning. The other one I never received. You know how promptly I reply to your epistles. I do not know all the riddles that are in your words, and why should I divulge your sufferings or thwartings to anyone else? Pascal says that man is malicious, and how well I know it. I should say that hurting others has become one of the national pastimes. Whatever you tell me I shall lock up in my heart.

I have felt for a very long time that you were unhappy. You should learn, please, to tell me the truth because when you don't the one you are being most false to is yourself. Your letter is a thousand fathoms deep, and how can I know how to be your friend when by guessing I may be plunging into shallows.

I had a three-hour dinner with Robert Hutchins a day after I arrived, and J. Laughlin told me that he went to the party given in honor of Bill Williams solely to see me again. Unfortunately, I arrived quite late for no other reason than that I feared to come too early. He, Laughlin informed me, was so vehement in my defense that a former president of a university, and now the head of one nearby, was unable to resist him, at least for the moment. I had met this president years ago and told him he was like Caracalla who had a morbid passion for casting up buildings. Not a good reminder of me in his eyes. Still he wants to see me right away, and maybe something will come of it. Anyway, I am grateful to Hutchins, a most charming and gifted nature.

I received so many tributes at the party for Williams that all I could say was what Myshkin said after a long period of tombed silence: "I thank you so very much for liking me."

There was Richard Eberhard, whom I had never known, who laureled me for the *Sorrows,* and Selden Rodman, another stranger, who said that he kept the *Sorrows* at his bedside. Josephine Herbst, a dear and old friend, ran into my arms and kissed me many times. Norman Pearson at Yale, who collects the letters of writers and has asked for mine, I don't know whether he has them or not, said that *Bottom Dogs* was the best piece of naturalistic fiction written in America. I told him I did not care for it. He said he wanted very much to write an introduction to a new edition of the book. Well, I mentioned it to Laughlin, but would hardly press him to do it. Laughlin is my good friend, but I don't try to urge him too much to reprint anything of mine. Curiously enough, he is quite content with what is happening to the *Sorrows.*

I was at Erwinna with Josephine Herbst where she has a lovely old Pennsylvania Dutch house, and just about nothing else. She mentioned that she had met you and that you cared for her book on Bartram which I think is done in a very clean and lovely prose, and I give her all homage for having written that. We stayed up talking until nearly one A.M., and she had the bedroom adjoining mine upstairs. There was also in the house the former wife of Delmore Schwartz, a very handsome woman, and we became quite sympathetic with one another very quickly. New Directions printed one book of hers which I never saw. Josephine's door to her bedchamber was open, and so was mine. I could hear how uneasy she was, and I myself was awake until four in the morning. I thought, perhaps, she had insomnia, and did not have the indelicacy to go into her room to find out things; she would have regarded such an act on my part as intrusive. When I came down about nine o'clock in the morning I took one look at Josephine's ashy face and was deeply troubled. Elizabeth, the young woman, and I drove at once to the town and I bought all sorts of canned juices for Josephine, and I told her to go to bed at once. She did, but by three in the afternoon she was vomiting and giving up blood, and we began to call all the bad doctors around the countryside. There were no good ones. I became more alarmed, for by then Josephine had become quite ill, and we couldn't get anyone. Elizabeth was doing the talking, and by then I went to the phone to speak to the wife of a physician. All the others whom Elizabeth had spoken to were busy and could not get out to the house. I appealed to her, and she promised that her husband would come out very soon, which he did. A well-fed face appeared; he came with a large case of pills, and gave Josephine some colored water, and other tablets and penicillin and promised that she would be all right by morning. I was sure he was a medical assassin and feared that if she worsened by two or three o'clock in the morning she might lose her life. Within a few minutes after the physician returned to his office I called him and asked that Josephine be admitted to the hospital at once. Luckily we got her there, and I stayed at the house until the next day and visited her at the hospital. She has pleurisy and pneumonia, but was getting marvelous attention. I then learned that this physician whom I so distrusted had been tried for killing one of his patients three years earlier and that his reputation was very bad. I shall not feel easy until I hear that she is out of danger.

Josephine is doing a book in which she says I am to be an important part. In her work at the Newberry Library she said that she had come across two letters of mine to Sherwood Anderson in which I rebuked the latter for his admiration of Thomas Wolfe. Of course, I don't remember the letters, though the incident, and Josephine had already asked Laughlin for permission to use the letters which she says were irrefutable replies to my late and wondrous friend, Sherwood.

Please tell me what is hindering you; stop being circumlocutious with me. What ails thee Hagar? I know, *absolutely,* that you are trying to hide in a bushel of wheat from the light. You can't do it.

I have been your devoted and steadfast friend, I hope I have; sometimes your letters to me are hot and then cold and then neither one nor the other. "Ye who are neither hot nor cold, ye shall spew them forth." I send you the same Letter to the Laodiceans, and beg you to be straight and open with me.

My warm love to you, Isabella,

New York
November 7, 1958

Dear Isabella:

I saw Robert M. Hutchins a couple of days ago, and after I assailed the offices of the Fund for the Republic, which look like a fancy department store or a cinema palace, and denounced the "eminent men" who surrounded him, he suggested that I write one of their booklets. He is a most charming man, and perhaps the only gifted man I have known who is in public life. But the booklets or chapbooks gotten out by the Fund for the Republic, and written by these famous nonentities, are inconceivably bad, and worse, nonhuman. I wrote him a lengthy epistle to tell him what hopeless and unimaginative men they were. Maybe I have spoken so pungently that he will not let me do one of these pamphlets which would give me, I believe, a few hundred dollars. I don't know because I did not ask him. But what else could I do? I like the man very much, and should I dishonor him by feigning to be what I am not?

I know you are homeless, as much of an Ishmael as I am, maybe not quite. For you have the tender and loving arms to receive you, but I can only embrace emptiness and phantasms. I earnestly pray, more than you know, that the man you now love is tender. If he is, you know I shall wait upon him as I do upon you, should the occasion arise.

I understand how hard it is for you to read; but what other viaticum have you now for your dissevered identity? How then, as Keats says, will you prove yourself upon your pulses? The simplest charwoman suffers all the days of her life and never comprehends her humiliations or knows why she drinks her vinegar and gall. You must find out, or again be potently hurt. Do not think, Isabella dear, that I talk to you as a wounded male. It is not the truth at all. I am only interested in your joys and raptures and in your quickening. Christ says the soul is as small as the cummin seed; it is even smaller than that, but we must find it. Also, I am neither noble, good, nor moral. I am just a certain moiety of dust that trembles so, and for some odd reason I can be very disinterested. I long ago gave over pursuing women either for my life or for my pleasure. If this love of yours is a benefit to you, it will be a great advantage to me also. I could never be so arrogant as to believe that I could have given you happiness. Were I younger I could have spoken so.

I am usually taken for a negative man with a rough heart. Do you know your friend, Karl Shapiro, told me that Henry Miller was really human and had a great vibrant yea, implying that I was not. I write him gentle epistles only to receive barbed replies. I had praised Miller more to please Karl. Of course, Miller now and then writes in a warm simple prose, and has some comprehension of our tragic and wounded earth. But to compare Miller with me is too bizarre! Once a gnome of the Muses had been praised, and was said to be far above Goethe. Goethe replied that the poet was very little in comparison to himself. However, Goethe added, it is not my fault; that I have so much genius is only an accident which Nature understands and I do not.

Speaking of writers, I broke my connection with Louis Zukofsky, whom I had aided very greatly. I once asked him to do me a kindness, to see a writer, not a poet or a man of letters, but a gifted man who has shown the connection between Dadaism and modern nihilism, and you know he wouldn't do it because this author is absolutely deaf and would be too burdensome for L.Z.! At one time I fought with Bill Williams over L.Z. and the latter said that I was interfering in his friendship with Williams! Oh God, what can one do what one ought not do, or not do what one should?

I must now write, dearest Isabella, to Josephine. She was to come here Friday, but after some dental surgery was too sick to appear, but will be here on the fourteenth. I got, as you know, the money for her, but failed to arrange the meeting between her and Sir Herbert. I was quite dismayed because Herbert had promised me that he would. He did not break his word to me, but could only *give* her an hour. When Read and I were at the Captain's Table my friend, Herbert, said to me: "I can only *give* you two hours," to which I replied, "We are giving each other our time, mine is worthless, and I had earnestly hoped yours was too." Take care, I warned him, lest you become pretentious. He is becoming too much of the public figure at the perilous cost of his wondrous gifts. For three years I have cudgeled him, telling him I did not care a straw about his books on art, but that he had to return to belles lettres. I had, in particular, strongly urged him to do a critical study of our beloved John Ruskin, and now he says he will do it and dedicate it to me. A very sweet man, Herbert Read, and I love him, but I have told him he must give up these absurd journeys to the United States to give some famous booby of the arts an award, and then fly back to London after a sojourn here of a week, or fall in the dust as Eliot has. I never cared very much for Eliot as a poet, but liked him as a man. I persuaded him, by being very wily, the meek Saint John the Baptist, to print *Chelsea Rooming House* in England. This was an enormity, for I did not ever like the book very much, but at that time I was very fond of Horace Gregory.

Let me hear from you often, Isabella dear, and please heed me. I must guard you as best I can, and, alas, what can we do for others, save vex them when we want to shield their bare, unhoused backs from the world which never gave one coat to the miserable acolytes of Pallas Athene.

With devoted love and my deepest thanks. I am ashamed to receive your gift.

New York
December 4, 1958

Isabella dear:

I wrote you at some length yesterday, and deeply petition you not to do anything until I see you. You must be the dove and the serpent, as you are a woman you will be the latter and since you have a great heart it will be simple for you to be the former. You must understand I have no hostility at all toward your husband. It is the ferocious situation that you are in that troubles me no less than Job on his dung heap. Nor do I wish you to steal any joy from your children. You must also teach them to comprehend hindrance and the sorrows of their parents. That your husband does not wish to relinquish you is hardly a fault in him. He is flesh and is very dismembered.

I finish my paper for Robert M. Hutchins in about ten days. He won't like it, I don't think. It is impossible to revivify the republic from a penthouse in the Lincoln Building! He believes in a withered legal approach, I in a human one. As long as the habits of the people are lunatic ten thousand more laws will be of no avail. This Aristotle, Lycurgus, and Montesquieu understood.

I wish, Isabella dear, that you would read a little. Do not imagine that I think one can embrace a book. Years ago I read with the utmost pagan pleasure the *Journal* of Marie Bashkirtshieff. Delacroix's *Journal* might quiet you a little. Do you know Jastrow's *The Song of Solomon* and also his enchanting book on Ecclesiastes, or the preacher of Jerusalem, Koheleth?

Should you feel very lacerated and want to talk to me I could come earlier to Chicago.

I must warn you again, don't fall into an idealistic orgy, and imagine that you and your husband can discuss this logically. Man is unreasonable all the days of his life, and he is hardly about to be rational when his wife tells him she prefers another man. "There are reasons of the heart of which Reason knows nothing," says Pascal.

I wish I were sure that the man you love has unusual character. Do not imagine that I doubt it. We are purblind Cimmerians, and what we imagine we see is only the abundance of love we give to others. When that wellspring is exhausted we wonder why we fell in love, or even thought that the other had a majesty of soul which were only those vapors that come up from the depths of our own longings.

You must have what you are, and cannot be content with a

sluggish ebb tide. Never for one moment imagine that I am at odds with your yearnings and your strong, festal need for those joys of Eros the eldest of all the gods. Should I not know? I have told you with absolute truth what my own predicament is, and sometimes Rlene looks at me with such compassions. Yesterday she said to me: "At least I am better for you than the four walls." Of course she is, far better, but I am fifty-eight, and you are forty-three, as much in your prime as Cressida or Dido, and I know that if I stay as I am, and where I am, that my cup too will overflow with gall and bitterness. I am not embittered against Rlene, not at all. I have nothing but the tenderest heart for her, and whether I leave her it will make no difference. She is a nun by nature, and devotes herself to my work with religious faith. She is an Ophelia without her erotical madness, and even in an unhinged mood could never bawl out ribald verses as Shakespeare's nymph does when Hamlet can never be hers.

Again, I beg you not to mention the name of the man you love to anybody at all. Nothing but more basilisk evil can come of that. Don't in an unguarded moment tell what must remain a secret sphinx in your own soul. Be as close-mouthed as the Pharaohs in their tombs.

I do my utmost to counsel you, Isabella dearest, and if my best is not good, please forgive me. My sole thought is: Guard Isabella, and at this time I have no other thoughts that seem as important as that.

I continue to read, eschewing the autobiography, but one of these mornings I shall pray to Elohim and to my Mother and commence the epitaphs, for what else is a confession if it be true, something you hope will not dishonor the remains of the author, and can be read with feeling and pain, the purgative sorrow, by the reader.

You know you have my devoted love, and that I would stand by you in anything. What is important is that you sigh now, and have those joys which too often are no more than the breathing of the Ephesian sod.

Always your loving friend,

Dear Isabella:

You must forgive me for sending the letters to Elmhurst. I was perplexed; on one letter you gave as a return address Elmhurst, which you had not done before, and on the other there was none. I felt it essential that you have reassuring words from me; I feared also that you might divulge the name of the person you so deeply love. You must also pardon me if I want you to have this felicity. I think I know the man you love, and if I am right I can tell you that it has not come to me through any gossip so don't be concerned. It only occurred to me yesterday. I fervently hope it is Allen Tate. I have the highest regard for him, and think he is one of the very few human beings in American Letters worth mentioning. I had just written him a long letter yesterday, and it then appeared odd that I for some inexplicable reason should be writing him so warmly, and at the same time not knowing that this man who comprehends the American dilemma in literature should be the one you dearly love. Should you by any chance not understand how deeply I am for this wedlock between you and him, know that I should also be deeply disappointed if it is not he. I want you to have the best, and he is that.

This is just a note. I am utterly worn out today, and I don't know why. The change from Spain to the United States has left me deeply frayed.

I have finished the paper on the American Trauma for Hutchins, and fear that it may be too iconoclastic for him. But I cannot write otherwise.

Your secret is entombed in my soul. Don't worry at all.

I give you both my blessings and love.

If I am right, then you must marry him. I know a little about his own lacerating wedlock, and I know yours. I can think of no two persons whom I would rather see together. I should not want to see him as tortured as Coleridge was, or you to relinquish rapture and completion that this man could give you.

New York
Tuesday, December 9, 1958

Dear Isabella:

I hope by the time this letter reaches you you will have that calm and delight of the Song of Songs. You must, I beg you, understand, why I used such an inane imperative, as, I demand. What is hopeless misery unto my soul is that I know I shall never reach another human being in this earth. Then, too, I feared greatly that you might fall in love with some sensitive nonentity. Should Allen Tate be the man you deeply love, and I repeat, I fervently pray that he is, then I no longer have any fears about you. His human tenderness is on the page, and the book never lies. And how few loving books we have produced; we are the ghosts of Europe and we stalk the new continent unburied, and as hurt as those who cry out their wounds in the fields of asphodels.

I repeat other caveats; if neither you nor he can secure a divorce, then you must flee to Europe. Gather up your children and go with him. Of course, I should like to see both of you married because I believe in ritual and the legends of the epithalamium. If you cannot do it now, there is no reason why mere legalistic obstacles should prevent you from going to him. Don't suffer more than you must. I must add that I know very little about Mr. Tate's life, private or otherwise. I admire him, and he has my affections, and now even more so if he loves you and you him. I am not a man of the world, and whatever my great defects are, and they are enormous, I do not smell of the world.

You cannot trust everybody. I have the least confidence in my own nature. No man fears himself enough, says Pascal. I would sooner give my soul to a gnat than to others. Do you know how many persons I have trusted, and helped and encouraged and how often I have been no more than the dust for their footprints? I shall never be shrewd, preferring to be the dupe, but I shall not overthrow the whole of Hebraic and Christian literature deeply grounded upon a tender, bleating misanthropy. I refuse to love everybody because I have not the strength to be deceived by that many. Let me then be decoyed by a few; it is enough, and may Christ bless the trimmer and he who is deceived, for we require the sharker if we are to weep in the grape-colored evening in Gethsemane.

I have not been imprudent, Isabella dear, you did give me the Elmhurst address in your last epistle, for I am not such a blockhead or so careless as to send you word there, but I thought you had relinquished your box, or were now instructing me to write you there. If you misdoubt my word, I shall send you the envelope.

I have been ailing since I came to America. The ulcer plagues me every day of my shabby earthen days. Meanwhile, I am making ready to give a lecture on the influence of the Bible on literature in the graduate school of New York University. That will give me a hundred dollars, so here and there I manage to get the lucre I need for breathing and the Pleiades, the books.

We leave here on the twenty-third for Detroit; Rlene's parents are paying the fare as we could not buy a house in Spain, even at such a niggard price as I mentioned, and make journeys. They are sweet, bourgeois people, but I could not remain in a kind of high-class mud lot glossed over with pecuniary grass for more than a few days. Should I meet a few people who are pleasant in Chicago I shall stay a week, two weeks, I don't know, maybe less. If you introduce me to some persons that will be more than good enough, and I hope I can stay with some people who have a beating heart. Otherwise, you have your own burdens, and must first take care of your life. In some ways I prefer to hide behind the epistle. "I was naked when I hid," Adam said to God. People often mistake my passion for some dogmatic Petrine rock. I would give my second coat to any man if he did not also want the one I had on my back, and if I could even by so doing gain his love. My whole life is a loveless failure.

My love,

New York
January 23, 1959

Dearest Isabella:

Your disconsolate letter arrived about three hours ago, and I hasten to send you what balm I can. It, alas, can be little, for what you need is Allen, a very dear person, and wondrously gifted. I cared for him at once, and Rlene felt the same about both of you. *The Forlorn Demon* came yesterday, and I fell upon the book at once, a work of genius, of course. Allen is about the only man in the United States I can talk to about letters, really is the one, and what bad luck for me that I had not met him many years earlier. I deeply prize his words to me. You know, Isabella dear, we labor all the days of our earth and sun, looking for those very rare souls who will give us laurels, and are in Elysium if we find one.

I shall be writing to Allen soon as I finish these words to you.

Now, I must again tell you why from the beginning I have told you to go to him. At the cost of seeming wood and rock rather than heart, I must urge you to join him at your earliest occasion, and you must create that. He is a frail man, as tender as the reed in the wind, but, alas, too as vulnerable to be shaken by sickness. If your children are flourishing, that is deeply good, and if they are good human beings they will accept you and Allen. Meantime, he might become ill in that bleak and foul climate at Leeds. This has been a great concern of mine, and despite repeated caveats you have not quite understood me. Morals somehow get into our lives, if the people involved are very dear, as both of you are. You have the health which he requires, and your strength and body will give him the energy which is the source of all hopes. I do not want you to stay in a homeless suburbia, trying to be great ethical dust, while this man wastes away in English bogs. I want you, too, to get him into the sun as soon as you can, but at all costs you must be at his side. I have no cause to boast about anything, but have I not given you wise counsel from the beginning; have I not when you were as purblind as the Cimmerians warned you against your own self-deception? I do not speak so to fatten my self-esteem. That matters very little to me. In the old rabbinic legends it is said that the gnat was created long before man, to show how unimportant the latter is. I am sure I am less than the gnat, but I have five hands and five toes, and an ambiguous head, and where there is supposed to be soul, there is maybe some Pythagorean circle of air and water, and with these I say to you: Go to him. Everything will come out all right, I am sure; God gives the wound, and God gives the balm, and nobody knows what may happen, as Cervantes has it.

I want to get this off to you, and I must send an epistle of opulent thanks to Allen for his Book, and the Words he wrote in them to me. They mean very much to me. The Kosmos has brought us together, and only the Kosmos can ultimately separate us, but in the meanwhile, I repeat, join him.

I hope Allen has already seen Herbert; you will love him too.

Rlene is deeply pleased that both of you were taken with her. She thanks you deeply and so do I.

Let me hear from you often, and you know I will always reply forthwith, with the speed of the Angels who hurried Lot and his daughters out of Sodom.

The autobiography unfolds; Rlene thinks it is the best work I have ever done. How do I know? I don't want to send it to Allen now, for I don't care to burden him with it at present. Moreover, I must go over it again, and plough under those words which are bad, ill-used, or chaff. Later, I shall be most grateful for his Intellectual Eyes, not to omit the Grace of his Heart. I like his face enormously, and were I Jehovah I should have selected the two of you for wedlock.

At the risk of being a bore, Isabella dearest, please don't stay in Elmhurst and tear him and yourself to pieces.

Rlene sends her love to you, and to Allen, and thinks you are both Angels.

With much love.

                              Always devotedly your friend,

_____

New York
September 15, 1959

Isabella dear:

I want to give you and Allen our deepest thanks for the charming cable. How delighted I am that you and Allen are now married. Wedlock is such a jocular impiety, and may you both be grandiose blasphemers.

We sent you a cable at once. We were at the El Guio Hotel at the time and pray that you got it.

I see that we are both in the same issue of the *Sewannee*. How pleasant, and what a doughty poem. The beginning of *The Looking Glass* is very strong; I admire the whole of it, very much. I earnestly hope that admirable poet, Allen, is writing now. Every time I meet somebody who wants to know anything about Literature I tell him to go forthwith to *The Man of Letters in the Modern World*. I can't cast out of my head that marvelous essay on Dr. Johnson, and have no intention of doing so. Hazlitt could not have done any better, nor Dryden. You know I am no fool about such things, at least if I am a fool I am a negative one.

I am making ruthless excisions in *Can These Bones Live* which should be reissued with drawings in January. My God, what a ninny one can be; I thought I had composed such clear firm lines only to discover that the grammar was often bad, the clauses shaky, and sometimes there were no verbs or subjects. If this book is not right this time, spite of flaws that are natural to erring flesh, I shall go down to Tartarus or to the pit of Erebus and ask Odysseus for right and just diction.

We bought a little wedding gift for you and Allen, but don't know where to send it. Tell Allen that when I hear from him I'll believe in God, and that otherwise I have nothing to sustain me but metaphysics and my own sweet defects, sweet or bitter, what is the difference. I have my trouble with that gifted and rare man. He is no passive feminine soul, and can write a letter. Why, by heaven, he is a writer, isn't he? I would swear that he is though were I asked for any recent evidence I would not have one epistle to prove it. If he is writing a remarkable poem I shall pardon him, no, I don't think so. If he has been lucky he must be generous, kind, delicate, considerate, good; he must, in short, have all the good qualities I have been looking for in my own nature. A bootless search I fear, and the only goodness that I have is that I try to be gentle, charitable, tender, but fall down in the dust each time.

Anyway, both of you have my love.

I did a rough exposé of Robert Graves, your specious warrior of the Muses, in *Twentieth Century, London,* which appeared about a fortnight ago. This taxidermist lion will roar, and could even bleed were he not exsanguious. I hope Allen will mend your taste.

letters to
Allen Tate

Soller de Mallorca
December 7, 1958

Dear Mr. Tate:

I am charmed by your most gracious letter and give you my deep thanks for what you have to say about *The Sorrows of Priapus.*

The same situations obtain everywhere. We have, or almost so, the universal dung heap, the united Babel of the world, and as Amiel said: We live in the epoch of the anthill. Every writer looks about with a kind of madness of the heart for another poet or author who will bring him that balm of Gilead by just reading him. The late Sherwood Anderson, who had warm, grassy flesh, received far more of Plato's honey in this life than either you or I, certainly far more than I. About 1939 he had fallen into a scathed and suffering obscurity. Once he wrote a little essay in which he said that every time he met a stranger who was interested in literature, or feigned to be, he announced his own name with some pulsing self-confidence. "I am Sherwood Anderson," he said, to which the other replied, "Oh, you're that famous man, Maxwell Anderson." So much for renown or infamy.

I have loved Longinus, as you do, since I was about twenty-four. By the bye, I tell everybody to read *The Man of Letters in the Modern World,* and have had some success here. I doubt that there is anything you say, and in remarkable English, without those grammatical aberrations that make for present-day sloth, nihilism, and street-gamin insolence, in your *Essays* that I don't at once include within my own heart. As you know, we suffer from the "cult of the big," and everyone wants to be a muralist,

an author of a book in a million words, unmindful that some of
the most precious savants of the Muses were comely and eternal
in the shortest poems or essays.

This is Sunday, that gray obituary festival, so that I am
not sending this to you or *The Sorrows of Priapus* until
tomorrow morning. I have rueful hands and cannot wrap a
package, and such a defect makes me more unreasonable than
man already is. But I shall mail it tomorrow with my gratitude
for your own Book. Any rare book that comes out of America
makes me that less solitary. Poor Hart, so torn, chose Lucifer as
his Symbol. He who goes to and fro in the earth. I read three
essays of yours on Hart Crane, and found not one moiety of
meanness in any of them. On the contrary, your human passion
for this tragic poet was always noble, and of course, nobly uttered.

The fell truth is that I have not yet done one line on the
autobiography; it requires months for me to heal the gap between reading and writing, and I am afraid to risk one line
without the help of the visionary sages of the past; so I go on
perusing and studying one volume after another, Saint Augustine, Saint-Simon, Josephus, Carlyle, Milton, Tacitus, Dio and
many others. But soon I must take the greatest hazard, put down
some words that I may assume someone else will care to know.

Mr. Stanley Burnshaw wants me to send you his abundant
appreciation for your kindness to him.

I am very troubled about Herbert; for several years I have
begged him to return to letters. I know the "ache of penury,"
and the devout discouragement there is in writing for a small
audience. There is no other way. Moreover, I have beseeched him
to do a chapbook on John Ruskin which he has now consented to
do, and he says he will dedicate the book to me, a very great
honor; such a tribute is our mountain of frankincense; as for
lucre, I have had the same poverty as you, and have lived most of
my days in Fleet Street as hapless Christopher Smart did. As
badly as Herbert needs money, there are those who require his
quiet, woodland style to ease them. I find little to placate me in
this brutish world in which Mammon is king, and what you call
"the idolatry of the means" is the touchstone of the multitude,

and when I speak of the crowd I mean the professor in the university no less than the street Arab.

I am glad, though, that you have found teaching at the University of Minnesota. So far I have been unable to get anything but chaff and wind, except a paper Robert M. Hutchins has asked me to do. I got that as a result of devout tactlessness. I read some of his pamphlets filled with the Stygian academic jargon, the education patois, and told him that the improper use of words was a species of depravity. Besides, I said such sentences are likely to send every man who looks at them to Tartarus at once. He asked me who were the people to write these booklets. I mentioned you, and Herbert, George Woodcock (a good yeoman of others' ideas, perhaps not an original imagination, but compared with the manslayers of English, of real worth). Are there no more? I thought of one or two more, and then said: "Don't blame me; I was luckless enough to be born in a century of woe, waste, and the apotheosis of trifles; I did not invent the age." I got five hundred dollars for the paper which we sorely needed.

Fort Meyers was also named after one of Rlene's ancestors. Meyers was a close friend of Robert E. Lee. Having been a warm admirer of your poetry for many years, not too many, since she is thirty-three, she would be delighted to meet you, and, of course, so would I.

The other day I was looking at some letters by Byron; the garbage about his life has obfuscated the poet. I found his remarks on Pope so absolutely sound, and he was not afraid to speak of sense when he mentioned Pope's verse, and with great admiration. I could not refrain from considering your own *Essays* which are preeminently sensible in an utterly senseless age. It was La Bruyère who said that sense is the first to decline in any period.

I only hope my own words to you show you the gratitude I feel for the honor you give me, and I may say I have the joy of returning your homage.

Please accept my devout thanks for your epistle, and, in like manner, my most sincere admiration. Would to God I had your technical knowledge of verse; but I don't mind at all leaving poetry to you, and continuing to do my best to write good prose.

La Bruyère says that a bad writer imagines he writes divinely, but that a good one hopes he can write tolerably well.

My warmest regards, and again my deepest appreciation of your Poems and Essays.

Soller de Mallorca
October 8, 1962

My dear Allen:

As for Cummings I shall make nothing of it; I thought little of him; he had a wizened mind, with peccant faults that did not enlarge his Muse. Nor am I of a mind to reread Faulkner's novels. Years ago, whenever I told somebody I could not read his later works, I was advised to peruse the third one he composed, the second, and the first. Finally, I read a dozen of his brutal, narrow-headed volumes and with the same dingy reward.

Now, I have not the scantiest intention of composing a polemic; let me say quite clearly that the essay on your work will be a tribute. I will do my utmost to convey the imperial value of your poems and literary criticism to the ignorant and obdurate Solymi in our stupid Parnassus. These people don't read you; they don't read. I met a woman about twenty-seven or so, a painter; her husband, a writer of two petulant verses in some small magazine. I asked her what she thought of Marsden Hartley. She had never heard of him! About a decade ago I said to Herbert that if four or five of us would band together as illuminati (we hope) we could rout the Philisters. They are a crafty lot; some of them I liked a great deal when I was a raw boy of letters. There was Edmund Wilson, who as a pachydermatous Marxist buried one book after another that was not dedicated to that draconian doctrine. When I knew nothing, or had even soiled that nothing I thought I understood, he regarded me as a proletarian priest of the novel. Then when I saw how venal and coarse this crew of Marxist angels was, nobody would even review a book of mine. I have had more gravediggers ready to inter a book of mine whenever it was published than anybody I know in

the States. I may be boastful, but the statement is not really a
gorged one. When Ford Madox Ford, whom both of us loved,
claimed in the *New York Herald Tribune* that a book of mine
was one of the three best in that year, that paper printed his
assertion but refused to give me a trench of two inches wide in
which to cast my volume. Now, I say all this, my dear friend, only
to indicate that I do not think that either you or I (unless my
brain is weak, which it is) should be the advocates of bestial
provincial scribblers like Dos Passos, Faulkner, Hemingway, and
those who have received the laurels while other books that are
truthful are starved to death in limbo. I have felt this very urgently and now for a generation. I know I made many craven
errors, and I resolved as early as '34 to be a man of letters, and to
be an eremite to do so. I am not so perverse as to tell you that I
relish the pose of a solitary. When I am dead I shall have all the
cloistral peace I require; but I must needs live so now, for I have
no choice. My good publisher, James Laughlin, does not want me
to live in the States; he fears that every time I meet a simpleton I
shall have one reader less. He is not paying to keep me here; it is
his strong inclination that I eschew the literary garbage of our
times. So I maintain a few epistolary friendships, with you,
Herbert, and some others, and that is my life or my death if you
wish to call it so, and I shan't contradict you.

Please don't be vexed with me if I mention a few things, here
and there, but of no grave matter. I agree with you that Swinburne was a poet who cannot be read with pleasure or much
advantage; but he had a critical intellect that was rare, and his
book on Ben Jonson I honor. Unless I am mistaken, you dismiss
him. Remember also, please, that when Walter Savage Landor
was as much of a recluse in Fiesole as I am in Soller de Mallorca,
who had eyes for his work except Swinburne and several others?
One of the most hapless dedications I have ever scanned is the
one by Landor to that wretched minion of nineteenth-century
England and America, Charles Dickens. Today, fools and churls
prate about Dickens as if he were a Paracelsus of literature. It is
abstruse nowadays to elevate commonplace souls.

I think, too, my dear Allen, that you dismiss Cicero summarily;
Cicero was no jackanapes simply canonized by the academies. He

comprehended the insolence of Diogenes, Crates, Zeno, sanctified by Dio Chrysostom. It has become quite popular to throw down Herodotus and Strabo; when I met Graves he said the former was a liar and the latter unreliable, which just describes the whole human race, including Robert Graves. What occurred to me at the time he vilified such heroes of books was, How does he know that Herodotus lied, and who told him that Strabo did not know what he was writing? Many people think that Aristotle was a wretched natural historian, and yet both Buffon and Alexander von Humboldt thought he had extraordinary knowledge about fish, the sea, the gestation of animals, and so on. I, myself, respect and revere the past, particularly what is most sacred in it. How can I so offend Aristotle, Herodotus, or Strabo? They have taught me a great deal and besides, now at the age of sixty-two, I am still learning how to compose one good sentence, and if I am unusually lucky I may be able to do it.

One has to have much good fortune in this world to have a friend, to know nothing in an oracular line or two, and to be sufficiently modest not to feign that it is possible to be what we call a literary man and at the same time to be an Egyptologist, a natural historian, and a Babylonian scholar. Sometimes I take risks but they are not of a negative kind; I would have said long before Schliemann had discovered Troy that that Asiatic and Sybaritic town had existed. The brain, even Homer's, is incapable of inventing very much, and our fingers, elbows, nose, and feet recognize the existence of certain things though we have no way of proving them. But when it comes to throwing down great men, which is the habit of Pound, Eliot, and Graves, I feel this is desecration, and I won't break open the tombs of venerable saints of thought. Eliot calls Blake an "homemade philosopher." How he comes by this I cannot surmise. I am sure that Eliot does not know that the marvelous mythology Blake employed was grounded upon Bryant's System of Mythology, a remarkable work. The title is not quite correct, and I have not the volume in Spain.

There is only one other small matter that I should call to your patient attention, your disdain of Stendhal. Maybe I am not correct in speaking so; I must go back to your essays; it will take me a fortnight anyway to jot down notes before I write a single line. Now, without the least wish to be overweening I believe you might have a rare esteem for Stendhal's book *On Love*; I think you would be most sympathetic with his scorn of our Atlantic, phlegmatic natures, and his dissection of the anatomy of love is done with a kind of intellection that you might honor.

What else, my dear friend? Nothing. Think you I am at odds with you; positively not. Or that I should set about to be a disadvantage to a man I admire and for whom I have opulent affection?

I have read *The Forlorn Demon, The Man of Letters in the Modern World*, and then the *Collected Essays*, and of course, the *Poems*, and so I have reread all of your work that I possess. In order to convey to readers such a marvelous corpus of literature I am also re-examining Donne, Milton, Ruskin, Dryden, Swift, Pope, Spenser, Hazlitt. There are besides these about fifty volumes altogether that I must go through before I feel ready to write. The truth is that I am a great coward before I dare venture one sentence. No man goes to the guillotine with greater apprehension than I sit down at my desk, no longer with a quill or a pen, but with a fell machine, and then dare hope that I shall not make Ten Plagues out of an essay I wish to devote to the very important works of my friend, Allen Tate. I know no other volumes in our country more significant than yours; maybe it was for that reason that I was upset when you were quoted as saying that Cummings had nobody who was his superior. If that be true, then my dear Allen, what are we? But I do not hold with this. Were you not immensely superior to the late Cummings I would not be breaking my head to pieces so that I should communicate this fact and myth to readers in America. Why bother then? We have a big sodality of bottleheads who have quaffed one drop of water from Hippocrene, and imagine that they are drunkards of letters.

To repeat, soon as I can finish the essay I shall mail it to you, so that if I put down anything that displeases you, or if you think something is redundant or ill-written, you will have my whole permission to throw it away. Besides, what have I left today but my life which Nature intends to cast away any moment. In short, the essay will be no argument, since in almost every essential value I agree with you.

Meantime, I am having my woes with my good publisher, James Laughlin: there is no hiatus between us; he has the greatest admiration for the autobiography, but he has had all sorts of people (I suspect persons you and I would regard as poeticules, and the refuse of newspaper ideas) ransacking the memoir, and each one has a new suggestion. The punctuation should be altered in some places, a niggish matter, and I don't care about that, and then the reader is not sure of the identities of the mother's suitors. She lived to be about seventy-three, and in that thwarted and tragic period she had had about five to six men who were interested in her. How anybody could confuse them, or imagine that the first or second was the last, I don't know. Then he is very troubled about the chronology; there are some pronouns too that are lacking. I had beseeched him to heal some of these mistakes himself or with the help of Rlene who labored over the manuscript for months. Then Herbert read it, and said he would not change anything except excise a dozen quotations, and make the author's note a part of the body of the memorial to which I readily agreed.

There is no controversy between Laughlin and myself; he is doing his utmost to make a book perfect. Can that be, considering that all flesh is filled with so many pores wherein are secreted multifarious errors? I have tried in every way to please him, and now I suggested that perhaps (were it not too burdensome for you) you might read it. Frankly, I did not wish to send it to you until galleys came from the printer; there is the consolation and the mysticism of the printed word; of course you cannot improve platitudes and scurvy writing, but if the book is good and truthful, and what else should I be writing a book for, I wished you to see it after it had come from the press. There is the citation from you, and so prefaced as to make no doubt as to my extremely high regard for you as our American poet (so I have put it), which I did not wish to convey to you until the value of the alphabet I had used was accented and elevated. Do I make myself clear; it is a cumbersome sentence I know, but I hope it is not unintelligible.

Another annoyance: I do not want to wallow in my own words continually; I think it has taken me four years to complete this book, and I cannot remember how many times I have rewritten it. At this point, I am beside myself, and I would not know what to repair, what was wrong, or how to mend it. Could I have the benefit of your intellect, it would be a mercy to me; and it would also allow me to go ahead with the work on you which at this time is a novelty for me, whereas the autobiography has become a stale and withered mistress with whom I wish to have no more connection, polite or otherwise. In short, I am done with that slut, my autobiography, and I wish she would go to the printer and let me be. To write about one's mother is too harrowing, and to follow her Ghost month in and month out and hear every morning the cock crowing the Logos is too great a pressure upon my mildewed and becrazed brain.

Believe me, my dear Allen, I am most grateful for your wish to help me; only insane people are independent; I need the consolation of your praise and a long statement from you about the autobiography would be a balm in Gilead, if there is such a curative herb there.

Rlene is now in Michigan gathering together my papers and notes and letters for the university that is interested in purchasing them. I say as little here as I asserted when my Ms. of essays was in the hands of the people of the University of Detroit. I think they kept my Ms. for a year, and I never had one word from them, or they from me, for the simple reason that until I had heard that there was some indecision I would not have known whom to write. I should have thought your marvelous letter would have sharpened their wits. But this is typical, as you know; the only authors who do not have such chagrins are liars, and I have had many. Soon as I have good tidings, if there be such, I shall tell you and Isabella straightway. Believe me, Rlene and I need the lucre and desperately. You can imagine what Gargantuan sums of gold I collect from my books. Now that Texas University has accepted a volume of verse I thought I would receive something, at least a jot more than nothing, but I have as my advance a pure nothing. In the midst of all this, I am involved in a lawsuit over the right-of-way through Rlene's and my land, and I have no alternative but to settle the claim, and to my adversary's advantage; besides, there are no victories, none I ever heard of, and I am not immune to rumors. You know, and please know it, that you have my highest admiration and love, and so has Isabella.

Your devoted friend,

Soller de Mallorca
January 12, 1963

Dear Allen:

I wrote your Isabella yesterday, and am still in a quandary as to how to prevent the rogues of our dollar literati from burying the autobiography. Both books have received advance plaudits and will have a heavy library sale. But I am not thinking of lucre which I sorely need, but plain, just honor. No university would ever give me any sort of advancement; I was lucky to be an instructor or a visiting lecturer in the graduate school, but for no more than a semester. I would not use that biggest of all American falsehoods, the college textbook. So that was the end of me. Years ago I was being considered for the department chairmanship of a Massachusetts university. After the president, who had a coffin face, had questioned me for three hours, he asked me whether I could get along with the nine professors in the English department. I promptly replied that I could not get along with nine people in the entire world.

So that was a debacle; then whether I wrote good or bad books I always had invisible foes who would not mention me. A couple of years ago, perhaps three or four, a professor gave a lecture on American Literature. After he had finished talking, one of his hearers asked him what about Edward Dahlberg. "Oh," he answered, "I am deeply indebted to Dahlberg." He composed a suety tome of about six hundred pages, and indeed he owed me much, but there was not a reference to me.

Now we are almost of the same age; our ideas are often very similar; you once said that I was fortunate; were I your adversary I should give you my ill luck. For no matter what I did it fell out ill. How can I at this point achieve nothing more than a *succès d'estime?* You say I have assailed thieves and liars in our miserable Parnassus. It is true; I must continue to do so; otherwise,

American Literature is just about hopeless. Once you told me that when you were asked whom did you admire, your retort was nobody. You are almost right. It's a feeble and perverse day. It would bore you to tell how many writers I have helped and who have for no other reason than that become my enemies. Either I must whore for fame, tell infernal falsehoods about gnomes who are fake, stuffed giants of literature, or be in my position. I will, if I must, take the conditions that are mine. But, my dear Allen, we have been friends, and you have helped me, and I pray that in the long essay I have done on the marvelous *The Forlorn Demon* I have been useful to you and to American Literature. I beg you now to do what you can to see to it that the autobiography and *Alms for Oblivion* are not cast in the garbage heap at Tophet. Most of my adversaries I have never met; write one truthful remark and you have sowed dragon's seeds. Am I to be the booty of the malice of an Irita Van Doren? My luck with the Van Dorens was never good. I knew Carl; he wrote a rotten volume on American Literature, all that nonsense about Freneau and Brockden Brown, a pair of pipers in the sewers of Helicon. But why tell you all the tedious details? It is a horrible irony that I who loathe the papers must somehow or other get my renown through them. I feel dirty in doing so, and in thinking that way. I suggested to Isabella that an appeal ought to be made to the Institute of Arts and Letters. That is their job if their work is not to be utterly drossy. They should protect the few truths that appear in books in the United States. I believe a fight ought to be made of it. What have we at our age to lose? Surely we have more vigor than the twenty-two-year-old boys who are now assistant professors, but they rule our ideas more fiercely than Khrushchev or some other murderous dictator. Literature in America is in the same ill health as it is in the Iron Curtain countries. The repression is as hard in the United States as it is in Yugoslavia. Each man must put on his ideological uniform or his books will be sure to face a firing squad.

We are living in a war period, when the health of the corporation nation depends upon the cult of sameness.

Laughlin is doing all that he can to make certain that the book* will have an audience. There is your wonderful statement

* *Because I Was Flesh*

and Herbert's; but alas, more must be done. What would Baudelaire have done without Gautier, or Stendhal without Balzac? Ten copies of Nietzsche's *Thus Spake Zarathustra* were sold, and Bach's works were found on wrapping paper in a butcher shop. It is always the same, but somehow or other, one must struggle so that it must not be. Were I to have the choice, be a celebrated nonentity or a seeker after truths and be alone, I should without hesitation choose the latter role. After all, only lonely souls have been my mentors. The crowd is untruth, says Kierkegaard. Perhaps the game is lost, for art is a tragic sport, but one must struggle to win. What? Death. Prometheus is bound to a rock with no shelter but snow, sleet, and hail, and his liver offered to the vulture, but each night his liver, the seat of contemplation, affection, and sorrow grows again. So solitary Aeschylus thought.

I am exceedingly sorry to hear that you were not well, but Isabella assures me that you will be strong again in a few days. As for me, I have been feeble, bed-ridden, and good-for-nothing for ten months. No time can I remember in my life when I did not study some wise author. Still, I have another book in my head, another Promethean failure, and if I have the health I shall do it. What else is there for me to do so that I shan't brood about my demise, for do we not write to forget that soon we will be nothing, and what else in an age of nihilism is there to worship but the god Nothing? He is the demiurge, the logos, and our murderer.

Live long, dear Allen, you and very dear Isabella, live long, my dear friend, and write some more wondrous poems.

As ever, my devoted love to you and your darling wife, Isabella.

Soller de Mallorca
January 28, 1964

Dear Allen:

I have your good letter and your enchanting words about some of my works. Had you not thought that the essay on *The Forlorn*

Demon was the best in the books I should have been crestfallen. It took nine months, and after I was finished with it, I furtively believed that what I had done might please you, and be of real use to American Literature. When I realized that I was offering a book on American Literature without the tribute to you that you deeply deserve, I was ashamed, and beseeched the editor to give me time to prepare the work and then to write the essay. That I would have such good luck with it I could not believe; Demetrius, the ancient rhetor, speaking of one writer, said that he put his words together so badly because he was so ill-natured.

Laughlin tells me that somebody who has a very high position at Bollingen is very impressed with *Because I Was Flesh*. Could I know who he is I might ask for a grant to write a volume of literary criticism going back to the ancients and emphasizing in particular Ruskin and Herbert Read. Too often friends honor each other in that congealed coffin called an epistle to the Laodiceans, but pay no public mention of them. And I should like to do something about this if I can. Of course, there are about half a dozen references to Herbert, and all laudatory, but what is that to Hecuba or to Herbert?

Now, my dear, good friend, it is most generous of you to propose me for membership in the Institute of Arts and Letters. The honor I have had for work done without the scantiest thought of my bread, soup, and fame has been niggish. Lucre is as legendary to me as Osiris. I thank you most wholeheartedly for all that you have done and for what you wish to do. Since disappointment has been my bride since childhood, another rejection will not make my wilderness any darker.

Texas has not yet given me a formal agreement for my papers, letters, and notes, and so on. I think there is a budgetary problem; you know Polonius Bursar. Did you ever know trustees of a university that did not want to put up a new building? This time it's a new library; what they have done with good books in the old library we can well surmise. Once at a party given in honor of a newly elected president of a Midwestern university, I said: "For God's sake, whatever you do, don't start building."

I wish to express my deepest appreciation to you for telling Laughlin what people he could send the autobiography to; I know it is rueful nonsense in me to crave renown in the garbage newspapers, but when they ignore my work, I must suffer to get another volume published. I am tired of my underground reputation. Ambrose Bierce used to say: "I am the most talked-about man in America; everybody mentions my obscurity."

Again, I thank you so much for liking my essay on *The Forlorn Demon.*

You and your darling Isabella have my devoted love, gratitude and admiration.

Your friend,

Soller de Mallorca
February 3, 1964

My dear Allen:

The other day I had word from James Laughlin that I should ask you how to go about asking the Bollingen people for a grant. I am a simpleton in such matters, and cannot draw up an aprioristic diagram of a book I intend to write. As Cervantes says, God gives the wound, and God gives the balm, and nobody knows what may happen. And that is the way it is with a book.

I have two different books in mind, one, as I told you, on adages à la Rochefoucauld, using American Indian myths as local color and American geography as scenery. But would such persons even give me a moment's notice, even though I might write a book that would be recollected? Then I thought of doing a volume on literary criticism (which really has its source in your marvelous query and essay, "Is Literary Criticism Possible?").

If you can advise me or write to somebody at Bollingen I should be very grateful to you, but then I fear I shall always be saying the same monotonous words to you: I thank you again.

Rlene arrives on the seventeenth or eighteenth of February, but we are impoverished. I have been ill for eleven months, and am taking daily injections for severe anemia, and because of the cost of doctors and medicines we are out of pocket. If you can think of any other foundations to which I could apply, please let me know.

Meantime, please pardon me for conveying to you Job's news. A man ought to guard his sorrows as he does a friend's secrets or a woman's favors.

My devoted love to you and Isabella, and need I say were you, Isabella, and Herbert not on the earth I should not have what little bravery is left in my glimmering spirit to live. Your constant friend,

I know the Institute of Arts and Letters have a fund for ill and penurious authors. They gave me some money about twelve years ago. Would it be too burdensome for you, my dear Allen, to write to them in my behalf?

Soller de Mallorca
February 24, 1964

Dear Allen:

I wrote to you and Isabella last week to thank you for your immense kindness to me. And so now I send you this letter to express my gratitude again. A check for eight hundred dollars came from the Institute of Arts and Letters. Laurence Pollinger wrote that he had placed *Because I Was Flesh* with Methuen. He also gave me enormous pleasure in telling me that he had found a publisher for *The Fathers*. There is word also that Piper Verlag will publish a German edition of the autobiography. All this means, I think, that I can get away from Soller in the fall, and live in digs at Dublin. I am sick unto death of this bucolic tedium, living in a Mediterranean town, where the sirocco blows all heads mad, and hope that a more bracing climate will give me vigor once more. I am as feeble as Pascal's pensive reed.

Am still thinking about a foundation that might give me a grant to do a book, one, as I mentioned to you, of adages à la Rochefoucauld. Though I never wrote for money, I had not resolved to be a beggar either, and this now frightens me greatly. So please don't blame me if I burden you, as I am doing, by asking you what foundation might make it possible for me, a

penurious maggot, to compose apothegms, without trembling
every hour for my bread. Lunatic prices obtain everywhere, and
if you have very little money you must be exceedingly agile to
keep alive, or not to go to Bedlam. My life is very frugal and
abstemious; aside from very simple commons, I need a tender
woman, a book, and walking. One who expects more than that
from this life is very likely to get less.

You are quite right, *Because I Was Flesh* will not bring me
much money. So no matter what I write, I shall be as wretched as
Lazarus, and now I must try not to be such a simpleton in this
world. Of course, my efforts there will be futile too. Had I any
sense, would I have been a writer? Once Lawrence said to me:
"Dahlberg, try not to be so unlucky." I tried, but now I am in
the middle of my sixty-third year, and misfortune bites my heels.
Nobody knows what the reasons may be, but the trustees at the
University of Texas have decided not to buy my Mss. The people
at Austin who wanted them, Dr. Roberts and Mr. Kim Taylor,
are sorely disappointed. My own feelings are broken pinions.

In the close future, I shall not write you such desponding
epistles; once I can return to work, and find some way of securing
enough money to write, I shall be far less afflicted with ennui,
which is a Mediterranean disease.

At the risk of boring you, my dear Allen, I thank you again.
Without your help *Alms for Oblivion* would not be published by
the University of Minnesota Press. It will also be tedious to say
once more that I was ill when the money came from you and
Isabella. God knows, only an insane man imagines he is independent; still it is hard to live without deceiving one's self a
little. We are dupes anyway, and when we take money from very
dear friends we then are sure that we are the deceivers. It is a
circle, Pascalean, as you might express it, or not, I do not
know.

Do let me hear from you, my dear Allen; what else can one
writer do now or at the time of Swift, but turn to another? I have
been acutely ill for a whole year, and I have never asked Laughlin for a penny, and be sure that he has never offered me one. His
cross, he thinks, is his money, and every author his conycatcher.
He is doing everything he can for the autobiography, but nothing for me. A rueful irony. Still I am his friend, and I believe in

his own furtive manner he considers himself mine, and he is. He enjoys the role of the despot; if I assail a writer he happens to like, he rails at me, and if I in any way attempt to tell him that this is the way I must live and write, he says I am querulous. About two years ago I met a very fine translator in Soller who denounced Pascal as an ill-natured man.

Soller de Mallorca
March 18, 1964

My dear Allen:

The doctor has advised me to leave Spain, and to find another climate. There is another matter also, money; we can no longer afford to maintain the house here. Meanwhile, Dominick Browne, the son of Lord Dranmore and Browne has offered us his cottage in Donegal on the northwest coast. So long as I lie beneath the debilitating Mallorcan skies I shall be as prone as Oblomov. I want to get back to work. Without the check from you and Isabella and the money from the Institute of Arts and Letters I could not do this. When Rlene arrived she showed me the autobiography; what amazed me were the names on the dust jacket; your own eminent name was no longer after Herbert's. Let me say quite simply I have never placed opportunity before the Truth. Had I known I would never have allowed this. Then there was a very long piece on seven of my books in the *New York Review of Books* (the date is March 19, 1964), and both Herbert and I are attacked because we wrote *Truth Is More Sacred*. That doesn't bother me at all. What troubles me is that in the review a Mr. Flint whom I know nothing about states that I "befriended Tate." Had he asserted that Allen Tate came to the rescue of Edward Dahlberg I should have been pleased. You know that once the book is published, what happens is out of your hands. To repeat, I don't mind taking the insults, but I grow sick if a very dear friend of mine is in any way harmed or humbled or not given abundant deference and courtesy.

I wrote you two to three letters, and sent one to your Isabella, and pray that you have received my full-hearted thanks. Now our dear and distinguished friend, Herbert, is going to help me get a Bollingen grant, so that, perhaps, if they allow me, I'll do the book on literary criticism (and let me be absolutely frank about it; had I not worked so long on your memorable *The Forlorn Demon,* the point of view I have would not have been in my mind; of course, I have always hated the alleged science of criticism, and consider the scientists of letters or of anything else as ignorant men), and I will there express my profound gratitude to you. Wherever I can refer to you, and do it as you so opulently deserve, I shall do it, so that you will know that I am no weathervane critic or friend.

If you have the time and the heart for it, please let me have some word from you. Could you also do anything about Bollingen, I cannot tell you how much I should thank you for that. I hope you and Isabella were not put off by the pain I felt in accepting money from you. I could not help so writing and feeling; please forgive me.

Both you and dearest Isabella have my devoted love, and you know, my dear Allen, what esteem I have for your work. "Know them by the fruits of their doings."

Your constant friend,

Dublin
April 20, 1964

My dear Allen:

Your good letter has been winged to me here, and as always I am grateful to hear that you are in fine health. I want to thank you very much for writing to Bollingen for me. *Because I Was Flesh* is doing well enough, but not exceptionally. Five thousand copies have been sold and a parcel of another five thousand have been bound, but spite of unusual notices the book lags. Laughlin says that the readers are mistaking the autobiography for serious literature!

Everything at Texas University is a bedlam; I had word from one, Kim Taylor, very friendly to me, and a warm adherent of my books, that the football coach has just been made a full professor and that his salary has been raised to twenty-four thousand dollars a year. Kim Taylor, the art director, who has designed some beautiful books, says he will work on the volume of poetry, *Cipango's Hinder Door* for nothing, and he should do a beautiful volume, provided now that the University of Minnesota takes it.

Dublin is damp, but bracing; it rains almost everywhere, and I have multifarious aches, but it is better now for me than Spain. I had to quit Soller or die; that may sound extravagant, but I was totally supine there, and could not, or would not, quit my bed, and had no palate for a book. The other day in a second-hand bookstore I came upon a complete set of Walter Savage Landor, the leaves still uncut, and the price fifty shillings; my soul flew to heaven, and I was imprudent enough to buy it, though I cannot afford to be alive, and it is too expensive to die.

Laughlin speaks of bringing out an *Edward Dahlberg Reader* in '66, and the complete *Sorrows* sometime in the future; I hate the word, future, it is nothing, the first day of creation, a terrible, satanic void, and what do I do in the meanwhile? A long and serious review is to appear in the June issue of the *Massachusetts Review;* they have accepted with delight two unpublished chapters of the *Sorrows* and four poems, for which I shall receive, if lucky, twenty-five dollars. Well, maybe the Bollingen Foundation will provide the lamb for Abraham, but that, as Herbert advises me, will take months, that is months for them to come to a decision.

Am enclosing my letter to the Bollingen people before sending it to them; if you think it is done in the right accent and tone, will you please, my dear friend, tell me, and then I shall mail it. I am sending a copy of it to Herbert too with the same motive in mind. Meanwhile, I am here, not by the grace of God but by the money you and Isabella gave me. God pardon all sinners, and particularly me, for I know not how to be virtuous.

Please know how devoted I am to you and Isabella; Rlene sends her love to both of you.

Dublin
May 8, 1964

My dear Allen:

I have revised the letter and thank you exceedingly for your suggestions. I also had a letter from Herbert and he thought I should make certain excisions which I have done.

Keep in good health; for I am relieved to hear that you are better once more. The change has been very good for me. I guess I have a northerly nature, for I am gross and unusually stupid in the Midi or when I am buffeted by the African sirocco. Almost every day I swim in the icy Irish sea, and I don't need any more injections and very few capsules. Moreover, I am writing, composing short essays and maxims, for I doubt that the guillotine is worse than idleness. Now I must once more express my deepest gratitude to you and dearest Isabella for making this journey possible. At this writing I pray that the Bollingen Foundation will give me a grant so that Rlene and I won't be beggars. Another university has offered to purchase my papers, but they tell me they are poor!

Alms for Oblivion has now appeared and as usual I cower, dreading that the book will not be noticed. After thirty years of obscurity you can understand my cowardice.

Otherwise, my life is nothing. I get up in the morning and say: "My God, I have to write, why?" and then later I declare: "Now I must go to the sea, and it is like a dagger in my back, and after I have gotten out of the water I must walk." I cling to life as tenaciously as anybody else, but abhor the daily routine, that devil, ennui, which so plagues me.

I thank you and thank you, my dear Allen, for being so gracious. I would rather have a friend than discover the northwest passage to Cathay, and you are a friend, both you and your marvelous wife, Isabella.

As always, with much love and devotion.

Dear Allen:

I asked Mr. Kim Taylor, advisor to publications at the University of Texas, to write you at Wellfleet and to send you word to Minneapolis also. He is very anxious to have your Introduction, and I don't mind repeating: and so am I, and very much so.

I have been writing maxims which I have sent to the University of Minnesota, but I don't know how many readers must approve them, and how can I please a brood of literary chimney-sweeps? For some while I have been thinking about a small novel on Mallorca, and then I am hesitant, because though I have no political doctrine, I may very likely be thrown out of Spain simply because I have told the truth. But an author has to write, and if he doesn't he begins to suffer from intellectual impotence, and that is a very severe punishment. We go to Golgotha every day we don't write, and each hour we do.

Now, my dear Allen, you are quite right about the letters I sent to you and Isabella. There are doubtless indiscretions that should be interred in sepulchers rather than in a volume. Should I read them, for it would be an Atalean nuisance for you and Isabella to examine them? Moreover, how many of them are trite I do not dare surmise. But do as you and Isabella see fit; you are far more discreet than I. I began life as a fool and shall surely die one.

God bless your premonitions, for I should like very much to get the Ingram Merrill grant, and if I do I shall again be indebted to you. But then only a churl thinks he is independent and owes no man gratitude. Your work has been very much on my mind, and that is the literal truth, and not epistolary flattery, and I feel I still have much to say about you that is buried somewhere in my torn spirit.

Please let me hear whether you have had a letter from Kim Taylor, and also what you and Isabella think I should do about the letters. A volume without missives sent to you and your darling wife, Isabella, would be a sherd.

Both of you, as always, have my devoted love and thanks, and thanks again. I forgot to tell you, Paul Carroll is editing the *Reader* for New Directions. Did you ever get the *Massachusetts Review* which I asked the editor to mail to you and Isabella?

Every time Laughlin visits some author he has published and whom I have attacked he sends me a few acerb phrases. The only way I can write literary criticism is first to find out at whose house Laughlin is staying. About a year or two ago he wrote: "You assailed Kenneth Rexroth, and think of it, I am now his guest in his apartment at San Francisco." A fortnight ago I had a letter from him coming from Rapallo. He had just left the divine scribbler Ezra Pound, and he informed me that what I had said about Pound who imagines he too drinks the waters at Hippocrene, was *shocking*. Poor Laughlin, for whom I have abundant affection, is always thinking about the grave, and if I suggest that he publish a new person, he replies: "Edward, I'm too tired, and old; I just can't do it." It's no pose. Always believe what a man tells you even if it is a lie. Ultimately, no one is capable of telling falsehoods about himself because the soul won't tolerate it.

Again with much love to your dearest Isabella.

Kansas City
June 9, 1965

My dear Allen:

I wrote Isabella an acerb letter, and I feel very sorry that I did it. You know I have been her friend and even mentor for years, and I feel she is repeating all the dingy, desiccated Marxisms which can only spoil her verse and damage her life. I have had the greatest feeling for Isabella, but I was sorely distressed when she invited me to the house for a *little* while; then she wrote me recently that she could not endure anybody for more than two days; I became angry. Believe me, whatever my defects are, and I know they are great, I can tolerate either or both of you, without thinking you are a heavy, doleful load upon my nervous system.

I found you enchanting company whether we were both torpid, stupid, or pensive. And I have the same feeling about Isabella.

I hope, my dear, good friend, that both of you will forgive me. I too am a cairn of sinning flesh, but one thing I do not do is to use other people's houses as an escape from my own woes or an asylum that could only be a burden to them. I have been the host, and many times, but seldom the guest. It is the way I prefer it. If you recall, I have on various occasions invited both of you to come and stay in the house at Mallorca, but always saying that I would be away if you decided to come. That was my way of informing both of you that I had no intention or wish to interfere with your privacies or to enlarge whatever ghostly griefs lie beneath the surface of those smiles which are themselves specters of another subterranean life we never comprehend.

Be sure, both of you, of my steadfast love and devotion. And forgive me if I have erred against either of you or both of you by writing Isabella in this vein.

Am at work on the novel; so far it is a lengthy syllogism, or I should say, solipsism. But then I am a lonely phantasm; though I am by no means without an instinct, I am sorely afraid to be with people.

But enough, my good, dear friend.

Both of you have my devotion and great affection, and apologies if you and Isabella think I owe them to both of you. It is, alas, not my first mistake; my life is a total and wretched error.

Kansas City
June 12, 1965

My dear Allen:

What is one to reply to such a letter as you send me? Zeus was known as the god of hospitality, and certainly a poet comprehends this. Would you like a close friend to ask you to come to his house for a little while and then write you that because the two of you were intimate you were intolerable except for a pair of days?

Allen, I don't know why you should be angry with me. Not one uncivil word had we exchanged while I was the guest of you and Isabella. Moreover, when we were alone you told me you were in absolute agreement with me about the Negro question.

Years before you met Isabella I was her mentor. Countless times I laid aside my own work to write and console her when she was unhappy and broken.

Pardon me for saying so, it does not make any sense to me that the nearer you are to the person the less you can stomach him, and that only strangers are really welcome as your guests for a great length of time. Dos Passos used to tell me that he preferred to talk to the grocer rather than converse with an author. But Dos Passos is a lowly clerk himself of literature, and his own conversation was never any addition to one's mind. But to hear a man of letters, like yourself, write in this vein startles me. You must have written in haste and with spleen, otherwise it is hard for me to believe that you could be so perverse. Please tell me plainly, how you would relish such an invitation?

What you call eccentricity is likely to be a dagger thrust into someone's soul. However, you are not stung because you did not receive the missive. I did.

Nor can I comprehend your dictatorial manner. You say that unless I allow my last epistle to be published, she will withdraw the other letters I wrote to her.

I am not the editor, and have exercised no influence over Paul Carroll. I don't even know what he will print or excise. Besides, what has our single misunderstanding to do with the literary quality of loving letters I sent to Isabella? What is involved here is belles lettres and not any temporary disagreement I have had with Isabella. There is also, my dear friend, a curious paradox in all of this. If the words I sent to Isabella are of real worth, and Paul decides to include them, who is honoring whom? Is Isabella giving me loud accolades because Paul publishes some remarkable letters I wrote to her! To say the least, this is an odd sort of literary criticism, and coming from you. What do we do? Punish one another, each giving the other limbo when he can, because three friends have had a disagreement?

Besides, Isabella had not written to me in a jocular vein. I wonder, also, if you would be willing to be the victim of such jocosity.

When I wrote to you (and without any rancor) it was my fervent hope that you would understand how a guest might feel if the hostess told him that he was welcome to her house provided he was sensible enough to rush off as rapidly as possible. May I ask you, and take this as a query from a simpleton, if you like, is white green, black yellow, and why do you and Isabella find those who are in your hearts insupportable whereas insipid acquaintances are welcome to be near you long as they wish? If this is true, our friends chill us, and give us the most implacable solitude. We don't want to bother with anyone whom we love, except to write them an occasional letter, and if the recipient is wounded by any phrase that has a sword's edge, we consider him a ninny for admitting it. Should we be dilated when a very dear friend tells us we would be a nuisance in her house were we so foolhardy as to stay there for more than two days? Is this really what the sages taught us?

Is it a symptom of abundant feeling to get rid of a friend with mercurial speed and a sign of jollity to tell him so? I then must not adopt such a credo for my life, but must as best I can be the acolyte of the great masters of the past. Tolstoy wrote a puissant chapter on human perversity, and since I was a young man, I resolved, no matter what the cost might be, to call a chagrin a humiliation, and not something jolly, and to say that bad is wicked, and not good.

Please bear in mind that I have not the scantiest thought of maiming you or Isabella as I feel I have been bruised. You cannot tell me how to feel, and I must say without equivocation that Isabella did not write this in a humorous vein.

This letter bears the signature of my spirit, and I will under no circumstances say I am somebody else, though it may be very difficult and even tragic to be what I am. Jehovah says, I AM that I AM, and though I am dust, and even less, I claim the same right.

Lonely as I feel my life to be, I prefer iconoclastic singleness of soul, apart from others, than to be cowardly and confess that Isabella or you is right. Not this time, my dear friend. I have

written several letters or more to you and Isabella, to explain my
feelings. It appears that in order to be a friend to you and
Isabella, that I must be a beggar, and accept the humiliation,
and say it is savory, though my flesh, my fingers, and my head, for
whatever they are worth, tell me I have been stabbed by an
unkind phrase.

I have never won any victories in this life, and am not such a
buffoon as to imagine that you will reply in a soft tone. Would
that it were true.

I expect nothing to come of this difference between us except a
cruel rupture. But it must be. You cannot, my dear Allen, tell me
what to do, or what epistles shall be included in the *Reader*,
though I have no power over what should be printed or excised.
Should it enlarge Isabella's life to demand that they be cast out,
she will have to do that, though I never thought it would come to
this, nor is there any intimation in any of my words to you or her
that this should be done. I should imagine, since you are a man
whose verse and criticism I highly admire, that what is important
is whether the letters I have written have some literary quality.
Do we throw each other's work away because in the course of
sixteen years or so we have one misunderstanding? No matter
what you say, or Isabella writes me, am I to be the tomb, the
wordless gnome who must, perforce, be acquiescent? I wish, to
repeat, that you should take my place. Ask yourself, whether you
would be joyful, if I offered you such an invitation?

Should there be another edition of *Alms for Oblivion,* should I
write you a dictatorial letter, demanding that if you don't recant,
I will exclude the essay on your marvelous book, *The Forlorn
Demon?* Is this, my dear friend, political letters?

I told Isabella that I would never go to her home again, and
there is not a tithe of spite in that remark. The simple truth is
that I cannot endure this kind of experience. My whole body
suffers, and I fear to do anything at all, answer you or be mute.
Besides, I deeply believe that people do more to their disadvantage than for their benefit. Self-destruction seems to be the black,
destroying angel of our age. Isabella writes me how lonely she is,
and then reminds me, for what cause I know not, that the sooner
a friend leaves her the better it is for her life. Should I swallow
this pellet of sagacity?

You, Isabella, and I have been very close in so many ways, and I cannot see what is to be gained by absolutely ignoring that an insult damages flesh and does not laurel it.

You and Isabella will have to make the decisions. You and she do what you think is right. I have no power over you, and you can admonish me, when I am wrong, but by God, I am not in this instance. Perhaps it will be my fate to belong to a group of one, but in that way nobody will be able to persuade me that what I believe is harmful is really a solace to my spirit.

The truth is one should not write in haste, and in answering you I have weighed my words, not as warily as Rhadamanthus could, but as best an error, like myself, can. I think, my dear Allen, were you willing to consider the whole matter more slowly you might see that anybody, unless he were a gnat or just pachydermatous skin, would find no comfort in the kind of letter you or Isabella have written me. My own to you was an entreaty, hardly an imperious command.

What also troubles me is that each one of us is absolutely separated from one another, and I think that is why we are producing such a meager literature. People have to be together in order to create a small commonweal of human letters. I had many differences with the late and noble Ford Madox Ford, but we found that no cause to part from one another. I even detested his wife, Biala, and that did not matter to him. What was important to him was a gifted intellect, and he believed I had one. We, on the contrary, have far more in common in values than Ford or I did, though I dearly loved the man. He always asked you to come and see him; had I been far riper I would have seen him far more often, and that would have been a balsam to me and added to my own perceptions.

I positively don't believe that the aristocrats of our miserable republic should be isolated from one another, and that the only persons who are companionable are strangers.

I write you this with many rueful, damp, and moldy emotions. I see in your reply a demise of our friendship which I always cherished. All I can say is live long, write some more magical verses, and Isabella must forgive me if I cannot accept punitive words from her. I have admonished her before, and that did not make the two of us spill blood, and I don't see why it should now. We had sharp differences over the Negro question, and you were on my side, but still the three of us were bound together by habit, learning, and love. I did not mean that Isabella was in the literal sense of the word a Marxist. But what I meant, and do assert, that it amounts to the same thing. One morning the dialecticians cry out for the Cubans, the next for the oppressed yellow race, who are now the power most to be feared, and then they weep over the terrible difficulties between white and black people. My own thought is that you don't ask a person about the pigmentation of his skin before you take him into your heart. Nor do you accept bulk races, or imagine that each Negro is a prodigy of goodness. I have told my American Negro friend, Harvey Cropper, not to be involved in racial strife. He will be a remarkable painter, not a fusty abstract fool, and besides, he cannot cure a problem insoluble at this time, and neither can I. I told him to paint, and that would be the simple for his days on this sorrowful earth. In the artistic world, the truthful people don't care what the color of a person is; what is significant is his work. As a matter of fact, we are fawning upon the Negro to such an extent that the worst scribblers are called geniuses just because they are black. Tell me, please, what difference is there in this cult of the Negro that now obtains among certain elements of the American populace and the nonsensical Marxism of the past, which did more harm to American Literature than anything else? And who was opposed to it? Who wrote the *Reactionary Essays* because he detested those Pygmies who were always wailing for one nation or another, and with the exception of a few persons, are they not all drossy? Of course, neither you nor I can be called reactionary; we just react, and I think that is what you had in mind, as a literary artist. I still tell Isabella to write poetry, and leave the Negro question to politicians and social welfare workers. Her involvement can only mar her verse, and I have told everybody I meet how gifted she is.

I pray that there is nothing in my retort that is wounding to your own sensibilities.

Let me give you my deep thanks for writing to the Rockefeller Foundation in my behalf.

We are, all of us, uneasy human animals, and when I received

Isabella's *eccentric* invitation, I knew that I should refuse it. But how do it, and not be offensive? Can you handle experience? I cannot. Should I commit an obtuse act, something intelligent comes of it, and if I endeavor to be good, I am bad.

What the two of you cannot know is that I fear going to other people's homes, and when I do, I leave as fast as I can, without seeming to be rude. It is not that I do not care deeply for my friends, or that I prefer to be with flimsy acquaintances rather than with the aristocratic intellects of our world. I dread unknowable disaster.

Both of you have my devoted love, which may be chaff, but it is better than the so-called wheat of the pharisaical stranger.

Your admiring friend,

letters to
Frank MacShane

Dear Mr. MacShane:

Your kind letter reached me a short while ago, and I am deeply sorry that I was not in New York at the time you were there. I loved Ford; he had the most tender heart of any man of letters I have ever known. He was supposed to have done the Introduction to my book, *Can These Bones Live,* and died several weeks after he had left his apartment at 10 Fifth Avenue.

Ford would meet you on Eighth Street, and ask you why you had not come to see him, or why you had not brought him a book you had written. One afternoon at the Brevoort, when it was a cheap Elysium for writers and artists, he said to me: "Let me be your literary agent; you get into too much trouble and are wild; you need someone like me to help you."

There have been some vulgar tales and gossip about Ford's lies. He said he had not consulted a single book or note for his *March of Literature.* Does it matter to me whether Don Quixote or Sancho Panza tells big windmill lies; that is chivalry of the soul. When he was dying, and I did not realize it, he was reading my Ms.

When good, precious Ford expired, I telephoned William Carlos Williams and suggested that we gather together and read some of his works and at least give the customary pusillanimous eulogy to the dead. Williams replied: "Death is a biological fact." I guess Bill Williams, now very ill and feeble, has a different point of view about the doleful fate of all flesh. Well, I don't say this with a bad heart towards Williams. We are all callow, and for the most part dead instead of quick in our attitudes toward the sorrows of others.

Ford used to give Thursday afternoons and always insisted that I come. He knew that I was likely to make some remark that would rouse hostile feelings in some upstart of letters, and he liked that. He would prod me, too, but always with joy in those tender, pelagic eyes, and never with malice.

This is a sparse and sterile note about a great man. Had he not been a genius because of his literary works, he would have been one because he had a paradisiacal heart. Sherwood [Anderson] who also told many artistic lies, which I admire, once said to me: "Ford, he is a big liar." But how little we know about our natures, generally blaming others for the faults we do not recognize in ourselves.

Forgive this fusty letter. It won't be of any use to you. But please know that I admire you for doing a critical biography of Ford.

Anyone who has radiant feelings about Ford Madox Ford is my friend.

Soller de Mallorca
July 9, 1961

Dear Mr. MacShane:

I must apologize for my meager letter to you. By the time your most courteous epistle reached me in Soller I thought it would be too late to write to you about Ford. Such a remark places another burden upon me. Will I be able to do any better now?

I had heard a good deal about Ford's legendary renown when I met him in his apartment which, I believe, was above the Rochambeau on Sixth Avenue at Eleventh Street. Quite raw, and gorged with Marxist boastfulness, I thought him old, flaccid, and porcine. A short time later I was one of a group of speakers on the platform at the New School for Social Research. We had come there to address a large audience and to organize a committee for indigent writers and artists. I suspect that the communist party had gotten the various people together. Anyway, I was rather startled to hear one celebrated man, who was talking to the persons in the hall, refer to me in the most complimentary manner. It was Ford who had turned toward me as he made this assertion.

Thereafter, I saw him on various occasions on Eighth Street; he had a slow, obese shuffle and his breathing was very hard. I looked at this Falstaffian bag of heaving clothes with some contempt. Could this be a demigod of letters? I had not read a single book of his. At about the same time, or maybe two or three years later, E. E. Cummings said to me: "What's the matter with Sherwood Anderson; how can a man allow his face to fall to pieces that way?" By then I was extremely vexed by such a pitiless view of hapless flesh. I recall looking at Cummings' puny, scathed countenance, and at his ineffectual nose.

Ford would stop me on Eighth Street or at lower Fifth Avenue and say: "When are you going to bring me your novels to read?" Imagine a man saying that to you today. He would either tell you that he was too busy to read your books because he was going abroad, beginning a volume himself, or trying to finish one. Ford stopped me on several occasions and repeated his query. Was I proud or stupid or just gauche? I came to his apartment one day and gave him my first two novels, *Bottom Dogs* and *From Flushing to Calvary*. When he had completed reading these he said: "What about the third one you wrote?" I gave him that also, and he told me that I was among the very few writers of autobiographical fiction who had succeeded in moving to a far less personal form of literature. He admired *Those Who Perish*, the third one, and later wrote a piece for *Forum* magazine on three neglected authors, William Carlos Williams, E. E. Cummings, and myself.

We had many arguments; he knew I was very passionate about books and a literary bigot, and he always did his best to raise my ire, and seldom failed. One day after one of my long iconoclastic fits, he said: "All Jews are nasty ikon-breakers." "What about Nietzsche?" I replied. I soon learned that his last wife Biala was a Jew. He cared for many authors I could not stomach, particularly Hemingway and also Faulkner. One day, his trousers very loose and his suspenders hanging down, he said while frying a pair of eggs in a skillet: "I think most of Shakespeare's plays were potboilers; certainly *Hamlet* was, and so was *Macbeth*." I thought this was a sacrilegious statement, but I thought about it afterwards a great deal.

Ford used to have Thursday afternoon teas at his apartment, 10 Fifth Avenue. He had two rooms, very sparsely furnished, a few secondhand chairs, a studio couch, a sofa for people who came for tea, Sutter's cookies, and outrageous declarations. It was perhaps the last literary salon in America, before virtually all of New York life was in the streets. The pair of wizened rooms were rented for sixty-five dollars a month. I went to these teas quite often, and Ford never failed to ask me to be sure to appear next week. Whether I made good or bad talk at these afternoons, he felt that if I were there there would not be sleepy conversation.

At the same time he wrote the *March of Literature* he told me when I was in his apartment that he had not consulted a single book to do this volume. He assured me that he had relied altogether on his memory. I remember when he said to me that swifts copulate on the wing, which I believe he got from *Selborne,* that wonderful nineteenth-century book on natural history. Ford had the reputation of being a liar. People either said he was fat or always lied. I received no other impression from Sherwood Anderson. Ford used to invite people to be a guest of his at a Southern manor which did not exist. Now what kind of lies were these? Ford had "windmills in his head"; if life could not provide him with the manor and the lucre his heart needed, why he had to invent them. Could he not be as generous as his nature demanded, why not indulge in apocryphal tales? Anderson too was a big liar, and he admitted it in his memoirs, but when he was sluggish, and far from a book, he forgot about his own inclinations. Who can impugn visionary perjuries of this sort?

About this time Dorothy Norman and I started a magazine called *Twice a Year.* At a party somewhere, in the neighborhood of Columbia University, I asked Ford whether he would not contribute to *Twice a Year,* maybe do a Paris Letter. He was going abroad and the party was in his honor. As always, he was most charming and modest notwithstanding some of his naïve

boasts. Ford sent me a piece which I could not read. Dorothy
Norman had agreed quite readily when I told her that Ford
would do something for each issue. I was exceedingly embar-
rassed. I was familiar with *Portraits from Life,* his *Personal Re-
membrances of Joseph Conrad,* and *Return to Yesterday,* and I
considered him a deeply experienced prose stylist. I was particularly moved by his portrait of "Stevie Crane," and though I have
never cared for Henry James I think he did a magical essay on
him. And who unless he were uncouth could be impervious to his
description of Turgenev?

The fault may have been mine; maybe Ford's ten-to-twelve-
page article for which he was to receive the kingly sum of fifty
dollars was very good. It takes a long time to misunderstand a
great person. In short, I gave the piece to Dorothy Norman and
she did not care for it at all. Then I said: "Will you please send
Ford the check; he needs the money." She refused. I had an
acrimonious two hours with Stieglitz pleading with him to persuade Dorothy Norman to pay Ford, but she would not do it.

Ford was very angry with me. I wrote him begging him not to
be vexed with me, saying that I was probably a fool in not being
able to appreciate what he had done, but not a knave. I had
parted with Dorothy Norman, withdrawn my own work, and
asked that my name be deleted from the magazine, although I
was responsible for the first issue.

I asked a friend to go to Ford and explain what had happened.
Then one day I saw him in front of the old Brevoort Hotel about
to get into a cab, and I ran after him, and told him I wanted to
see him. He was not too pleased and reluctantly consented.

He forgave me, and one day at his apartment, William Carlos
Williams, Ford, and I were talking about Pound's Fascism and
Jew-baiting. Both Ford and Williams were very distressed. Suddenly, Ford turned to me, and said: "Why don't we start a
group, meet, say once a month, in order to get Bill Williams'
books published?" I replied with much exuberance, and Ford
thought, and then said: "How about a name? What do you think
of calling the group the Friends of William Carlos Williams?" I
said I considered it a very good name. Ford drew up a list of
names of people whom he thought we should invite to join.

Among these were Paul Rosenfeld, Anderson, Marsden Hartley, Stieglitz, the painter Elizabeth Sparhawk Jones, altogether about fifty. I asked him to expunge some of the names as I said there is no point in getting together the enemies of literature to be the friends of the very authors they have been suppressing. Ford smiled; he had not had so many obscure protégés whose cause he had advanced against so many Philisters without appreciating my feeling. The young, valiant James Laughlin was also a member of the group. We met once a month at the Downtown Gallery on Thirteenth Street. There were I believe three dinners given for three authors, Williams, Cummings, and myself. Ford presided at all these meetings, and I must say a wonderful galaxy of genuine people in the arts attended these affairs. I say this because it could have been a piece of Dada nonsense, or worse, something for poeticules.

Cummings refused to attend the dinner given in his honor which I felt was most discourteous and even base. The third one was given to me, and I read from a Ms., later to be published as *Can These Bones Live*. As a result of these felicitous evenings once a month Ford got publishers interested in Williams and was himself responsible for the publication of Williams' *The White Mule*. After my own reading I was told that Ford had persuaded a woman to give fifteen hundred dollars as a prize for the best piece of work done up till that time, and that I was to receive this money.

Shortly thereafter, I brought the finished Ms. to Ford and he read it. What I did not know then was that he was dying. One day he walked with me across the street from 10 Fifth Avenue to the Brevoort, and told me I had written a book of genius, and after paying me so many delightful compliments he advised me to have nothing to do with publishers. He said that I was too wild, too forthright, and could only be my worst adversary. Some while before Harrison Smith had bought the *Saturday Review*, and I had urged him to employ Ford as the literary editor. Of course, he had no intention of doing that; far too shrewd, he was interested in a business sheet of letters. I had antagonized him as I was quite put out when he refused to take such an opportunity.

Ford told me that day that he would be my literary agent; I

was then not thirty-nine, my development had been most sluggish, and my star had already fallen into the dust. I did not know
how to thank this man whom I had once looked upon as a
decayed gentleman of quondam arts, asthmatic and obscenely
gross in bulk. That day I had the occasion to look at his eyes;
Lawrence, whom Ford disliked, had spoken of Ford who had the
"dove-gray eyes of the Shulamite." He had the large Mediterranean orbs of Astarte; but no matter. Lawrence had gotten the
man, and it was the truth. One never knows where a man's
genius is, in his hands, cheeks, or in that great upland forehead
of Ford's, or the eyes of Anderson, which resembled those of the
cow-goddess Io.

I asked Ford whether he would write the Introduction, and he
told me how proud he would be to do that. He took the Ms. with
him when he sailed for France, and three weeks later a great man
had died in Deauville. I was utterly prone when I read the
obituary notice in the *Tribune*. I had lost the most steadfast
friend I had ever had in literature. Most authors are a perfidious
lot, weathervane critics, but not this good, savory identity.

Ford had very little money, and I can say that I heard of no
one who spoke of his books at all, saying that they were either
good or ill. I never heard anybody mention the Tietjens books. I
must freely own that I had not read them myself. It is a hard
statement for me to make since I loved Ford, and never tried to
exploit his outrageously kind heart. I did not have the chance to,
had I been so boorish; he had already offered to do everything
for me.

You doubtless know of the New Directions memorial issue to
Ford; I wrote a piece there, and maybe you saw my tender words
about him in *Can These Bones Live*.

Like Sherwood Anderson at that period, Ford was a fabulous
name in literature, but a forsaken one. I never even recollect that
Anderson ever referred to a single book that Ford had written.
Despite Ford's long essay on Dreiser in *Portraits from Life*
Dreiser never once spoke to me of any book by Ford.

I am almost positive that the *March of Literature* was remain-
dered. Again, I must be regarded as being no less base than those
I mention. I had not read the volume either. For some reason or

other I got the impression that it was an academic anthology of literature, and I abhor anthologies. I tell you this because I believe it conveys the apathy toward this genius.

Even when Knopf did the Tietjens books they were a failure; that is my impression. Ford represented a pleasant, expatriate fable; everybody feigned to admire him, but not only was he neither read nor misread; most of his books were not known to those whom he helped. And Ford was the Archangel of every obscurian, every illuminated waif of the Muses who could not get into a magazine or into a book. I know he was poor because I used to go to see his widow, Biala, simply out of respect for Ford. I thought this was a marriage of convenience too. She did not get money out of this, but she did derive a social literary position that meant a great deal to her. She had come from the dumps of Provincetown, where she had painted and starved. Ford, of course, arranged to get her a one-man show, and it was a big affair that I attended. However, much as I disrelish this woman, it must be said that she lived at least for some years after his demise in a loft on Twenty-third Street off Lexington Avenue. I doubt that even now the revenue from Ford's books could be much more than metaphysical.

He was a close friend of Allen Tate's, an intimate friend of mine, whom I did not know then. And I should find it hard to believe that he could have indulged too much in what Randolph Bourne called "the new orthodoxies of propaganda." Still, he was an ardent advocate of my own Marxist novel, *Those Who Perish*. But he associated with all sorts of people at the end, Padraic Colum, as Roman Catholic as Tate was in those days. But I cannot speak with any assurance. He detested Nazism, and I believe he wanted to die before another world war took place, before France was destroyed. He had as poor luck with his books as he had with women in the fag end of his great heartbreak life. I know he had asked a fine, buxom, and rather demented wench, Polly Boyden, of Chicago, to marry him, but she refused.

I don't go to Deya, and I see almost nobody here; I am not wooing solitude, but that is the way it has turned out. I was in Palma in '54, I think, spring, and am very sorry that I did not see you then.

I have jotted these things down in great haste, and I don't know whether I have said anything of use to you or not. But you can believe that I have the most ardent love of Ford, his works, his life. Once Unamuno said: "I am not a Cervantist; I am a Quixotist." It is a beautiful distinction, and it fits Ford Madox Ford; he was everybody's warrior; as far as I am concerned he had no faults, or if he had any I wish to God that I could borrow them, for I could live better with his defects than I can with my alleged virtues.

You have, be sure, my deepest and friendliest sympathy and regard. Would to heaven that I could be more useful; the truth is that we never see people at all; we imagine we do, not even clever enough to realize that we do not know anything about ourselves, either. And that is why we are so coarse; we are too phlegmatic to be valiant or even charitable enough to perceive a great man.

letters to
Stanley Burnshaw

Dear Stanley:

I have thought about you a great deal. You can have no doubts about my affections for you, but I could not accept one of your epistles which troubled me greatly. Ultimately, I don't care whether Dudley Fitts or you or Josephine Herbst care about my work or not. I mention the three only as examples. I tried to placate Fitts because he was exceedingly kind; I am not endeavoring to be any sort of tactician with him, you, or anybody else. Were I that kind of devil I should not have written *Truth Is More Sacred*. I felt that you were pusillanimous; the problems are too heavy to be dismissed by you as "excellent reading" as though you were a scribbler for the press. What need have I of a friend who spends more than half a letter praising a trifling article on Wallace Stevens, a very niggish poet, and who passes over a book that took me a lustrum of pain, reading, and writing, to compose. You told me you were uneasy because some of your remarks which I used (for your advantage, I thought) would bring about an estrangement between you and Herbert Read, but did not appear to be qualmish when you said you were more sympathetic with his point of view than with mine (what point of view?). Then I must needs ask you, what is the groundwork of our affections, and how could you so fervently admire *Can These Bones Live* and *The Sorrows of Priapus*, and speak so to me. Why should you find yourself so cool in writing to me when you are fearful that if you spoke in a similar way or expressed yourself as you had about Eliot that you would deeply annoy Herbert Read? As for myself, I do not care a straw whether my vision and my truth are too heavy for Read's back or not. He wrote a perfidious epistle on Eliot, which had absolutely nothing to do with literary criticism, no matter what canons you might imagine you could refer to or what invisible Jacob's Ladder you might climb to ascend to Angelic Contemplation. You don't in the name of charity impugn one friend while you viciously assail another, and even at that without adducing the least evidence that might prove that you had any reason to maintain that Eliot is not a *mungrell versifier*.

I do not, moreover, care for the overworldly aesthetical treatment that obtains in our refined, but effete textbooks on literature. Nor do I place my heart in false scales, which you must do every time you endeavor to weigh the importance of a poet by considering to what extent he represents his times. Any vile newspaper is also a mirror of the times, and if you take one thousand gutter papers together and bind them, you have a modern novel. One man told me that I had to be familiar with Pascal's controversies to comprehend the *Pensées*; he also advised me that the great Pascal had a sour disposition and was much given to heated disputes. So was Swift, who said that he hoped to make his fame by controversy. As for myself, I have in so many ways a feeling of revulsion about being known that I have not the least cause to continue writing save that I have nothing better to do with my life.

If you are the bridegroom of oblivion, as you have told me so often, what does it matter to you whether your truths bother Herbert Read or not? You have to abide by what you think. Do you imagine that I could write such a book and not know what a load of Tyre it would be upon my head, and how I would sow dragon's teeth by doing it?

I owe Herbert Read some genuine thanks, but he owes me something too, two dedications to two books. At the time, Read, who had desired the pleasure of such a tribute, advised me that it would be inexpedient for me to express my feelings for him and in such a public way, since he was going to write about the book. I paid not the least heed to such counsel as I never had. Moreover, Read has not written a whole book in twenty years, with the exception of those horror volumes on art. I have rebuked him for twenty years but as a friend.

Read is a lovely stylist, or has been; I do not here attempt to comprehend the metaphysics of a person, the riddle of another nature, how he will unfold or if he will. He has involved himself more and more in art, Jung, and heaped upon his prose style all the thorns and briers of psychology which are the tares of modern English. Doubtless he has had a subterranean rancor against me, for each time he brought out a volume he omitted my name, and I pointed out that he would rather mention the *Hudson Review* (he quarreled with the editor later, anyway, and never referred to that periodical again) than speak of me. I stand by a man, and am not such a fusty or clever liar as to feign to admire him privately; and his essays on me are of a privy sort since he refused to include them in any volume of his, or even to intimate that I exist. That is one of the principal reasons that I insisted on bringing your name into the volume, and someday, when you realize that I have told the truth about poets and that Read was guided by the most craven of gods, self-interest, you will have a different opinion of the epistles and of me. That you don't now does not matter except that you know I have taken a perilous position without regard to fame or expediency or people, and their mass shibboleths, and you should be the first to come to my defense. Do you know that Baudelaire could not get Saint-Beuve to write about him for no other cause than that he was a controversial figure and that that old codger of letters simply did not care to risk his reputation.

Josephine Herbst, who has told me how great her admiration is for me, had the effrontery to say that after reading my essay on *Moby-Dick* she had to revise her whole idea regarding me, and my work. Maybe now you may have some moiety of comprehension regarding my own vexation with you. What you feel about me and my iconoclasm is deeply related to your own brave vision. You cannot be a parcel of the whole Pound and Eliot perfidy in literature, and be an advocate of a *Hero of Silence*. You fall or get up after falling every day of your life by removing yourself from such mangy jades of our new Hellas.

To repeat, the temporal conception of a poet is false; when I read François Villon I do not have to be familiar with his times in order to value him as a poet; I do not have to know all the bile and bitterness of his life to comprehend his great visionary

malice (unlike Eliot, a simpering, peevish man with abundant
vile feelings about Donne, Blake, and Hobbes, all his superior
cherubim by far); I do not feign that I have no rancor in my
heart against my enemies. I have, but I am also far more interested in understanding what I am doing when I write, though I
do not know why I write or for whom, to allow ill feeling to
stand in the way of my perceptions. I might impugn a man I did
not like were he a bad writer, but never if he were a good one. I
don't like Robert Graves, and refused to shake hands with him
when I was in Mallorca some time in 1954 because I thought he
was an ambitious charlatan. Read had expressed his great reluctance even to write about him. Graves had attacked Read, and
the latter said that he did not consider Graves worthy of being
included in our book. I replied that I didn't think Pound and
Eliot were either, but that we had certain didactic tasks to per-
form, and that we had to be of use to students and to apprentices
in literature.

It was my duty, and is, to sweep the dung out of the Augean
stables of literature, and that is what I did. What did Read do?
Instead of saying even in a word or two what Graves was, or in
place of not bothering altogether, he praised him! Why? The
answer is simple; Read is a very timorous man, and has a reputation to protect, lectures at sundry colleges, a position as one of
the directors of Routledge although they will not allow him to
select one book a year that he believes is worth a reader's good
and honest eyes. I go into the world as a writer as naked as I
shall be when I go out of it. Does that mean I have no interest in
being known, or that I desire to print books that will be thrown
into some pauper's grave or necropolis for books? It only means
that I won't pay Judas' price for a reputation, because I do not
care for posterity, for one matter, and for another, it would not
make a great deal of difference to me should I finish *Because I
Was Flesh* and then disappear. Can you understand why Congreve was so bored when Voltaire came to England to talk about
his plays that he refused to discuss them or letters at all? I who
do not share your feelings, and am not deliberately looking in
the streets for alms for oblivion, understand him.

I now have a kidney infection, and sorely troubled about that;

I came to Dublin for blowy weather; I had fallen into a sick inertia in Spain that was more like death than breathing even the Ephesian sod.

I shall stay here, God willing, as the Scripture saith, until the money is used up, or go to the west Irish coast when the cold days have come to a close. I do not know.

Laughlin abused me greatly too for assailing Eliot, asserting that what I said about him was now to my disadvantage. He has been a steadfast friend, like yourself, up till the publication of *Truth Is More Sacred*. After an exchange of many epistles in which this fine man accused me also of being uncharitable while he wrote me the most uncivil, and unmerciful letters, I no longer bridled my own tongue, but suggested that his own words, so uncharitable and even savage at moments, should be scrutinized by him. In short, it is all healed, and I hope so, for I never had a dispute with this man in the fourteen years that he has published verse, essays, and books of mine.

I suppose we ought to compose a poem as if our souls were about to be required by the Angel of Death, and if somebody, noddle or fool or shrewd nature for one cause or another happens not to mislike it, consider that the poor, bitter bread of this world. To imagine that you want obscurity, and that nothing on this earth would give you more opulent satisfaction, shows an impoverished understanding of yourself. Let us begin by admitting that we are ambitious, vain, stupid, liars, fools and will hang a friend for a button on one's shirt, and then maybe there is some jot of hope for us. The other way is too dangerous.

Now to other matters: I am very much honored by your dedication to me, and do admire the poem very much. I have always thought that if you could separate yourself from the market place, Holt, Eliot, Pound, and Wallace Stevens, and hoaxing aesthetics, that you would be a remarkable poet; I have said a pure, Arctic visionary. Though I believe a man ought to be as hot as Giordano Bruno who has said that not even the snows of the Alps could cool him, I am not impervious to all sorts of natures provided they are not mundane. I hate the world; William Carlos Williams, who has some talent, once had it in a single volume, but has a mean grudging culture, says that one ought to love the world; I might as well advise a man to run barefoot through the streets, eating nothing but herbs, lentils, and bread made of roots and tree bark in order to be pure and ascetic enough to embrace a lawyer, a beadle, or a pimp.

You have not sent me the proofs of the *Moby-Dick* essay. I accept almost every suggestion and excision you have made; though I cannot include your scorn for the writers of the Restoration. It is not very sensible to throw away Wycherley, Will Congreve, Dryden, Etherege, while you espouse the small, brittle puns, and the scatological jokes of Pound and Eliot. In short, we are not brave because we admire Homer, which any dunce can now do, though if he had met him, he would have taken him for an illiterate singer of low ballads and a blind beggar; it is far better to make a mistake about the gnomes who are only strong enough to chase cranes on the River Strymon—that is, if it be an error to take them for the dwarfs that they are—than to lard your own nature with all their foul droppings. We are the times, whether we will it or not, and what we are looking for is a hero or an epical antihero, if that makes any sense, and not the epigones of letters.

I hope this letter, too often written in words poorly chosen, will explain in some sort my own feeling.

It was a deep relief to hear that you are in sound health.

My love and friendship.

Dublin
November 15, 1961

Dear Stanley:

Your long epistle arrived here yesterday, and the very lovely poem dedicated to me for which I give you my deepest thanks. Now I should tell you that I find discord between us a maiming experience. Spite of my great fondness for you, and admiration for your gifts, I am troubled by your contradictions. First, you tell me, Stanley, that you do not talk about your work. But, Stanley, in the letter I received from you when I was in Spain, you spent half of a lengthy letter on an article you wrote when you were a radical boy of letters, and dismissed a great book that took me a lustrum of reading and writing with "excellent reading," and "I am more sympathetic with Herbert Read's point of view than yours." I read the article, and I have not the least disagreement with you regarding your viewpoint on Wallace Stevens. I read *Harmonium* in '29 or '30, and did not find it the kind of viaticum I look for in poetry. I have never had any interest since then in this deceased vice president of an insurance company.

I look for a whole body and intelligence in a man's work, and if a bad person, or a savagely mediocre one, like Eliot or Pound, has done a few scattered lines, that is not enough for me to excuse the basilisk influence he has had on an infernal generation of zero minds, in part, made so by such polysyllabic illiterates. You say I scream, so did Ruskin, and Jeremiah, and Unamuno, all of whom I have read for years, and aside from the defects of my own identity, I must have learned to shriek from them; but the eagle does so too, and lives in a mountain eyrie, where I pine to nest, and all sorts of truthful books are noises of one kind or another. Coleridge was hardly a quiet man, and Hazlitt was waspish. No more; what I am saying is that I must do this because I have certain didactic principles that I abide by, to my peril or not.

You say you hate reviews and criticism, and yet some marvelous work has been done by savants without which our lives would be more niggard than they are. And you are so grateful when your work is reviewed by Read or Josephine Herbst, and I imagine they gave you more than one hundred and fifty words which you seem to think is sufficient to cover a work that took me as long to consummate as it did for Jacob to acquire Leah, and maybe I have never gained anything in this world but Leah, but I don't think you or I can be so clever as to write about a serious and honest book in so few words. But these are some of the contradictions I mean, Stanley; you are ecstatic when others pay heed to your work, but think you should not bother about anybody else's books. Now I have an enormous distaste for deceit and chicane, and though I understand your feeling and even

when you regard yourself as a bridegroom of oblivion, I also
know that the heart is much too guileful for either of us to be
content with just that. Sure, I am at this writing quite sick in my
bowels when I consider what fame is, and how you come by it.
Herbert Read, some of whose books I deeply admire, is not getting an honorary degree from a college for his probity; were that
so we would both have received all sorts of honors years ago. Nor
does Eliot or Pound or any of the other Myrmidons of letters
become well known because they are even as indifferent-honest as
Hamlet. Now, you are very upset by Allen, but when you read
Read's last envenomed epistle which had little or nothing to do
with literature or with Eliot, but was an adder's hiss, you are not
quick enough to grasp what is occurring. Do you really believe
that Read, doing a book with a man whose prose style he com-
pares with Sir Thomas Browne and Robert Burton, deserves that
kind of bile? I may not enjoy it, but I consider it even as I think
about the lilies or the cockatrice, and wonder why there is one
and also the other.

When you advise me that you are more sympathetic with
Herbert Read's point of view than with mine, I must needs ask
you what point of view? Now let me not take advantage of you
by reminding you again that I had to tether your wrath against
Read so that he would be of some real use to you. I have no
invidious meaning when I say this, any more than I had when I
told you that I used your quotations because I honored them,
and felt that they were your truths, and that if I mentioned you,
quoted you, it would be of some advantage to you, since I have
been your advocate for a long while, speaking of you warmly
to Read, Josephine, and to Isabella and Allen. You ask me do I
know Allen's essay on Eliot; my reply and it is not a canting one,
is no, though I have read many of his essays and find some of them
genuinely gifted as I have said. He told me that he thought *The
Sacred Wood* flimsy, and though I believe I told him I had the
most pelting regard for Eliot's doggerel, I do not recall what he
said. Read too wrote a very prolix essay on Pound, which I
commenced to read, and it so galled my soul and bowels that I
left off.

I had felt that notwithstanding certain differences in temperament, we were quite close, and I can assure you that you will never enjoy that intimacy with Read as you have with me. He is too busy, and that as I have said innumerable times is the greatest malady of our century or of Pascal's for that matter. He will do you a service, for he is a most courteous soul, and even write an introduction for you, which he will forget about and have an agreeable pair of hours with you, and then rush off for a meeting with the Bollingen boys or go to a college for fools and rogues for another degree.

I do not care whether Eliot represents his times or not, but I do care whether John Webster does or to a lesser extent Bunyan does. I go to the best for my temporal as well as my angelic experiences. And to repeat, I cannot begin to read the best poems that have been composed, and have no time to waste on rogues of Helicon simply because they managed to get off a good line now and then.

I thought a great deal of your marvelous acuity in your long letter to me regarding the Melville essay, and though I hardly blame you for reprinting your article on Stevens in the *Sewanee* and am delighted that you were given first place, the piece is far beneath you. Some of your lackadaisical clichés and use of French words bother me; we should employ foreign words very seldom. Tolstoy felt this and so did John Dryden whose *Dramatic Essays* are extraordinary, and which received the least amount of attention in their time, as a matter of fact, were utterly neglected. I am referring to words like ambience, and a lot of the claptrap of the academics which a poet like you should severely eschew. Ben Jonson has quite a catalogue of such heavy, cumbersome words in his *Poetasters*.

Of course, when I picked up *Poetry,* most of what I read of the other versifiers, if they can be called that, gave me jaundice. You have purity of line, but I think, Stanley, you must go farther; now, please, don't be annoyed with me; you did a beautiful and very wondrous rendering of Mallarmé. You cannot push your own sensibilities beyond certain confines without symbols which you will make your own. You will deepen your line so; just as Jonson does, though he fails more often than not maybe for the same reason, because his line is too stuffed while yours is too bare.

You rely, I think, too greatly upon yourself. For years I have beseeched you to go to the ancients or to some masters, just as you have chosen Mallarmé, which is wonderful. He went to others too, as Vergil went to Homer and Dante to Homer. Otherwise you get no more out of a poem, really pure as yours is, but private rather than artistic experiences, or shall I say, to be quite banal myself, a plural instead of a single experience.

I know, Stanley, I cannot persuade you to take a book of mine to your bosom if you cannot. Maybe you are in part right when you say my work should appear by itself, but then if that is so, we cannot appear in periodicals, as you do in *Sewanee* or in *Poetry*, and I should feel deeply sorry if you did not. I do not think you want, despite your genuine disgust with shrewd and monied souls, and also mine, Gehenna as a poet. You wish to be read, and you desire speech with some soul as lonely as your own, and as surrounded as all of us are by wild, tangled forests which prevent us from ever crossing over to the boundaries of another person. If one could only comprehend one person, that would be the miracle perhaps of greater worth than the knowledge that there is a God, or equal to it. But one cannot. It takes years and years to misunderstand another one, and a great deal of drudgery, and I am just as much of a charwoman in this respect as anybody else.

All this goes to you, Stanley, with love and admiration, and I do wish you would not be so contradictory. You did speak disparagingly of the Restoration writers. You may be quite right in saying that I should remove the quotations, but I cited them because they have flesh and pulses, even their teasing, shallow, babbling lines, while Melville had not. Still, to repeat, your close work on the *Moby-Dick* essay resulted in great advantages to me, and if I ask you to send it to me here, that does not mean that I shall do much meddling with your labor, maybe little or none, but certainly little. I trust you in many ways, and wish I could trust you altogether, if I had the nature to have that much confidence in a single soul. I can tell you that I scarcely trust myself at all, and should imagine that I was gross and base if I did.

At this writing what have I to brag about? *Bottom Dogs* has been republished. I did not even know it till yesterday, and I have never seen page proofs even of the short introduction I did attacking the book. I imagine my own words are not much good; I also cited Josephine. I do this whenever I can and I certainly would not do it unless I believed in the lines or had real genuine feeling for the author.

Your drumbling comments about Herbert and me still bite my veins. Why should Read praise Graves when he told me he despised him, and did not consider him worth our attention? Or why should he assert that I am garbling the Platonic Socrates when I quote Plato who says: "Truth is more sacred than Friendship." Now Read, at the outset, when I suggested the book to him, said quite meekly that I knew much more about the ancients than he did, and then he takes such an obvious remark which anyone knowing the least bit about Socrates would know and says that I am misusing the quotation. Socrates reprehended Alcibiades and Critias, one of the thirty tyrants, and both his friends. But people are terribly perverse; Graves says in the beginning of *The White Goddess* that he abhors homosexuals, and then in a review in an English paper about four or five years ago suggested that Aldington ought to be horsewhipped because he showed what a pathic T. E. Lawrence was. Or how, to go back to Read, can one be just when you defend one friend by attacking another? Oh well, the whole matter is a bore, and you are quite right, Stanley, I should not waste my strength in all this, and write the best I can, and now that I am ailing, and have God knows what kind of serious disorder, I have blood cells and albumen in my kidneys, and have to go to hospital Monday or Tuesday for X-rays, and I spent so much of my money on the house so that I have to guard my shillings. Who has any sense, not I, and I pray Stanley that you do not misunderstand me; I rejoice in your separation from Holt; believe me, you cannot do the work you are best fitted for, poetry, and be engaged all day long, even three days or more, in idiotic commerce. Never think I do not have genuine feeling for your gifts, and only despair that as close as I feel to you I should get no more than a miser's pence in words about a book that caused me much suffering, and now hatred and derision from boobs and scoundrels.

I wait further word from Laughlin, a very good man; we had quite a dispute, the first one in fourteen or fifteen years; I never minded his critical suggestions, some of them exceedingly good, but when he tried to deprive me of the liberty of my own judgments and feelings I could no longer bridle my tongue—one should, I know—and I must here beg your pardon, Stanley, for writing you an acrimonious letter. I know I should write you in composure, and do nothing to offend you, for I do not wish to. You must realize that whether you are more solitary than I am, or I than you, I do not know, I write you far more than anybody else except Rlene now. But even here I hardly send her such a long garrulous letter, and I fear tiresome too, for I am sick, and in a very despondent mood. Much of the autobiography is already chaff in my mouth; how can I heal naturalism by ritual, by the gods, or by nature, lichen, hawthorn, sumac, Tantalus, Sisyphus, all of which can be affected and false too if that does not become my own living loaf.

Stanley, you have done me many kindnesses, and I was only dismayed because of your barest mention of my book, and I am not unmindful of your wonderful dedication of your pure poem (I can't read the other things there; what dross and offal from the Augean stables do I find in that magazine). Please again forgive me if any of my remarks supposed to be criticism only fret you. Maybe I should not do it at all. I wish I knew at this time what to do. I don't; I sit in a room and suck my own paws, and a thousand untold griefs and follies, and wonder if I can write one line that comes from Potosi where it is said that grass does not grow because wherever there is gold and silver it is barren.

Again, my love and deep thanks, Stanley, for the dedication.

This is a fissured reply; would that it were more reasonable, but I have not the patience for logic, which has nothing to do with our acts and the imaginings of our erring hearts. I wanted to tell you also how close I feel to you when you write about Santa Teresa, the Jewess of Avila, a prodigious seer though I confess that too much humility and an avowal of a plethora of sins (though the body and the mind are the biggest sins) vex me. When she is not the sister of Christ, and her lines are not the customary trash of the Church, I admire her. I am genuinely sorry that Valerie is so far from you. I don't like San Francisco as a place for such a tender, warm mammal. Could we only commit the mistakes for others instead of our own, one might not be a fool every day and each hour.

I did *not* ask the publisher to send you *Bottom Dogs* because I think you have better things to do than to be reading a first novel of mine.

Dublin
January 3, 1962

Dear Stanley:

I was very glad to get your letter, and give you all my thanks for your concern with my health. Of course, you are right, Stanley, disputation is sterile. When you tell me that you know yourself better than I know you, my simple reply is that I don't know anything about anybody. Were I to go to Delphi and to be told, Know Thyself, I should hear it with the greatest confusion, and were I asked what I knew about myself, what good clear words would I have to say about myself? I would, my good friend, contrary to your lucid feelings about your own nature, assert that I am not meek, am egregiously vain, peevish, querulous, ambitious, and while disclosing all my defects would have to freely own that I was being outrageously charming in admitting what a monster I am.

You are, with all good and affectionate regard for you, a chameleon nature. I don't know where I stand or where you do. Years ago you sent me your book of verse wanting very much my opinion of it. Then when we became friends, you were eager to have Herbert Read read it, so that you might gain his esteem for it. Naturally, it was my utmost desire to please you, for contrary to my irascible identity, I like very much to please my very few friends, though I sometimes think that if I went that far for my foes I should fare much better in this world.

Now after a year of letter-writing to Herbert Read, I got him to engage his interest in you, and arranged a meeting between the two of you, while you, Stanley, were seething, boiling, and were a furnace of wrath, for all of which I do not blame you one tittle. What I now find culpable in you is that you tell me you have no regard for Herbert's ideas on you. You tell me the only three people you respect or whose conceptions of your verse you have feeling for are Allen Tate, Frost, and Cummings, all of whom have praised you, no doubt. We love ourselves, it is an infernal truth, and I wish it were a lie.

Now another matter comes to mind; you wrote me a short while ago that you were more sympathetic with Herbert Read's point of view than mine. So now, my stable and staunch friend, if you care more for Herbert Read's reactions to your work, though you do not really care a straw for his reflections regarding your poems, where do I, poor gnome, Edward Dahlberg, fit into this dismal picture? I guess I don't. Why you ever courted or solicited my responses which you never wanted, is just another Sphinx without riddles.

You might be surprised to learn how many have been deeply affected by *Can These Bones Live*; few have ever made any acknowledgments to me, but if you are a quick and clever reader, you should have seen that a poor wight like myself has affected many a writer in America, some you genuinely esteem.

Now, your disgust with such a dwarf of merchandizing letters as Rahv I altogether appreciate. While you were being the iconoclastic editor of *New Masses*, after it was reorganized, the communists would not even put my name on the masthead. When it was to be made into a journalistic rag, three people were very disconcerted, Kunitz, Freeman, and myself, and at the meeting only one person made a vehement protest, myself, the other two were pusillanimous.

As for Rahv, I assailed him about thirty years ago as an oleaginous churl; I was asked to found the *Partisan Review*, and when Rahv and Phelps, now Phillips, came in, I walked out, and my name has never been mentioned in that high church of the comma and semicolon. You see, you can get into the *Partisan Review*, hobnob with Trilling, and all the other impostors of literature, but I cannot. No book of mine, because I am such a belly pragmatist, has been reviewed in the *Partisan Review*, the *Saturday Review* (until Hicks' piece, and he has been waiting to lay hands on a volume of mine for thirty years), the *Herald Tribune*, while you, my brave and stalwart man, can.

I had hoped you would not take my acerb remarks about a piece you had written a generation ago with much solemnity. You interest me as a poet, and my recent criticism of you was really positive, what I wanted you to do is to make an addition to your vision. I think your translation, if it is not really your own poem, is brilliant, and I admire it exceedingly. The use of Idumean heightens the entire vision, takes it out of the Valley of Hinnom, out of drab, particular experience and transforms it into a plural vision, all the experiences of other seers that pulse in such a magnificent poem which I attribute to Mallarmé and you. Again, I wish to give you my deepest thanks for honoring me with the poem which came out of a warm, adhesive talk we had together. It gives me pleasure to repeat that, because I care very much for the poem, and care very much for the dedication.

As for Cummings, I find him a tedious urchin and street gamin of versification. I never liked him personally, because he is a shallowpate, with a little nose stuck up in the air like a puffed-up weasel of Parnassus. Allen I am exceedingly fond of, and admire, but his association with people like Trilling and Rahv put me off, and I find it even now baffling to care so much for a man I had formerly distrusted because he consorted with persons I consider evil. Too, I could not get a book of mine examined in the *Kenyon Review*, and Allen was a very close friend of Ransom's. Ransom had written to Ford Madox Ford that I was a prophet but that he was *afraid* to publish a segment of *Can These Bones Live*; consequently he did not have the book or any other volume of mine reviewed there before or after that time.

Now, I don't trouble with book reviews, but if I am to get published at all—remember I was not a vice president of Henry Holt—I must not have my books interred as they are by many savage simpletons. I turn to you, Stanley, not for a book review but for literary criticism, quite a different matter. Baudelaire was most disconsolate when he could not get people to defend *Les*

Fleurs du Mal, and Congreve says it is the duty of poets to protect the Muses, and sacred poems and works by those who are wholly concerned with telling the truth.

As for your own work, it satisfies me, but not enough; I want you to break the Cordilleras, to thaw the cold regions of Potosi, to get therefrom either silver ore or grass, as the latter does not grow where such metals are abundant. As the friend of your nature and your own minerals and fruits in Paradise, I must do what I am doing. Have I not been after you to disentangle yourself with business since we have been friends? Tell a man to do a good thing, and he will do it and forget that you have advised him to do it, but not forget to hate you for having irritated him by giving him wise counsel.

Now I am exceedingly fond of Herbert Read; but he threw me into the ditch; a quick-witted man here who read the book* saw that at once. You are so sharp about people who compromise, and Read confesses that he and Eliot have made many compromises, but he states quite explicitly that I have not. And if you knew all the facts about my association with people, and you can hardly say that I carry on a wily connection with you, annoying you, and being your gadfly as I have been Read's, you might begin to ask yourself who is the iconoclast.

Read and I discussed our book; the volume was my idea; he had been savagely attacked by Graves, and said that Graves should not be included in our volume because he was not a man of letters, good or bad. How startled I was then when Read praised Graves. How surprised was I when Read, who freely owned that I knew far more about Greek literature and philosophy than he, should take the title which came out of one of my epistles, and say that I had mutilated Plato's words. Now, anybody who has any intimate familiarity with the Socratic life, grounded upon Plato's works, Xenophon's *Memorabilia,* and Grote's marvelous portrait—of a man who did not, according to his own words, regard himself as the hero of dialectics, and who though he loved friends, was continually reprehending Alcibiades and Critias the tyrant—could not possibly make such a charge.

* *Truth Is More Sacred*

It was the publisher who took the title from my own quotation, and Read agreed to it, after which he claimed that I had misused it. He did not read the books for our volume, and he freely owns it, says that he could not reread them, more, he admits that he is only the devil's advocate, in this book of ours, and he agrees with virtually everything I say, until we get to the Eliot essay, and that touched his wallet, lectures, reputation, position with regard to academics. For over thirty-two years I have known this man, and he has done me many kindnesses, save the one that I required most, and which has to do with imponderables, and only marginally with fame and lucre; he has written introductions, two, and one essay, beautifully written about *The Sorrows of Priapus*. But in every book that Read writes I am not only not mentioned; one could ask is there such a man as Edward Dahlberg, a writer? It is no accident to bury a man whom you say you greatly admire, and whom you rank with Browne and Burton, and to be his embalmer for twenty-five years. The introductions have never gotten into the books, nor any hint of my work. Am I clear now? Am I peevish or just too self-loving? Was not the great Edmund Spenser brokenhearted at the end of his life because he was obscure? Being truthfully acknowledged by your own peers is quite another matter from being thought a gilded or gelded guttersnipe of Hellas in the penny papers.

Now when I first met Allen Tate he said that until he had met me he had regarded Herbert Read as the most learned man of letters in the world.

To return to Read and to you; I did not believe that you were as eager to be obscure as you say; true or not, I could have been the sort of friend who took you at your word and as your friend buried your work to make sure that you had all the oblivion you craved. But knowing how I have been lacerated by people who gave me privy esteem and who each time they published a book did not mention me, I wanted to be straight and plain and not subtle with you. Let my foes be my undertakers, and not my friends. In short, I went far out of way, asking you many times to give me quotations I could use, that is, quotes from you, so that I could honor you, and without wounding your self-esteem, bring you more into the sunlight. Were you the adherent of Herbert's viewpoint, rather than mine, then it should have been only just of you to say so, and tell me that I think Eliot is a plagiary, but you agree with Read, and believe that he will be remembered. Yea, by Dunciads and fools and poeticules, and should not be recollected by you or Read, for that matter. I took every risk and hazard, but should not have been the victim of Herbert's venom. I could easily take care of him in a battle of wits or learning, or anybody else in the Anglo-American world of letters for that matter. It does not matter, but it is true.

Anyway, Stanley, far from being your adversary when I reprehended you for dismissing my book like a book reviewer, with "excellent reading," I was only wounded by you. You will, I pray, live long enough to see me wholly redeemed; literary criticism of the highest order is not as most Poloniuses imagine, good-natured; look at Hazlitt's, or Dryden's magnificent dramatic essays, and Dryden frankly confesses that he is waspish, or consider the contumely of Dr. Johnson, or Swift's acerb *Battle of the Books*, the *Drapier's Letters*, or *The Art of Sinking in Poetry*, or Pope's *Dunciad*. Well, I need go no farther.

If you wish to be so unjust with me as I feel you have been, then you are as purblind as the Cimmerians, and live in a Bosporus fog.

You are my friend, Stanley, and I have fought with more people than you can know about your work. I will fight for you at the risk of irritating you, but will not allow you to maul a book that took a lustrum of tribulation and discernment to do. I am not a boy now, and I know my faults, what books of mine should be cast into Tophet, most of them, but be sure several of my works shall be recollected, and with justice; others will be reprinted, alas, because fools will mistake what is bad in them for what is good.

Please, and without any nonsense read the ancients; you have a wonderful feeling for the line, and Allen can tell you far more about that than I can, and so can you, but I know a good poem, just as I know where the wild thyme blows.

I hope with this, you know, goes my deep appreciation of what you are, as a poet and my friend.

Meantime, you have my love, Stanley, and for heaven's sake don't be ailing as I am, every week some new malaise, but I had to get to new weather, and be hard by headlands, a gray, pensive sea, rocks that have enough virtue in them to cure us of melancholia and the diseases of the soul.

Again your devoted friend,

Dublin
January 27, 1962

Dear Stanley:

I am always delighted to have your letters; how do you come to the opinion that I have no high regard for your taste and understanding of literature. Many times we had dinner together, and we were always of the same mind about authors.

Have had no correspondence either with Allen or Isabella for the past six months, and now an unexpected missive comes from Allen with the following manna and quail on *Truth Is More Sacred*: ". . . a very fine book the argument of which I shall not take sides in, for I see much in both sides. Your great chapter on Pound and Eliot (pp. 169–208) I consider a masterly piece of polemics, and you convince me about Pound; but perhaps that is because I need no convincing. What does convince me, and what the chapter convinces me about, is a great prose style which is all your own and which I wholly accept, not for its 'opinion' but for its passion and elegance."

I was exceedingly grateful to get that from Allen, and I had good reason to hope for great interest and even esteem from you. But I hardly got a dog's morsel. I think our situation is the reverse of what you say it is. I go far out of my way battling with people for you, whilst you spend most of a long letter telling me about an article you wrote thirty years ago, or less. Well, I don't blame you for printing it any more than I blame myself for publishing *Bottom Dogs* again, but at least I did not prate about it to you, but told you quite candidly, and without any cant, that I wouldn't trouble your mind with the volume.

You ought to be a literary bigot; cast a poet into sheol, if most of his work is garbage, even if he had done a few good lines.

Such a posture of mind will be better for your own afflatus. Otherwise, you will go about pecking words here and there in the big dunghill of present-day Parnassus, and you will be sure to get some of the excrement on yourself, and worse on your own poems. That is why I said, Eliot even sinks in a line that is good in another poet. Long while ago I said that a truth in the mouth of Pontius Pilate is always a lie. And I came upon a similar thought in Pascal. In short, you've got to trust the whole poet; that does not mean that all his poems are of equal worth; but it does mean that the lesser as well as the major lines come from a person you have confidence in, and that is the whole quiddity of our dispute.

I am here, my dear Stanley, because it rains most of the time, and I stay indoors and work! Too much sun and a lazy Mediterranean sea are too much for indolent human flesh to endure.

I shall doubtless stay here until summer anyway.

If you will, please, take my advice, and reread the ancients and the fifteenth- and sixteenth-century writers, as well as Chaucer; I am sure that will sharpen and quicken your own Pisgah vision. Now is that derision? If it is then I despise myself; well, many times I do. Particularly, when I write you querulous letters.

Let me, please, see page proofs of the *Moby-Dick* essay as soon as you can. Again I want to thank you deeply for your intellectual labor on that essay, and I am convinced that you are in almost all cases more correct than I in your emendations and excisions.

Be sure, Stanley, that I have the fondest regard for you, and your genuine abilities as a poet and a critical intellect.

Your devoted friend,

Soller de Mallorca
February 10, 1963

Dear Stanley:

Your very lengthy and deeply good letter has just come, and I want to give you my immense thanks for the labor devoted to the

Ms.* Why, my dear Stanley, you should imagine that I would be rancorous I do not know. Your suggestions seem most sound and reasonable. What ailed me was that the Ms. has been edited since July 1st; had the memoir gone to you at once and you had gone over it, as you have, and in such a small space of time, I should have been profoundly relieved, and of course, exceedingly grateful. I shall wait for Rlene to arrive to take up the various suggestions you have made. The delay has nothing to do with any reluctance on my part to accept what you say; if you recall when you corrected the *Moby-Dick* essay, I told you I was too enervated to know what I was doing. True, I could surmise that what you had done was right. Now, with a book of this sort, can you imagine how debilitated I am? The sun is utterly extinguished in my poor mind at this point. Far from wishing to argue with you, as you fear, I don't even have the ability or strength to do anything but follow your counsel, and wait until Rlene comes and points out to me just what I should do and where it should be done. It is terrible to continue reading your own work, and to reshape it, even so little as you suggest.

What you say about the book means a great deal to me; again, at this juncture I ceased to have any thoughts about it, good or ill, because I no longer knew.

I told Josephine you were going over the autobiography very closely, and I can say here that I deem what you have done a marvelous act of friendship.

If I repeat myself, let me say I am helpless after I have finished an essay or a book, and am blind as the Cimmerians. It is not that I have such animal arrogance about it as you think. I don't know what to think at all.

Please don't think I am evading any of your queries by not replying to them. The plain truth is that I shall probably accept most if not all of your corrections. Naturally, I shall ask James to send you galleys, so that you will see that I do this, in order that you may know how deeply I appreciate your task.

Now, as for Hebrew spellings, I was under the impression that I had gotten them, most of them, from Ginzberg's *Legends of the*

* *Because I Was Flesh*

Jews, a beautiful piece of scholarship; I had relied on other Hebraists too, but I may have misspelled some of the words. I don't know. As for Eve the Serpent, though I attributed this to Clement of Alexandria, he in turn borrowed a great deal of this sort of learning from the ancient rabbis. To give you an example: I did one silly thing; I attributed the title of the autobiography to Saint Augustine who did not trouble to offer it as a quotation from the Book of Psalms. That was my ignorance, and the general stupidity of our age.

Though I have little feeling for the modern grammarians, you are right in asserting that the punctuation ought to be consistent. But what would you think if you read Dekker's Plague Pamphlets? The spelling varies, the commas and semicolons are the consequence of rhythm and may appear haphazard to you. But I am taking your advice, not because I care what the scribblers in the press will say, but because I imagine you are right and that I ought to follow you. I read with great care, as I told you, *The Poem Itself.* And although I felt that Henri Peyre did wonderful translations of Mallarmé, I thought his lovely work was somewhat tarnished by drossy pedantry, an overelaborate attention to punctuation. However, your spirit pervades the book, and I want to tell you how greatly impressed I am with it. If you recall, I said I had not read much of it when you gave me the volume, but I brought it to Spain, and spent a great deal of time over it. That somebody else has received the laurels for your insights, and for making available the French Symbolist poets in an English that I could read and even love, sorely vexes me. However, do not let any remarks about my own on metrics and punctuation give you the impression that I do not care very deeply for the work. I do, and make no doubt about it. I am doing an essay now on the limitations of literary criticism, and if I can refer to *The Poem Itself* I will do so, and give you the honor that belongs *only to you* and not to somebody else. If I am not redundant, and if I am let it be, this is the first time I have been able to enjoy Baudelaire in English; there is only the other translation of "Correspondence" done by Allen Tate that I care for as much.

I feel this is a trifling epistle, and a pittance of thanks for so much that you have done for the Ms. I want to make a few acknowledgments in the autobiography, and I should like to mention you unless you object.

Am deeply sorry to hear that you have been ill; I have been plagued with a rheumatic back; a moiety of the reason for a barren letter is that I am as lost as Osiris was without his sacrum, and that I am tired, because it is evening, but I could not repress the strong wish to reply to you forthwith so that you would have my answer in the next four days.

Soon as Rlene gets here we will go over all your very fine questions, emendations, and thoughts, and I shall write you again to tell you, without any doubt, that I have accepted them. Only one misgiving I have; how can I write an intelligent paragraph that will take care of some of the years I did not mention; should we utter what we hardly recollect, and what is vapory or even in the waters of Lethe, should that be dredged up? This is the only doubt I have. I don't remember everything, or if I do, never felt that it was important enough to include. I need not remind you of the old platitude that art is selection, and I don't like to rely on any commonplace canon. But if you don't feel something piercingly, is it not a fault to imagine that you can write about it with enough strength to capture a hearer? Where you say I am "overrich," you are probably right. I hate the modern exclusion of ancient lore, and the glories of myth with which we can fill the holes. Be sure, I am in no mood to argue with you, Stanley; I am too deeply indebted to you.

My deepest thanks and my love. Your grateful friend.

Index